Marx's economic predictions

Fred M. Gottheil is Associate
Professor of Economics at the
University of Illinois.
A Canadian, he was educated
at McGill University and Duke
University. He has published a
number of professional articles,
and is a member of the
executive committee of the
Association for
Comparative Economics.

Marx's economic predictions

by Fred M. Gottheil

Northwestern University Press • Evanston • 1966

FRED M. GOTTHEIL *is associate professor of economics at the*
University of Illinois. A Canadian, he was educated at McGill University
and Duke University. He is author of several professional articles and
is a member of the executive committee of the Association for
Comparative Economics.

to Diane

Preface

NEXT YEAR—1967—marks the centennial of Marx's *Das Kapital,* and in these hundred years a prodigious quantity of economic analysis has been devoted to it. University libraries have in their stacks, if not on their reserve shelves, scores of titles, including such definitive ones as *The Meaning of Marx, What Marx Really Meant,* and *A New Look at Marx.* This book makes no pretense of being "A Newer Look at What Marx Really, Really Meant." Its purpose, rather, is to test Marx's predictions as logical derivatives of his economic system. There is no foul play here. Marx, I am sure, would invite such a test, for he considered his major contribution to be the development of an economic theory of capitalism that could be used to foretell future events. In his own Preface to the first German edition of *Capital,* Marx promises his readers that he will uncover the natural laws of capitalist development which work "with iron necessity toward inevitable results." "The country that is more developed industrially," he writes, "only shows to the less developed, the image of its own future."

Marx's economic analysis of capitalism can be, and has been, "translated" into modern economic terminology. For example, his "organic composition of capital" is, in fact, akin to the capital-output ratio; his "moral depreciation" is technological obsolescence; his "simple reproduction" is the stationary state. But I see little to be gained by such translations. Marx's concepts are clearly defined and should not be burdensome to the interested reader. In this way I hope to avoid the very probable and understandable charges of incorrect translation and misuse.

A note concerning reference procedures used in this book. All titles of Marxian works are abbreviated, e.g., *Capital,* Volume II, page 300, is written C. II, 300. A list of these abbreviated titles will be found on page xiii. All page numbers refer to the editions of Marx's works listed in the Bibliography on page 208. So as not to overburden the book with footnotes, these references are for the most part incorporated directly into the text. Since the evaluation of Marx's predictions is based on a critical analysis of his economic system, constant reference is made in the evaluations to material developed in preceding chapters, and these references (e.g., "Chap. 2, sec. 3") are also placed within the body of the text. *The Theories of Surplus Value* is cited as Volume IV of *Capital.*

In the construction of his theories Marx frequently expresses specific economic relationships in algebraic form, e.g., $P = k + p'k$. The book attempts, whenever possible, to reproduce the Marxian equations in their original form. Other economic relationships which are expressed in Marx's work literally are rewritten here in algebraic form. A list of these symbols will be found on page xv.

My indebtedness to Dr. Joseph J. Spengler and Dr. Calvin B. Hoover of Duke University cannot be adequately expressed. It was Dr. Spengler who suggested the need for an intensive study of Marx's predictions and who supervised my dissertation, from which this book emerges. Dr. Hoover not only provided invaluable constructive criticism but has been a much appreciated source of encouragement.

The substance of section 1 of Chapter 11 of this book appeared in article form in the *Canadian Journal of Economics and Political Science.* I would like to thank the editors of the *Journal* for permitting me the use of the material. Also, I would like to express my appreciation to Mrs. Virginia C. Seidman for her very careful editing of the manuscript. The usual caveat holds.

FRED M. GOTTHEIL

Urbana, Illinois
April 28, 1966

Contents

Part II: Marxian Predictions

Abbreviated titles

For full bibliographic data on these titles, see the Bibliography on p. 208.

List of symbols

C	*commodity	MR	money rent
M	*money	d	*differential rent
c	*constant capital	r	*absolute rent
v	*variable capital	C_{pm}^{l}	*commodity capital
s	*surplus value	$...P...$	*production process
s/v	*rate of surplus value	t_p	time of production
s'	*rate of surplus value	t_c	time of circulation
$s/c + v$	*specific rate of profit	k_c	expenses of circula-
$c/c + v$	*organic composition		tion
	of capital	k_p	expenses of produc-
k	*cost price		tion
p'	*average rate of profit	t	turnover of capital
P	*prices of production	n	*number of capital
L	working day		turnovers
S	*surplus labor time	cK	circulating capital
P	*value of labor power	fK	fixed capital
n	*number of laborers	K_e	capital employed
d_m	moral depreciation	K_o	capital outlay
S_e	surplus profits	S'	*annual rate of surplus
i	*interest		value
i'	rate of interest	S	*annual surplus value
CV	capital value	a	accumulation
y	fixed income per pe-	g	percentage of surplus
	riod		value devoted to
GR	ground rent		accumulation
		w	prevailing wage rate

*Marx's own symbols

Part I: Marxian theory

1

Introduction

JOSEPH A. SCHUMPETER, in the opening pages of his *Capitalism, Socialism, and Democracy,* refers to Karl Marx as, among other things, a prophet.[1] Prophets do not usually excel in professional learning, yet, Schumpeter writes, Marx's economic analyses are not vulnerable to a charge of want of scholarship or training in the technique of theoretical analysis; still, he continues, a part of Marx's success, though a very minor part, is attributable to the "barrelful of white-hot phrases, of impassioned accusations, and wrathful gesticulations, ready for use on any platform, that he put at the disposal of his flock." [2]

Some economic writers, when discussing the Marxian ventures into the prophetic realms of economics, are inclined to discount *in toto* any respectability that may be attached to Karl Marx, the economist. The vigorous charges leveled against the Marxian pretensions to predictive ability are exemplified in the writings of such men as Ludwig von Mises, who writes:

> The materialist conception is scientifically worthless; moreover Marx never worked it out exactly but propounded it in various incompatible forms. . . . Marxism is against logic, against science and against the activities of thought itself. . . . Its outstanding principle is the prohibition of thought and inquiry, especially as applied to the institutions and workings of the socialist economy.[3]

Other economic writers, however, reviewing Marxian contributions in this area, provide a less devastating account of the "prophet." Perhaps more sympathetic to Marxian thought, they prefer to draw a distinction

1. J. A. Schumpeter, *Capitalism, Socialism, and Democracy* (New York: Harper & Bros., 1942), p. 5.
2. *Ibid.,* p. 5.
3. L. von Mises, *Socialism* (New Haven: Yale University Press, 1951), pp. 459–60.

3

between the German economist and a mere rambling soothsayer, ascribing to Marx what Leontief calls the unique quality of a "character-reader." [4] Like the experienced layman, gifted with "character-reading," whose prognostications on individual behavior often prove more accurate than those advanced by the professional psychologist, Karl Marx was able to apply his vast fund of empirical knowledge of the capitalist system to the formulation of specific predictions which, as time revealed, contained much substance. Although Marx was truly a great character-reader of the capitalist system, Leontief asserts, his rational theories generally "do not hold water." [5]

There remains, however, still a third school of economists writing on Marx who look upon his predictions not as a resultant of irresponsible charges or mere character-reading ability, but as logical derivatives of a consistent theory of economic evolution. This group expounds the theory of scientific socialism and attributes to Marx the discovery of its universal laws. Oscar Lange writes:

Thus a "law of development" of the capitalist system is established. Hence the anticipation of the future course of events as deduced from the Marxian theory is not a mechanical extrapolation of a purely empirical trend, but an anticipation based on the recognition of a law of development and is, with certain reservations, not less stringent than the anticipation based on the static theory of economic equilibrium such as, for instance, the anticipation that a rise in price leads, under certain circumstances, to a decline in the amount of the commodity demanded.[6]

This present study attempts to evaluate the Marxian economic predictions. The object here is not to pronounce judgment on the accuracy of the predictions in the historical sense but rather to determine the bases upon which the predictions were made and then to evaluate the predictions as derivatives from the assumed bases. This presents no tautology. If the predictor asserts that the predictions he makes evolve from a theoretical structure which he himself constructs, a legitimate test of the predictions is to assess them as logical resultants of this theoretical structure. To test the predictions against the real world, it should be noted, is not to test the predictions but rather the reality of the theoretical structure. This, however, is not the purpose of this book.

Both Schumpeter and Leontief, and indeed von Mises, would agree

4. W. Leontief, "Marxian Economics for Present-Day Economic Theory," *American Economic Review*, XXVIII, 8.

5. *Ibid.*, p. 9.

6. O. Lange, "Marxian Economics and Modern Economic Theory," *Review of Economic Studies*, II (June, 1935), 193.

with Lange that Marx *professed* to have developed a theoretical system from which his prophecies were derived. Marx's constant attack upon "unscientific" utopian socialism and upon the vulgar economics of the English classical school, as well as his claim to have discovered the natural laws of social evolution, renders this point beyond debate. To evaluate the Marxian predictions as logical derivatives of an economic system, however, the system itself must first be explicitly developed. This is attempted in Part I. Here, the Marxian theories of price, profit, interest, capital circulation, and capital accumulation are examined. In each case, emphasis is placed on making explicit the underlying assumptions of the theory and tracing through its development as Marx himself presented it. No attempt is made to "reconstruct" or transform the theories into terms of "orthodox economics." Nor is the purpose an attempt to reconcile his conflicting theories or to expound lengthily on his inconsistencies, although the inconsistencies are made explicit. To do so would defeat the aim of Part I, which is to provide an exposition of the Marxian economic system. The chapters in Part I, it must be emphasized, do not, therefore, examine the predictions. They merely present the base upon which the study of the predictions will be made.

In brief, Chapter 2 deals with the Marxian theory of price. Here, the salient relationships between labor, value, and price are expounded. Chapter 3 examines the most important aspect of capitalist production —the formation of profit. Included in the Marxian exposition of profit is his theory on innovations. Chapters 4 and 5 examine the Marxian theories of interest and rent. The major consideration here, as in the earlier chapters, is the analysis of those variables which, Marx states, determine the magnitudes of these surplus derivatives. Chapter 6 deals with the Marxian theory of capital circulation. Here the various Marxian reproduction schemata are examined. Capital circulation, or the reproduction of capital in the capitalist economy, constitutes the basis of the Marxian economic system. The economic system is further developed in Chapter 7, dealing with the theory of capital accumulation. In this, the final chapter of Part I, the simple-reproduction model developed in Chapter 6 is expanded to incorporate economic growth into the Marxian system.

The preparatory work for the analysis of the Marxian economic prediction has thus been established. The evaluation of his predictions as logical derivatives of his economic system can now be undertaken. This is the task of Part II. Here all predictions which Marx explicitly makes in the volumes of *Capital, The Communist Manifesto, The Poverty of Philosophy, A Contribution to the Critique of Political Economy, The German Ideology, The Civil War in France, The Class Struggles in*

France, The Critique of the Gotha Programme, published addresses, essays, articles, and correspondence are analyzed. In each case, an attempt is made to trace the prediction to its origin—the Marxian economic system—and to test it for internal consistency within this system. The test involves two considerations: (1) analysis of the specific theories which Marx integrates to develop the prediction in question, and (2) analysis of those relationships which are developed in the Marxian system and are relevant to the prediction but which Marx fails to incorporate. The Marxian predictions fall into three categories: (1) *primary,* defined as those predictions affecting the major determinants of the capitalist system, (2) *secondary,* those predictions which relate to the development of the primary predictions, and (3) *specific,* those predictions which concern specific dates, names, and events.

Chapter 8, the most significant in Part II, evaluates the predictions on the falling rate of profit and the increasing organic compositions of capital. Secondary predictions, such as the continuing decline in labor skills, the increasing capital turnovers per year, the falling rate of interest, and the decline in ground rent, are incorporated into the analysis of the profit-rate prediction. In Chapter 9 the Marxian predictions on the development of the world market and the internationalization of the capitalist mode of production are evaluated. Among the secondary predictions considered is the forecasting of the geographical polarization of the world's economies into areas of specifically agricultural and industrial production. Chapter 10 evaluates the Marxian predictions related to the increasing instability of the capitalist economy, the growing concentration of capital, and the transformation of a production organization based on atomistic capital units into one based on the development of joint-stock companies. Chapter 11 concerns itself primarily with an analysis of the Marxian predictions on the increasing misery of the proletariat and the development of class struggle. These predictions follow directly from the predictions on the falling value of subsistence, the expansion of the industrial reserve army, the polarization of classes into bourgeoisie and proletariat, and the emergence of class consciousness. Chapter 12 completes the analysis of Marxian predictions with an evaluation of Marx's prophecies on the proletarian revolution and the emergence of the communist society.

The book concludes with a short summary chapter dealing with a general evaluation of Marxian predictions and the theoretical structure from which they are derived.

2

Price

THE PURPOSE OF THIS CHAPTER is to examine Marxian price theory. In the analysis of price, emphasis is placed on the development of the Marxian labor theory of value and its significance to commodity exchange. The evolution of price from value is examined in a series of three approximations. Here, major attention is focused on making explicit the assumptions and variables incorporated in each approximation. The chapter also includes an exposition of the salient Marxian concepts of commodity production.

(1) MARXIAN ANALYSIS
OF THE COMMODITY

The study of political economy begins in the Marxian system with the study of the *commodity*. According to Marx, the commodity has definite historical dimensions which are based on the institution of social exchange (C. I, 99).[1] An article produced for immediate consumption is defined by Marx as a *product*. Produced for exchange, however, the article becomes a commodity. The world of commodities is, therefore, a world of exchange; and exchange, Marx explains, is a definite social relation among men (C. I, 83).

Analytically, the commodity presents itself as the complex of two things: use value and exchange value.[2] The *utility* of the commodity

1. I.e., *Capital*, Volume I, page 99. Titles of Marx's works are abbreviated in all text and footnote references. A list of these abbreviations will be found on page xiii. Page numbers cited refer to the editions of Marx's works listed in the Bibliography on page 208.
2. In the section, "Notes on the History of the Theory of the Commodity," Marx states, "The analysis of commodities according to their two-fold aspect of use-value and exchange-value . . . is the result of a century and a half of critical study by the classical school of political economy which dates from William Petty

defines its specific *use value,* which is realized only in final consumption. Although use value is necessary, it is not a sufficient property of the commodity:

Suppose, we have a commodity whose use-value is that of a diamond. We can not tell by looking at the diamond that it is a commodity. *When it serves as a use-value,* aesthetic or mechanical, on the breast of a harlot, or in the hand of the glasscutter, *it is a diamond and not a commodity* [CPE, 20; italics added].

Use values thus have no independent existence within the Marxian framework of commodity analysis. They serve only as the "material depositories of exchange value" (C. I, 43). *Exchange value* is the essence of the commodity; it is the "fundamental law of modern political economy" (CPE, 62); it "presents itself as a quantitative relation, as a proportion in which values in use of one sort, are exchanged for those of another sort" (C. I, 43). The conceptual development of commodity exchange value is the crucial piece of abstraction in Marxian price theory:

A given commodity, e.g., a quarter of wheat is exchanged for x blacking, y silk, or z gold, &c,—in short, for other commodities in the most different proportions. Instead of one exchange value, the wheat has, therefore, a great many. But since x blacking, y silk or z gold &c, each represent the exchange value of one quarter of wheat, x blacking, y silk, or z gold &c, must as exchange values be replaceable by each other, or equal to each other [C. I, 43].

The equating of blacking, silk, and gold, it must be noted, is derived not as the logical resultant of any scientific investigation undertaken by Marx but merely from a postulate which he makes and accepts as a self-evident truth. That each commodity represents one quarter of wheat and that the exchange values of each must be equal is merely definition. The expression of this commodity equation or definition is, however, critical to the development of Marxian value theory. It provides the bases upon which exchange value and labor are associated:

Let us take two commodities, e.g., corn and iron . . . in which a given quantity of corn is equated to some quantity of iron: e.g., 1 quarter corn $= x$ cwt. iron. What does this equation tell us? [It tells us that] there exists in equal quantities something common to both [C. I, 43].

The discovery of a "common substance" once again does not follow logically from any theoretical examination. It exists merely as the

---

in England and Boisguillebert in France and closes with Ricardo in the former country and Sismondi in the latter" (CPE, 56).

second postulate in Marx's commodity analysis. The transformation or reduction of value to labor, however, depends upon the establishment of the common-substance equation. Marx says:

If then we leave out of consideration the use-value of commodities, they have only one common property left, that of *being products of labor* [C. I, 44; italics added].

It is a physiological fact, that they [useful kinds of labor] are functions of the human organism, and that each such function, whatever may be its nature or form, is essentially the expenditure of human brain, nerves, muscles etc. [C. I, 82].

The recent scientific discovery, that the products of labor, so far as they are values, are but material expressions of the human labor spent in their production, marks, indeed, an epoch in the history of the development of the human race [C. I, 85].

Here, too, identification of the common substance as labor results not from logic but from choice.[3] Indeed, Marx himself refers to the development of value in terms of tautologies:

Since the exchange value of the commodities is . . . nothing but a material expression of a specific social form of labor, it is a tautology to say that labor is the only source of exchange value. . . . Similarly, it is a tautology to say that matter in its natural state has no exchange value, because it does not contain any labor [CPE, 31–32].

The utility of the labor concept as the embodiment of value depends upon five basic assumptions which Marx, with varying degrees of success, incorporates into his analysis:

1. The labor materialized in all commodities is reducible to a common factor defined as *human labor in the abstract* (C. I, 45).
2. Labor can be measured in *units of time* (C. I, 45).
3. Only *socially necessary labor time* is represented as value (C. I, 45, 46).
4. The variety of labor skills is subject to cardinal measurement in units of unskilled labor.
5. Expenditure of labor must satisfy a definite social want (C. I, 54).

Marx was less successful in solving the reduction of varied labor skills to the common unit of measurement than he was at any other stage in

3. The obvious alternative to labor as the "common substance" in commodities is nature. This Marx considers but dismisses with an argument which is itself based on the predetermination of value by labor. Therefore, simply by definition, Marx is able to write, "Since exchange value is a definite social manner of expressing the amount of labor bestowed upon an object, Nature has no more to do with it, than it has in fixing the course of exchange" (C. I, 94).

his development of the labor theory of value. While reducibility is essential to the theory, the best Marx can provide is this:

Experience shows that this reduction is constantly being made. . . . The different proportions in which different sorts of labor are reduced to unskilled labor as their standard, are established by a social process that goes on behind the back of their producers, and, consequently, appear to be fixed by custom. For simplicity's sake we shall henceforth account every kind of labor to be unskilled, simple labor; by this we do no more than save ourselves the trouble of making the reduction [C. I, 51–52].

Marx poses the same vital question (and answer) in the *Critique:*

But how about skilled labor which rises above the level of average labor by its high intensity, by its greater specific gravity? This kind of labor resolves itself into unskilled labor composing it; it is simple labor of a higher intensity, so that one day of skilled labor, e.g., may equal three days of unskilled labor. This is not the place to discover the laws regulating this reduction. It is clear, however, that such reduction does take place [CPE, 25].

That reduction is constantly being made and established by social process provides no solution to the problem of reducibility. And to assume reducibility for "simplicity's sake" or to "save ourselves trouble" is tantamount to ignoring the very existence of the problem. In still an earlier work, *The Poverty of Philosophy,* the problem was raised. Here, however, a solution is offered which apparently is dropped in the later works:

Does labor time, as the measure of value, suppose at least that the days are *equivalent,* and that one man's day is worth as much as another's? No. Let us suppose that a jeweller's day is equivalent to three days of a weaver . . . ; to apply such a measure we must have a comparative scale of the different working days: *it is competition that sets up the scale* [PP, 58; italics added].

At this point in the analysis the concept of reducibility must be accepted as a Marxian postulate, but with the qualification here understood.

(2) THE LABOR THEORY OF VALUE

The basis for the labor theory of value has been established. Commodities are valued according to the quantity of socially necessary abstract human labor they possess. The earlier equating of blacking, silk, and gold represents the equality of labor time expended in each commodity. Equivalents in exchange, in the Marxian system, are equivalents in labor content, i.e., 20 yards of linen are equivalent to 1 coat because each contains equal amounts of labor time. Exchange value between any two commodities thus appears to be an accidental and purely relative relation. When the expenditure of labor time on one commodity, i.e., linen, changes, the exchange value by definition changes. The introduction of the power loom in England, reducing the labor input in a given quantity of yarn, reduced as well the exchange value of the yarn (C. I, 46).

The necessary labor time expended in a particular commodity depends upon the productiveness of labor. An increase in the productiveness of labor reduces the labor-time requirement in the production of the commodity. Consequently, changes in factors which affect the productiveness of labor, viz., the efficiency of labor, the state of technology, and the social organization of production, indirectly affect value relations (C. I, 47). Marx states the labor theory of value in the following simple maxim: "The value of a commodity, therefore, varies directly as the quantity, and inversely as the productiveness, of the labor incorporated in it" (C. I, 47).

The Smithian value paradox is resolved in the simple Marxian solution. Air and water possess use values, that is, they satisfy some definite social want. However, due to their unique accessibility, they demand no expenditure of labor time in their production and consequently bear no value. Diamonds, on the other hand, as commodities not only satisfy the use-value criterion but bear a relatively high value because of their "very rare occurrence on the earth's surface, and hence their discovery costs, on the average, a great deal of labor-time" (C. I, 47). Marx speculates that if we could succeed at a small expenditure of labor in converting carbon into diamonds, their value might fall below that of bricks.

(3) COMMODITIES IN CIRCULATION: SIMPLE EXCHANGE

The purpose of exchange in the Marxian system is the realization of commodity use values. Once a commodity has found a "resting place" where it can serve as a use value, it falls out of the sphere of exchange into that of consumption (C. I, 117). The *metamorphosis of the commodity,* as it moves or circulates from production to consumption, is symbolized by Marx in the generalized form

$$C—M—C$$

where the C's represent qualitatively different commodities containing equal quantities of materialized labor, and M, money, possessing the same labor content, acts as the medium of exchange.

Tracing the evolutionary process of production from "production for consumption" to "production for exchange," Marx shows that in the latter the producer is not concerned with satisfying his wants directly (in contradistinction to the producer for consumption) but with producing commodities that, although containing no personal use value, satisfy wants of other producers. These "nonuse-value" commodities, produced and owned by the producer, are, however, his means of accumulating or commanding, through exchange, commodities that do satisfy his own wants, i.e., contain use values (C. I, 97). The institution of "production for exchange" thus introduces a temporal separation between the production-satisfaction relations, destroying the automaticity of use-value realization. Production for exchange creates potential use values which are realized only by the complete metamorphosis of the commodities.

Consider the process of circulation, C_1—M—C_2. The producer of C_1, namely P_1, exchanges C_1, which contains no use value to him, for its labor equivalent in terms of money, M, the medium of exchange. This act constitutes the first metamorphosis, the *sale* (C. I, 119). With M, P_1 at any time makes a second exchange of M for some other commodity, C_2, which contains an equal quantity of labor and a definite use value to P_1. This act constitutes the second or concluding metamorphosis of the commodity, the *purchase* (C. I, 123).[4]

(4) COMMODITIES IN PRODUCTION: EXPANDED EXCHANGE

The metamorphosis of commodities in simple exchange characterizes the circulation of all commodities. In all cases, the circulation of commodities from producer to consumer entails only a transfer of commodity ownership, having no effect whatever on the exchange value of the commodity itself (C. I, 175). The purpose of the sale is the monetization of the exchange value. The purpose of the purchase is consumption, the realization of its use value. Consequently, in the

---

4. A similar process of circulation, or metamorphosis, of commodities can be illustrated for the producer of C_2, namely P_2, who gives up the nonuse value C_2 for the definite use value C_1. However, C_2 may purchase C_3, C_4, or C_5 instead of C_1. This will have no effect on C_1 or on its metamorphosis since it will be taken off the market by P_3, P_4, or P_5, by definition of C_1 containing some use value.

process of circulation the coat maintains its exchange value while it becomes a use value. Such is the case with blacking, silk, gold, coffee, tea, etc.

In the Marxian world of commodities, labor is included. However, the metamorphosis of this commodity, Marx asserts, is unique. The purchaser of labor comes into possession of a commodity whose use value, unlike any other use value, possesses the peculiar property of being a source of value and whose actual consumption is itself an embodiment of labor and consequently a creation of value (C. I, 186).[5] This uniqueness, Marx states, is understood only by the purchaser of labor, the capitalist. This distinction between labor and other commodities, he writes, is the beginning to an understanding of capitalist production (C. I, 174).

The capitalist enters the commodity market to purchase the commodity labor, which Marx calls labor power, with the money equivalent of the labor power's exchange value. According to the labor theory of value, the exchange value of labor power is determined by the labor time necessary for its production—in other words, the labor time incorporated in the laborer's *means of subsistence* (C. I, 189). The means of subsistence must

be sufficient to maintain him in his normal state as a laboring individual. His natural wants, such as food, clothing, fuel, and housing vary according to climatic and other physical conditions of his country. On the other hand, the number and extent of his so-called necessary wants, as also the modes of satisfying them, are themselves the product of historical development, and depend therefore to a great extent on the degree of civilization of a country, more particularly on the conditions under which, and consequently on the habits and degree of comfort in which, the class of free laborers has been formed [C. I, 190].

Performing as a use value, labor power is removed from the process of circulation and enters the process of production.[6] Here, Marx explains, man and nature participate, with the former, on his own accord, starting, regulating, and controlling the material reaction between himself and nature (C. I, 197). In this process the laborer, employing

5. "So far as the advance of capital is concerned, labor-power *counts as a value.* But in the process of production, labor-power performs the function of *creating value*" (C. III, 41).
6. The purchase of the labor power was made solely with the intent of utilizing the labor power in production. The production process, or labor process, exhibits two characteristics: (1) laborers work under the control of the capitalist, and (2) the product is the property of the capitalist, not that of the laborer, its immediate producer (C. I, 206).

specific instruments of production, alters the material worked upon. The process disappears in the product; the latter is the use value. The labor power, expended in the process, has materialized itself in its subject (C. I, 201).

When the product of the labor power re-enters the process of circulation, which it must, the metamorphosis is completed with its sale. The commodity now has an enhanced exchange value, increased by the newly created value. The total metamorphosis of the labor commodity can be symbolized by the inverted form of exchange,

$$M—C—M'$$

where M is the money advanced in the purchase of labor power, M' is the money equivalent of the exchange value of the product of labor, and C is the commodity created by the labor power. Because of the significance of the process of production in this analysis, the expanded form can be written as:

$$M—C \ldots C'—M'$$

where C represents the labor power, C' the resulting commodity or *product of labor,* and $C \ldots C'$ the process of production. The C in the production process Marx calls commodity *capital:*

It is a commodity-*capital,* as distinguished from a simpler commodity, 1) because it is pregnant with surplus-value, so that the realization of its value is simultaneously a realization of surplus-value. . . . 2) It is a commodity-*capital,* because its function as a commodity is a phase in its process of reproduction as capital [C. III, 402].

The quantitative difference, ΔM, the "increment or excess over the original value," Marx calls *surplus value* (C. I, 168). The surplus value is a product solely of the productive process, as distinct from the process of circulation. It is created only within the sphere of production where the commodity labor power, possessing that power to create value, is employed.

Surplus value emerges without violating the laws of exchange (C. I, 217). The seller of the labor power, Marx maintains, was not defrauded. Marx takes special care to indicate the legality of the sale of the labor power. He makes the following assumptions to support the so-called justice of the labor-commodity exchange: (a) there exists no relationship between the seller and buyer, i.e., both operate as free agents on the market, (b) the seller must be the sole owner of the capacity for labor, (c) the sale of the labor power is only for a definite duration of time, and (d) labor is considered by both parties as a commodity (C. I, 186).

What the laborer sells is not the product of the labor power but the labor itself:

The seller of labor-power, like the seller of any other commodity, realizes its exchange-value, and parts with its use-value. He cannot take the one without giving the other. The use-value of labor-power, or in other words, labor, belongs just as little to its seller, as the use-value of oil after it has been sold belongs to the dealer who has sold it [C. I, 216].

The laborer receives, in return for the sale of the labor power, its exchange-value equivalent, the means of subsistence. The capitalist, selling the product of labor, $C'—M'$, likewise is not in any manner a victim of fraud. He receives money, M', in exchange for a use value whose exchange value incorporated both the paid and unpaid labor time.

(5) MARXIAN THEORY OF PRICE

(a) FIRST APPROXIMATION

The abstraction of commodity exchange value into the categories of paid and unpaid labor, labor and surplus labor, or value and surplus value constitutes the primary division of the commodity. A further distinction, relating to the component structure of the commodity, is made, however, concerning the form in which labor enters the commodity. In the preceding analysis, the commodity was created in the process of production by the application of labor power and physical instruments which Marx now defines as *means of production* (C. I, 201). This distinction between labor power and instrument is paramount in the Marxian system. Exchange value evolves from both forms of applied labor, viz., the "living" labor power and the "past" or "dead" labor manifest in the means of production. The former Marx defines as *variable capital,* the latter as *constant capital* (C. I, 232).

The only form of labor capable of value *creation,* however, is the variable capital, i.e., labor power. The conversion of the means of production into the commodity transfers its own exchange value and no more. The exchange value of the means of production is determined not by the labor process into which it enters but by that out of which it issued as a commodity (C. I, 229). Its exchange value becomes realized only when it is employed in the production process as a use value, that is, in conjunction with living labor:

A machine which does not serve the purposes of labor, is useless. In addition, it falls prey to the destructive influence of natural forces. Iron rusts and wood rots. . . . Living labor must seize upon these things and rouse them from their death-sleep, change them from mere possible use-values into real and effective ones . . . ; their contact with living labor, is the sole means by which they can be made to retain their character of use-values, and be utilized [C. I, 203–4].

Division of "paid" labor into its constant and variable proportions is of particular significance in Marxian value analysis, for it illustrates the proposition that all surplus is derived only from the application of labor power. The composition of commodity value is symbolized by:

$$C = c + v + s \tag{2.1}$$

where c represents constant capital, or the value of the means of production used up in the labor process, v represents variable capital or the value of the labor power applied to the process, and s, surplus value, the value created by labor power in production.

The $c + v + s$ formulation is significant, not only as a value structure of a particular commodity, but also as the structural formulation of particular processes of production. Its application thus extends to both the micro and macro spheres of Marxian political economy. While the value of the commodity may remain constant, its component ratio, $c:v:s$, may undergo alteration. These alterations, though revealing significant tendencies in the economy, are hidden when value determination is restricted merely to quantitative measurement of labor, that is, without regard to the labor form.

Considering the structural organization of commodity production, certain basic relationships can be made explicit. Surplus value (s) is expressed solely as a function of variable capital (v). The ratio s/v Marx calls the *rate of surplus value*. In his development of the rate-of-surplus-value concept Marx assumes an expenditure of 90 in variable capital and equates constant capital to zero:

We have now the value produced ($v + s$). Given the new value produced = £180, which sum consequently represents the whole labor expended during the process, then subtracting from it £90, the value of the variable capital, we have remaining £90, the amount of surplus-value. This sum of £90 or s expresses the absolute quantity of surplus value produced. The relative quantity produced, or the increase per cent. of the variable capital, is determined, it is plain, by the ratio of the surplus-value to the variable capital, or is expressed by s/v. In our example this ratio is 90/90, which gives an increase of 100%. This relative increase in the value of the variable capital, or the relative magnitude of the surplus-value, I call, "The rate of surplus-value" [C. I, 239].

In an alternative formulation of s/v Marx introduces the concept of the working day. Its minimum-maximum limits are determined by the number of hours which the laborer must necessarily work for his own maintenance and the minimum time that a man requires for physical regeneration (C. I, 256). That part of the working day in which labor power is employed to reproduce its daily exchange value (subsistence) Marx calls *necessary labor*. The remainder of the working day thus constitutes *surplus labor:*

Both ratios, s/v and *surplus labor/necessary labor* express the same thing in different ways; in the one case by reference to materialized incorporated labor, in the other by reference to living fluent labor.
The rate of surplus-value is therefore an exact expression for the *degree of exploitation* of labor-power by capital, or of the laborer by the capitalist [C. I, 241; italics added].

The precise division of the working day into necessary and surplus labor depends upon the productiveness of labor, which is a function of what Marx calls the *organic composition of capital, $c/c + v$,* measuring the value relationship between the constant capital and total capital outlay, i.e., constant and variable (C. III, 248). The productiveness of labor, Marx shows, varies directly with the organic composition of capital and inversely to the value of the commodity:

The degree of the productivity of labor, in a given society, is expressed in the relative extent of the means of production that one laborer, during a given time, with the same tension of labor-power, turns into products [C. I, 681–82].

An analysis and comparison of the prices of commodities produced by handicrafts or manufacturers, and of the prices of the same commodities produced by machinery, shows generally that, in the product of machinery, the value due to the instruments of labor, increases relatively, but decreases absolutely [C. I, 426].

The relation between surplus and total capital outlay Marx calls the *rate of profit, $s/(c + v)$* (C. III, 55). A careful distinction must be made at this point. The rate of profit is calculated not on the expenditure of capital in production but on the advance of capital. When the turnover of capital is unitary, then the quantity of capital expended on production is equal to the quantity of capital advanced.

In producing commodity C_1, with a capital structure of $80c + 20v$ and a rate of surplus value of 100 per cent, the exchange value of C_1

would be $80c + 20v + 20s$, or 120. The organic composition of capital in this case would be 80/100 or 80 per cent; the rate of profit would be 20/100 or 20 per cent.

Recall that the simple exchange C_1—M—C_2 reflects the exchange of equal quantities of labor. Since commodity prices are equated to commodity exchange values, relative prices must reflect the relative quantities of labor contained in the commodities. Marx, however, further defines the market by assuming equal rates of surplus value in all processes of production (industries) [7] (eq. 2.2) and equal rates of profit in all processes, due to the forces of *competition* (eq. 2.3). Thus:

$$\frac{s_1}{v_1} = \frac{s_2}{v_2} = \frac{s_3}{v_3} \cdots = \frac{s_n}{v_n} \qquad (2.2)$$

$$\frac{s_1}{(c + v)_1} = \frac{s_2}{(c + v)_2} \cdots = \frac{s_n}{(c + v)_n} \qquad (2.3)$$

These assumptions, however, *imply* yet another namely, equal organic composition of capital in all production processes:

$$\frac{c_1}{(c + v)_1} = \frac{c_2}{(c + v)_2} \cdots = \frac{c_n}{(c + v)_n} \qquad (2.4)$$

That all industries are not characterized by identical organic compositions of capital is conceded by Marx. The internal consistency of the Marxian theory of price, however, demands this equation (eq. 2.4) *if* the theory professes to relate commodity prices to their labor contents and if equal rates of profit and surplus value in all industries are assumed. While the identity between price and labor is implicit in Marx's exposition of simple exchange, in his "developed" theory of price the identity serves merely as an "approximation." Here individual commodity prices tend to equate individual commodity values but in fact do not, and the necessity of assuming equal organic compositions of capital no longer prevails under these conditions.

(b) SECOND APPROXIMATION

Marx's examination of price theory is divided into two distinct studies: (1) the analysis of the scientific laws of value creation and (2) the study of value creation as it appears to the capitalist. While surplus value is created solely by the application of variable capital in the production process, to the capitalist the distinction between the variable

7. Marx was aware of differing rates of surplus value. However, to explain certain movements of other variables in the model, he abstracted from varying rates of surplus values. This assumption and its significance to the model are discussed in Chapter 8.

and constant capitals "disappears" (C. III, 44). The capitalist discovers that he cannot exploit the labor unless he advances, at the same time, the material requirements for the incorporation of this labor, i.e., the means of production. He is not as much interested, Marx shows, in the "science of production" as he is in the return on his investment; consequently he regards the surplus value as a product not simply of the variable factor but of the total capital he advanced.

Commodity value has previously been expressed in terms of "living" and "dead" labor, symbolized by $c + (v + s)$; but to the capitalist, commodity value is portrayed by $(c + v) + s$, where $c + v$ represents the total capital outlay necessary to realize the surplus value, s. Marx denotes this distinction by defining the surplus value which appears as a result of total capital outlay as *profit* (C. III, 49). The capital advanced to produce this profit Marx calls the *cost price* (k) (C. III, 39), and in another passage he says:

The capitalist understands well enough that this increment of value has its genesis in the productive manipulations of capital, that it is generated out of the capital. . . . So far as the capital assimilated in production is concerned, the surplus-value seems to arise equally from all its different elements consisting of means of production and labor. For all these elements contribute equally to the formation of the cost-price. All of them add their values, which are advanced as capital, to the value of the product, and they are not distinguished as constant and variable magnitudes [C. III, 47].

Marx recites the capitalist's argument:

We do not know anything of the way in which its surplus-portion . . . is formed . . . ; the surplus arises from a given value, because this value was advanced in the form of productive capital, no matter whether in the form of labor or of means of production [C. III, 48].

The value of the commodity is thus made equal to the sum of cost price (k) and profit (p). The relation between profit and cost price, p/k, Marx calls the *rate of profit*, which corresponds to the earlier formulation of the Marxian profit rate:

$$\frac{s}{c + v} = \frac{p}{k} \tag{2.5}$$

That the organic composition of capital, $c/c + v$, in the various *spheres of production* [8] differs was readily acknowledged by Marx.

8. Marx defines a particular industry as a "sphere of production." Thus a production process which characterizes an industry falls into the classification of a sphere in the Marxian system.

Indeed, it is this realization of differing capital compositions which dictates the deviation of an individual commodity's price from its exchange value or labor content. The composition of capital, measuring the proportion of its active and passive parts—of the variable and constant capital—is determined by both technical and value considerations. By "technical," Marx means:

A definite quantity of labor-power, represented by a definite number of laborers, is required for the purpose of producing a definite quantity of products, for instance in one day, and thereby to consume productively, by setting in motion, a definite quantity of means of production, machinery, raw materials, etc. A definite number of laborers corresponds to a definite quantity of means of production, so that a definite quantity of living labor corresponds to a definite quantity of materialized labor in means of production [C. III, 171–72].

The development of the Marxian theory of price from the first approximation, i.e., value theory, postulates the following:

1. Equal rates of surplus value in all spheres of production.
2. A constant working day in all spheres of production.
3. Equality of wages in all spheres of production.
4. Perfect mobility in the product and factor markets.
5. A competitive market structure.
6. A unitary rate of capital turnover in all spheres of production (C. III, 181).[9]

On the basis of these assumptions, the rates of profit resulting from equal investments of capital in any two spheres of production, i.e., A and B, depend upon their respective organic compositions. If the capital structure of sphere A is $90c + 10v$, the resulting commodity value, assuming the rate of surplus value to be 100 per cent, is $90c + 10v + 10s$, or 110. If sphere B, however, with the same outlay, is characterized by an organic composition of $10c + 90v$, the resulting commodity value becomes $10c + 90v + 90s$, or 190. The rate of profit in the one case would be 10 per cent, in the other 90 per cent (C. III, 177). This situation Marx believes is intolerable in capitalist society. He writes: "A difference in the average rate of profit of the various lines of industry does not exist in reality, and could not exist without abolishing the entire system of capitalist production" (C. III, 181). The capitalist operating in the competitive market is not at all interested in the functional relationship of the capital components. He is solely concerned with the return on his investment, and the cost price, k, does

9. The theory of capital turnover is discussed in Chapter 6.

not show any such functional distinction. Competition among capitalists, Marx argues, must force the rates of profit in the various spheres to equality (C. III, 212).

The reconciliation by Marx of the differing organic compositions of capital and the equality of the rate of profit is accomplished by the transformation of profit to *average profit,* rate of profit to the *average* (or *general*) *rate of profit,* and value to *price of production* (C. III, 182–86).

The Marxian transformation from value to price is demonstrated in Table 1, which sets up five different spheres of production, each charac-

Table 1

Sphere	Capitals	Rate of Surplus Value	Surplus Value	Value of Product	Rate of Profit
I	80c 20v	100%	20	120	20%
II	70c 30v	100%	30	130	30%
III	60c 40v	100%	40	140	40%
IV	85c 15v	100%	15	115	15%
V	95c 5v	100%	5	105	5%

Source: C. III, 183.

terized by a unique organic composition of capital. The capital composition of each particular sphere is itself an average of varying compositions. This is probably Marx's most explicit recognition of variable technical coefficients of production: "The rates of profit in every sphere of production, considered by itself, have previously been reduced to so many average rates of profit" (C. III, 185; see also C. I, 671).

The total capital investment in all spheres is 500. The summation of the surplus values produced by all spheres is 110, and the resulting total value of all commodities is 610. If each sphere is considered as a separate department of a greater single capital, i.e., 500, then the *average composition* of this single or social capital is 390c + 110v or, in terms of percentages, 78c + 22v. In this case, the *average surplus value* of the social capital would be 22, the average rate of profit would be 22 per cent, and the product of each 100 advanced capitals would be sold at 122 (C. III, 184).

While the capital outlay in each individual sphere is 100, it does not necessarily follow that the cost price of each sphere is also 100. This equation, Marx points out, would only occur if the total constant capital in each sphere were used up completely in the process of production. If, however, only part of the constant capital were transferred to the

Table 2

Sphere	Capitals	Surplus Value	Rate of Profit	Used-up c	Value of Commodity	Cost Price
I	80c 20v	20	20%	50	90	70
II	70c 30v	30	30%	51	111	81
III	60c 40v	40	40%	51	131	91
IV	85c 15v	15	15%	10	70	55
V	95c 5v	5	5%	10	20	15
Total	390c 110v	110				
Average	78c 22v	22	22%			

Source: C. III, 185.

product, the resulting cost price would be less than the capital advanced. This is illustrated in Table 2. The determination of the general rate of profit, however, is independent of this factor. As Marx says:

But this is immaterial so far as the rate of profit is concerned. Whether the 80c transfer the value of 80, or 50, or 5, to the annual product, whether the annual product is consequently 80c + 20v + 20s = 120, or 50c + 20v + 20s = 90, or 5c + 20v + 20s = 45, in all of these cases the excess of value of the product over its cost-price is 20, and in every case these 20 are calculated on a capital of 100 in ascertaining the rate of profit [C. III, 184].

Thus, assuming the average rate of profit at 22 per cent, the prices of individual commodities in each sphere can be determined.

Table 3

Sphere	Capitals	Surplus Value	Value	Cost Price of Commodity	Price of Commodity	Rate of Profit	Deviation of Price from Value
I	80c 20v	20	90	70	92	22%	+ 2
II	70c 30v	30	111	81	103	22%	− 8
III	60c 40v	40	131	91	113	22%	−18
IV	85c 15v	15	70	55	77	22%	+ 7
V	95c 5v	5	20	15	37	22%	+17

Source: C. III, 185.

In sphere I, the commodity price of 92, shown in column 6, Table 3, represents the summation of the cost price 70 (col. 5) and the average profit 22 (col. 7). The determination of the cost price 70 refers back to Table 2, where cost price represents the summation of the used-up constant capital 50 (col. 5) and the variable capital 20 (col. 2).

These prices, P, defined by Marx as *prices of production*, "arise by drawing the average of the various rates of profit in the different spheres of production and adding this average to the cost-prices of the different spheres of production" (C. III, 185).

The reconciliation between equality of the profit rate and differing organic compositions of capital is made.[10] It should be noted, however, that the concept of the Marxian rate of profit has, in the process of value-price transformation, undergone a qualitative change. The rate of profit, associated with a particular sphere, $s/c + v$, Marx now calls the *special rate of profit* (C. III, 186). That rate of profit which establishes equality in the economic system Marx calls the *general* or *average rate of profit:*

While the capitalists in the various spheres of production re-cover the value of the capital consumed in the production of their commodities through the sale of these, they do not secure the surplus-value, and consequently the profit, created in their own sphere by the production of these commodities, but only as much surplus-value, and profit, as falls to the share of every aliquot part of the total social capital out of the total social surplus-value, or social profit produced by the total capital of society in all the spheres of production [C. III, 186–87].

The transformation is formalized in the following stages:

$$\text{Commodity value} \quad = c + v + s \qquad (2.1)$$
$$= (c + v) + s$$
$$\text{Prices of production} = k + p \qquad (2.6)$$
$$= k + p'k \qquad (2.7)$$

When the specific organic composition of capital equals the social composition; then

$$s = p$$
$$p' = s/c + v$$
$$C = P$$

In cases, however, where the specific composition is higher than the social; then

10. It should be noted here that Marx's conversion of value to price affects his later development of capital reproduction (see Chaps. 6 and 7). The simple-reproduction equilibrium situation, which Marx constructs in Volume II of *Capital,* deals with the intraclass commodity exchange, not in terms of price, but in terms of value. Had he attempted the conversion of value to price in this context, the equilibrium solution to the simple-reproduction scheme could not have been achieved. Attempts have been made by Marxists to reconcile the transformation within the Marxian simple-reproduction model. This problem is commonly referred to as "the transformation problem" in the literature on Marx.

$$s < p$$
$$p' > s/c + v$$
$$C < P$$

This is illustrated in column 8, Table 3, spheres I, IV, and V. In specific spheres of lower than social composition,

$$s > p$$
$$p' < s/c + v$$
$$C > P$$

as indicated in spheres II and III.

Identification of the Marxian theory of value with his theory of price is thus misleading. Only in the unrealistic case of one organic composition of capital in the economy does the equality between value and price hold true. The Marxian price theory, however, is not restricted to this situation. Individual commodity prices consequently differ from their values in the Marxian system, i.e., from the labor time embodied in them, although some "approximation" to value is suggested:

Whatever may be the way in which the prices of the various commodities are first fixed or mutually regulated, the law of value always dominates their movements. If the labor time required for the production of these commodities is reduced, prices fall; if it is increased, prices rise, other circumstances remaining the same [C. III, 208].

The assumption that the commodities of the various spheres of production are sold at their values implies, of course, only that their value is the center of gravity around which prices fluctuate, and around which their rise and fall tends to an equilibrium [C. III, 209–10].

(c) THIRD APPROXIMATION

The price of a commodity existing on the market at any point in time, i.e., the market price, is equated to the commodity's price of production only in the equilibrium market, i.e., a market characterized by a demand for and supply of the commodity under ordinary circumstances (C. III, 210). Unless the market is in equilibrium, the market price, a function of demand and supply relations, would tend to deviate from its price of production or *market value* (C. III, 210).

The theory of the market price, a short-run phenomenon in the Marxian system, necessitates an inquiry into the demand and supply conditions prevailing on the market. Marx must consequently qualify his treatment of demand as it had appeared in value theory, where he equated it simply with use value. Thus he writes:

To say that a commodity has a use-value is merely to say that it satisfies some social want. So long as we are dealing simply with individual commodities, we could assume that the demand for any one commodity—its price implying its quantity—existed without inquiring into the extent to which this demand required satisfaction. But this question of the extent of a certain demand becomes essential, whenever the product of some entire line of production is placed on one side, and the social demand for it on the other. In that case it becomes necessary to consider the *amount*, the *quantity*, of this social demand [C. III, 218; italics added].

In the elaboration of the Marxian demand analysis, the concepts of *ordinary demand, strong demand, and weak demand* are developed to identify the varying demands that meet a supply of commodities at their market values (C. III, 211). At any given time the "connection" between society's demand for a commodity and the quantity made available through production is considered by Marx to be purely "accidental" (C. III, 220). When the quantity of a particular commodity demanded is equal to the commodity supply, the demand is defined as "ordinary," and the market price, reflecting the demand-supply equation, coincides with the commodity's market value. When the market price of a commodity is greater than its market value, "demand exceeds the ordinary, or the supply falls below it" (C. III, 211). If, however, demand is weak compared to supply, then the market price falls below market value (C. III, 217). The institution of the competitive market structure, Marx writes, establishes equilibrium in the long run, i.e., the equation of market price and value:

In order that the market-prices of identical commodities, which however are produced under different individual circumstances, may correspond to the market-value, may not differ from it by exceeding or falling below it, it is necessary that the different sellers should exert sufficient pressure upon one another to bring that quantity of commodities on the market which social requirements demand, in other words, that quantity of commodities whose market-value society can pay [C. III, 213] . . . ; this price of production is . . . the center of gravity around which the daily market-prices tend to fluctuate and tend to balance one another within definite periods [C. III, 211].

When the market price exceeds the market value, certain producers earn greater than surplus value, i.e., *surplus profits*,[11] which induce more producers to enter the production process. When the market price falls short of the market value, certain producers receive less than

---

11. The concept of surplus profits is developed in Chap. 3, sec. 4.

the average surplus value and are consequently shifted out of the production of the commodity, reducing the supply and bringing the market price into accord with the market value, and equilibrium is achieved.

The deviation of market price from market value results not only from daily changes in the demand and supply functions but from changes in the market values themselves:

If the market-value is changed, then there will also be a change in the conditions under which the total quantity of commodities can be sold. If the market-value falls, then the average social demand increases . . . and can absorb a larger quantity of commodities within certain limits. If the market-value rises, then the solvent social demand for commodities is reduced and smaller quantities of them are absorbed [C. III, 213].

The determination of the Marxian equilibrium price thus results from the interaction of the demand and supply functions with the market values or prices of production:

Hence, if supply and demand regulate the market-price, or rather the deviations of market-price from market-values, it is true, on the other hand, that the market-value regulates the proportions of supply and demand or the center around which supply and demand cause the market-prices to fluctuate [C. III, 213].

At this point, the Marxian demand analysis is refined to the explicit recognition of the functional relationship between price and quantity demanded, i.e., "the quantity demanded . . . is very elastic and changing" (C. III, 222). Marx writes:

"Social demand". . . that which regulates the principle of demand, is essentially conditioned on the mutual relations of the different economic classes and their relative economic positions [C. III, 214].

If the means of subsistence were cheaper, or money-wages higher, the laborers would buy more of them, and a greater "social demand" would be manifested . . . ; if cotton were cheaper, the demand of the capitalists for it would increase [C. III, 222].

It is a mistake to say that the consumption of necessities of life does not grow with their cheapening. The abolition of the corn laws in England proved the reverse [C. III, 769].

In this way Marx was able to compare the "effective" demand with the actual social need:

The limits within which the need *for commodities on the market,* the demand, differs quantitatively from the *actual social need,* [vary] naturally considerably for different commodities; in other words, the difference between the demanded quantity of commodities and that quantity which would be demanded, if the money-prices of the commodities, or other conditions concerning the money or living of the buyers, were different [C. III, 222–23].

(6) CONCLUSION

The Marxian theory of price, as developed in *Capital,* particularly in Volume I and the earlier parts of Volume III, shows an evolutionary process from the crude value theory of the first volume, where price is identified with labor content and demand with use value, to a more "realistic" interpretation of price, i.e., prices of production, which permits varying organic compositions of capital, and finally to the third stage, where Marx recognizes, and attempts to include, the market forces of supply and demand.

The concept of price which is incorporated in the analysis of the Marxian economic system is, without exception, the prices-of-production concept developed in the second approximation and defined as equilibrium price (market price = market value) in the third approximation. It is this price, not the labor theory of value, that prevails even in the communist society that Marx envisaged (CGP, 30). Marx makes the important distinction between surplus value and profit, between the "scientific" and the "superficial" approaches to the understanding of commodity production. Here Marx shows that, although surplus value is created solely by variable capital, the capitalists conceive of it as a product of total capital outlay. Yet Marx had earlier made explicit the functional relationship between the organic composition of capital and the productiveness of labor (Chap. 2, sec. 5). This relationship is critical in the Marxian economic model and will be expanded upon in Chapters 3 and 8.

3

Profit and innovation

MARX'S THEORIES of profit and innovation are elaborations of his more general theory of commodity valuation. Surplus is one component part of value. This surplus or profit or exploitation—Marx uses all three terms—emerges, in his system, in two basic forms: as absolute surplus value and as relative surplus value. They are distinguished by their sources. This chapter is primarily concerned with the formation of these surpluses. Marx's definition of profit and its connection with property relations precedes the discussion of profit formation. The chapter concludes with an examination of Marx's theory of innovation and its relation to profit formation.

(1) THE CONCEPT OF PROFIT

The existence of profit in the Marxian system presupposes only one condition, namely, the development of the state of industrial arts to that point where the laborer in the course of a day's work can, and is compelled to, produce a greater supply of commodities than is necessary for his daily subsistence and the reproduction of the means of production used up in the process (C. I, 232; cf. C. III, 741). Any monetary gain made outside the production process, i.e., in the process of circulation, by capitalists or other nonproducing agents, through the manipulations of commodity prices, does not constitute, in Marx's system, the creation of profit:

> The upholders of the delusion that surplus-value has its origin in a nominal rise of prices or in the privilege which the seller has of selling too dear, must assume the existence of a class that only buys and does not sell, i.e., only consumes and does not produce. . . . To sell commodities above their values to such a class, is only to crib back again a part of the money previously

28

given to it. . . . The capitalist class, as a whole, in any country, cannot over-reach themselves. . . . If equivalents are exchanged, no surplus-value results, and if non-equivalents are exchanged, still no surplus-value. Circulation, or the exchange of commodities, begets no value [C. I, 180–82].

The restriction of the Marxian concept of profit to the production process also excludes from profit the return on *merchant's capital,* which he defines as capital employed in the process of circulation to finance the sale of commodities (C. III, 331). While merchant's capital claims a share in the profits of enterprise, it cannot create profit (C. I, 182–83). As Marx states, in another passage:

Merchant's capital is simply capital performing its function in the sphere of circulation. The process of circulation is a phase of the total process of reproduction. But no value is produced in the process of circulation, and therefore, no surplus-value. Nothing takes place there but change of form of the same mass of values. In fact, nothing occurs there but the metamorphosis of commodities, and this has nothing to do either with the creation or with the transformation of values. If surplus-value is realized by the sale of the produced commodities, it is only because that surplus-value already existed in them [C. III, 329].

Profit formation is also independent of property or class relations. Marx writes, "If instead of working for the capitalist, he [the laborer] worked independently . . . he would . . . still be obliged to labor for the same number of hours, in order to produce the value of his labor-power" (C. I, 240). The expenditure of labor time over and above this minimum alone creates the surplus value or profit. The existence of profit in the Marxian system depends, consequently, upon purely technical rather than political considerations. Marx continues: "It is every bit as important, for a correct understanding of surplus-value, to conceive it as a mere congelation of surplus labor-time, as nothing but materialized labor" (C. I, 241).

(2) PROFIT AND PROPERTY RELATIONS

That profit takes the form of an unearned increment in the distribution of income is merely a manifestation of certain property relations existing in the economic system. If the ownership of the means of production were in the hands of the laboring class, the element of profit would none the less appear (C. III, 733):

Capital has not invented surplus-labor. Whenever a part of society possesses the monopoly of the means of production, the laborer, free or not free, must add to the working time necessary for his own maintenance an extra working time in order to produce the means of subsistence for the owners of the means of production, whether the proprietor be the Athenian, . . . Etruscan theocrat, civis Romanus, Norman baron, American slave owner, Wallachian Boyard, modern landlord or capitalist [C. I, 259–60].

The essential difference between the various economic forms of society, between, for instance, a society based on slave labor, and one based on wage labor, lies only in the mode in which this surplus-labor is in each case extracted from the actual producer, the laborer [C. I, 241].

The identification of profit with particular property-owning classes, Marx claims, is established through the development of certain historical processes (C. II, 40). The institution of private property in the means of production, Marx suggests, originated with the separation—by means of direct expropriation—of the product from its producer. The evolution of private property in the Marxian sense thus suggests the Brissot dictum, "property is theft" (PP, 220). The institution of the bourgeois propertied class, Marx explains, was accomplished through the use of force, often through legislation (C. I, 628). Private property, as the antithesis of social collective property, emerged with the expropriation of land from the great mass of people. This "fearful and painful expropriation of the mass of the people," Marx writes, "forms the prelude to the history of capital" (C. I, 835). Elsewhere he says:

In actual history it is notorious that conquest, enslavement, robbery, murder, briefly force, play the great part [C. I, 785]; . . . freedmen became sellers of themselves only after they had been robbed of all their own means of production, and of all the guarantees of existence afforded by the old feudal arrangements And the history of this, this expropriation, is written in the annals of mankind in letters of blood and fire [C. I, 786]. The advance made by the 18th century shows itself in this, that the law itself becomes now the instrument of the theft of the people's land [C. I, 796].

It comprises a series of forcible methods, of which we have passed in review only those that have been epoch-making as methods of the primitive accumulation of capital. The expropriation of the immediate producers was accomplished with merciless Vandalism, and under the stimulus of passions the most infamous, the most sordid, the pettiest, the most meanly odious [C. I, 835–36].

The capitalists' claim to profit is a claim of property rights. Because the capitalist *owns* the means of production, and consequently the production process, the product resulting from the process becomes his property.[1] The fact that the laborer contracts to work twelve hours per day for the capitalist and needs only six hours for maintenance is, Marx states, "a piece of good luck for the buyer, but by no means an injury to the seller" (C. I, 216; cf. C. I, 186). The distinction between the slave and capitalist economies is drawn on the basis of property rights of the original producer, i.e., the laborer. In the capitalist economy the laborer is a free agent who "must constantly look upon his labor-power as his own property" (C. I, 186).[2]

The formation of profit in the Marxian system thus appears as a residual component of exchange value, its distribution depending strictly upon property relations. Deriving profit on this basis, Marx is able to dismiss as vain bourgeois apologies the "abstinence" and "reward" theories of profit. Surplus product, he argues, results not from the abstinence of the capitalist but from the employment of the laborer (C. I, 651). Capitalist consumption grows with his capital accumulation, without one necessarily restricting the other. That capital "conservation" requires constant efforts to resist the temptation of consuming it is, Marx states, merely a childish attempt by vulgar economists to justify the capitalists' appropriation of the laborer's produce (C. I, 655). Elsewhere he writes:

Consider my abstinence; I might have played ducks and drakes with the 15 shillings; but instead of that I consumed it productively, and made yarn with it; . . . whatever may be the merit of his abstinence, there is nothing wherewith specially to remuner-

1. A distinction is drawn here between the ownership of the means of production or production process and ownership of money capital that is materialized in the process. Marx writes, "The investing capital derives his claim to profits of enterprise, and consequently the profit of enterprise itself, not from his ownership of capital, but from its production function as distinguished from the form, in which it is only inert property" (C. III, 446).

2. While Marx recognized the outward appearances of the freedom of contract and property rights in the capitalist economy, he also recognized the institutional framework within which these rights and freedoms were manifest. "Individual consumption provides, on the one hand, the means for their maintenance and reproduction; on the other hand, it secures by the annihilation of the necessaries of life, the continued reappearance of the workman in the labor-market . . . ; the wage-laborer is bound to his owner by invisible threads. The appearance of independence is kept up by means of constant change of employers, and by the fictio juris of contract" (C. I, 628). In the *Critique of the Gotha Programme,* Marx dissolves the distinction between wage and slave labor: ". . . the system of wage-labour is a system of slavery and to wit of a slavery which becomes more arduous in measure as the social productive forces of labour develop, whether the worker receives better or worse payment for his labour" (CGP, 41).

ate it, *because the value of the product is merely the sum of the values of the commodities that were thrown into the process of production.* Let him therefore console himself with the reflection that virtue is its own reward [C. I, 214; my italics].

And, in another passage, he says:

The simple dictates of humanity therefore plainly enjoin the release of the capitalist from this martyrdom and temptation, in the same way that the Georgian slave-owner was lately delivered, by the abolition of slavery, from the painful dilemma, whether to squander the surplus-product lashed out of his niggers, entirely in champagne, or whether to reconvert a part of it, into more niggers and more land [C. I, 655].

The functioning of the credit system, which facilitates the operation or expansion of the production process, depends upon several factors, among them, public savings. Marx writes, "The last illusion of the capitalist system, to the effect that capital is the fruit of one's own labor and saving, is thereby destroyed" (C. III, 597).

Marx even more briefly dismisses the theory of profit as reward for service:

Our friend, up to this time so purse-proud, suddenly assumes the modest demeanour of his own workman, and exclaims: "Have I myself not worked? Have I not performed the labor of superintendence and of overlooking the spinner? And does not this labor, too, create value?" His overlooker and his manager try to hide their smiles. Meanwhile, after a hearty laugh, he re-assumes his usual mien [C. I, 215].

In his analysis of interest, Marx draws the distinction between the industrial capitalist and the money capitalist; the former owns and controls the production process, the latter owns the actual capital fund. This separation, Marx writes, affords the industrial capitalist the opportunity of claiming profit as reward for service in contradistinction to the money capitalist. This claim, too, Marx finds unacceptable, saying of the industrial capitalist that

his brain necessarily conceives the idea, that his profit of enterprise, far from being in opposition to wage-labor and representing only the unpaid labor of others, is rather itself *wages of labor.* . . . The fact that his function as a capitalist consists in creating surplus-value . . . is entirely forgotten over the contrast, that the interest falls to the share of the capitalist, even if he does not perform any capitalist function and is merely the owner of capital. . . . The antagonistic form of the two parts, into which profit, or surplus-value is divided, leads him to forget, that both parts are surplus-value, and that this division does not alter the nature, origin and living conditions of surplus-value [C. III, 447].

The real separation of ownership and control of the production process is examined by Marx. The service provided by the controllers is recognized as wages of superintendence but is "entirely differentiated from the profit and assumes the form of wages for skilled labor" (C. III, 454). Consequently, Marx is able to write that "not the industrial capitalist, but the industrial managers are the souls of our industrial system" (C. III, 454).

(3) DETERMINATION OF THE MAGNITUDE OF PROFIT

"If we now compare the two processes of producing value and creating surplus-value, we see that the latter is nothing but the continuation of the former beyond a definite point" (C. I, 218). Recall that, in the formation of the expanded exchange,

$$M—C\ldots.. C'—M'$$

the difference between M' and M represented surplus value (Chap. 2, sec. 4). This exchange notation can be expressed with value equivalents

$$M—(c + v)\ldots[(c + v) + s]—M'$$

The variable s equals the change in M.

In analyzing the factors related to the production of surplus value, Marx rewrites the $c + v + s$ notation to incorporate the concept of the working day, L, into profit analysis, thus:

$$
\begin{aligned}
C &= c + v + s & \text{(2.1)} \\
&= c + L \\
s &= L - v & \text{(3.1)}
\end{aligned}
$$

Eq. (3.1) represents surplus value per laborer. It is simply that part of the working day, L, not devoted to v, the reproduction of the value of labor power. Marx distinguishes between surplus value resulting from changes in the length of the working day and surplus value resulting from changes in the value of labor power. The former he defines as absolute, the latter as relative, surplus value.

(a) ABSOLUTE SURPLUS VALUE: $s = f(L)$

(i) DETERMINATION OF THE WORKING DAY

"What is the working day? What is the length of time during which capital may consume the labor power whose daily value it buys? How far may the working day be extended beyond the working time necessary for the reproduction of the labor power itself?" (C. I, 290).

The working day, Marx notes, is upper-bounded. Clearly, it cannot exceed 24 hours. Apart from the time necessary for daily subsistence, the laborer must also rest, sleep, and in general revitalize his energies (C. I, 256). The minimum working day, on the other hand, is described as simply the subsistence time plus some minimal surplus value. Without such a surplus, no capitalist production is undertaken (C. I, 256). But Marx never quantifies this minimal surplus value.

The actual working day falls somewhere within this range. It may be, Marx speculates, 8 or 18 hours (C. I, 257). Its precise length varies with time, space, the supply of labor, and, on occasion, political influence. For example, he writes:

This organization of proletarians into a class . . . compels legislative recognition of particular interests of the workers, by taking advantage of the divisions among the bourgeoisie itself. Thus the ten-hour bill in England was carried [CM, 21–22].

In economies where legal limitations on the working day are set by government, capitalists maneuver around them by adding minutes before and after the legal workday and by trimming the legally specified time for meals. Marx quotes from the *Reports of the Inspectors of Factories:* " 'If you allow me,' said a highly respectable master to me, 'to work only ten minutes a day overtime, you put one thousand a year in my pocket. Moments are the elements of profit' " (C. I, 267). This is absolute surplus value.

Marx reproduces a table (C. I, 265) submitted by the inspector of factories illustrating the method of extracting extra hours of work:

Before 6 A.M.	15 minutes
After 6 P.M.	15 "
At breakfast time	10 "
At dinner time	20 "
	60 minutes
Five days	300 "
On Saturday before 6 A.M.	15 "
At breakfast time	10 "
After 2 P.M.	15 "
	40 minutes
Total weekly	340 minutes

Marx also discusses the formulation of the working day in the context of "two competing rights": the rights of the capitalist to prolong the working day to its maximum length, and the rights of the laborer to reduce the working day to one of "definite normal duration." Between these rights, force decides (C. I, 259). This force becomes the essence of class conflict:

Hence is it that in the history of capitalist production, the determination of what is a working day, presents itself as the result of a struggle, a struggle between collective capital, i.e., the class of capitalists, and collective labor, i.e., the working class [C. I, 259].

(ii) THE NORMAL WORKING DAY

The concept of the normal working day is peculiar to Marx's analysis of value and profit. It relates the length of the working day to that time which will produce, in the long run, the greatest surplus to the capitalist class. Consider Marx's development of the concept.

The determination of the normal working day depends upon the establishment of a specific working life-span for the laborer. Marx estimates this span at 30 years (C. I, 258).[3] The value of labor power per day is then $1/(365 \times 30)$ or $1/10950$ of his total labor power. If, by extending the working day, the capitalist uses up in one day a quantity of labor power greater than that which the laborer can restore in three, or, in other words, if he consumes the laborer's lifetime labor power in 10 instead of 30 years, the daily value of labor power should be $1/3650$ instead of $1/10950$ of the total labor power. But if the capitalist exploits labor so that working span is 10 years, why then does Marx assume the average span at 30 years? Nowhere does he introduce into the analysis the replenishing of the labor supply.

To the extent that capitalists succeed in extending the working day beyond a specific limit, they deplete the labor supply. There are costs involved in replenishing this supply which must be subtracted from the additions to surplus generated by the working-day extension. If these costs exceed the additional surplus, the extension is uneconomic. In this context Marx compares the prolongation of the working day in slave and nonslave economies. In the slave system excessive exploitation of slave labor is consistent, Marx argues, with the conditions of the labor market

3. The 30-year working span of the laborer is nowhere explained by Marx. It must therefore be treated merely as an assumption introduced into the system. While Marx fails to provide any scientific basis for the selection of 30 years, he emphatically rejects the ethical implication that it may suggest (C. I, 258). However, in dealing with the political struggle for the normal working day, morality becomes the only substantial basis for the Marxian argument (C. I, 291).

which he describes as "teeming preserves" (C. I, 292). He quotes J. Cairnes's *The Slave Power* to illustrate:

The rice grounds of Georgia, or the swamps of the Mississippi may be fatally injurious to the human constitution; but the waste of human life which the cultivation of these districts necessitates, is not so great that it cannot be repaired from the teeming preserves of Virginia and Kentucky. . . . It is accordingly a maxim of slave management, in slave-importing countries, that the most effective economy is that which takes out of the human chattel in the shortest space of time the utmost amount of exertion it is capable of putting forth [C. I, 292–93].

The exploitation was carried to such an extent that "as the export of cotton became of vital interest to these states, the over-working of the negro and sometimes the using up of his life in 7 years of labor became a factor in a calculated and calculating system" (C. I, 260). On the other hand, such unrestrained extensions of the working day in a nonslave system, Marx argues, would be generally unprofitable. Setting the working day at some "normal duration" (C. I, 258) or "rational dimension" (VPP, 108) is the best strategy for maximizing profits. The tendency, however, is to transgress this normal duration. For while limitation of the working day maximizes aggregate surplus for the capitalist class, each capitalist, operating independently, takes as given the supply of labor and extends the day beyond the normal time in an attempt to increase individual surplus.

(b) RELATIVE SURPLUS VALUE: $s = f(v)$

The application of machinery to production is one of the most important factors influencing the magnitude of relative surplus value. Although itself not a source of value, constant capital none the less affects the productiveness of labor. The labor productivity determines the allocation of the working day between labor power and surplus:

The value of commodities is in inverse ratio to the productiveness of labor. And so, too, the value of the labor-power, because it depends on the values of commodities. Relative surplus value is, on the contrary, directly proportional to that productiveness. It rises with rising and falls with falling productiveness [C. I, 350].[4]

4. And Marx continues: "If, in consequence of increased productiveness, the value of the necessities of life fall, and the value of a day's labor-power be thereby reduced from five shillings to three, the surplus value increases from one shilling to three. Ten hours were necessary for the reproduction of the value of labor-

Marx defines productiveness of labor as "an alteration in the labor process of such a kind as to shorten the labor time socially necessary for the production of a commodity, and to endow a given quantity of labor with the power of producing a greater quantity of use-value" (C. I, 345). Modern machinery, Marx claims, has already given rise to an increase in the productiveness of labor of an "extraordinary degree" (C. I, 422). The maximum relative surplus value resulting from the employment of machinery is determined at that point where the labor expenses incurred in the manufacturing of the machine are equal to the relative surplus value forthcoming from the machine's employment (C. I, 426–27).

But greater utilization of machinery also affects the quality of the labor power employed. As technology advances, reliance upon muscular power diminishes, and this permits employment of women and children. As more members of the family join the labor force, the value of labor power, measured by the provision for family subsistence, depreciates:

To purchase the labor-power of a family of four workers may, perhaps, cost more than it formerly did to purchase the labor-power of the head of the family, but, in return, four days' labor takes the place of one, and their price falls in proportion to the excess of the surplus-labor of four over the surplus-labor of one. In order that the family may live, four people must now, not only labor, but expend surplus-labor for the capitalist. Thus, we see, that machinery, while augmenting the human material that forms the principal object of capital's exploiting power, at the same time raises the degree of exploitation [C. I, 431–32].

Changes in the physical composition of the laborer's subsistence or in the prices of those commodities that constitute subsistence directly affect the value of labor power (C. III, 98). Marx writes:

The cheapened commodity . . . causes only a pro tanto fall in the value of labor-power, a fall proportional to the extent of that

---

power; now only six are required. Four hours have been set free, and can be annexed to the domain of surplus-labor" (C. I, 350–51). Throughout the first and third volumes of *Capital*, Marx repeatedly makes this point. Yet, in the Preface to *Capital*, Vol. III, Engels criticizes Professor Julius Wolf for making this same observation on Marx's analysis. Engels writes, "Furthermore, the assertion that according to Marx, relative surplus-value increases in proportion as the constant capital is augmented while the variable capital decreases, is so astounding that it defies all parliamentarian language. And finally Mr. Julius Wolf demonstrates in every line that he has neither relatively nor absolutely the least understanding of relative or absolute surplus-value" (C. III, 26–27).

commodity's employment in the reproduction of labor-power. Shirts, for instance, are a necessary means of subsistence, but are only one out of many. The totality of the necessaries of life consists, however, of various commodities, each a product of a distinct industry; and the value of each of those commodities enters as a component part into the value of labor-power. This latter value decreases with a decrease in the labor-time necessary for its reproduction; the total decrease being the sum of all the different curtailments of labor-time effected in those various and distinct industries. . . . Whenever an individual capitalist cheapens shirts . . . he by no means necessarily aims at reducing the value of labor-power and shortening, pro tanto, the necessary labor-time. But it is only in so far as he ultimately contributes to this result, that he assists in raising the general rate of surplus-value [C. I, 346–47].

Marx cites a historical case. The capitalists urged the working class to support the repeal of the Corn Laws, promising them, in return for their support, the enactment of the Ten Hour Bill. The repeal in effect lowered the prices of staple commodities, which thereby reduced the value of labor power (C. I, 308). To the extent that the value of labor power falls, relative surplus value is augmented.

The advent of modern industry also introduces modifications in the social organization of production from which emerge greater quantities of relative surplus value (C. I, 353). Efficiency in social organization, Marx states, is a function of the division of labor or the degree of cooperation in the production process. Increases in the number of laborers employed in a process permit greater specialization and, consequently, increased relative surplus value:

$$s = f(v[n])$$

Marx enumerates the factors underlying the "powers of cooperation" which tend to heighten labor productiveness and relative surplus value:

1. The increase in the mechanical forces of labor (C. I, 361).
2. The extension of the "sphere of action" over a greater space (C. I, 360).
3. The contraction of the field of production relative to the scale of production (C. I, 360).
4. The setting, at critical moments, of large masses of laborers to work (C. I, 360).
5. The excitement of emulation between individuals, which raises their animal spirits (C. I, 358).

6. The impression of continuity on all operations (C. I, 361).
7. The simultaneous performance of different operations (C. I, 359).
8. The economization of the means of production by use in common (C. I, 356).
9. The development of the character of average social labor from individual labor (C. I, 355).
10. Reconversion of the waste products of production into new elements of production (C. III, 95).

The extent to which each of the above factors becomes operative in the production process depends upon the individual sphere, the social environment, and the efficiency of management (C. III, 100). Factors which Marx considers as part of the social environment include the physical assemblage in one locale, the density of population, and the existence of sufficient capital stock in the hands of one capitalist or group of capitalists working together.

Too, the adoption of machinery and the extension of division of labor have adverse effects upon labor skills. The shift from handicraft to manufacture tends to reduce occupational skills to "a class of so-called unskilled laborers" (C. I, 384). The cost of apprenticeship, Marx observes, is inversely related to the degree of specialization. Thus, as these costs decline, the value of labor power falls. He writes:

The fall in the value of labor-power, caused by the disappearance or diminution of the expense of apprenticeship, implies a direct increase of surplus-value for the benefit of capital; *for everything that shortens the necessary labor-time required for the reproduction of labor-power, extends the domain of surplus-labor* [C. I, 385; italics added].

The prolongation of the working day also provides for lower managerial labor costs and therefore greater relative surplus value (C. III, 94).

Although monetary values are merely reflectors of the real world and as such cannot contribute to surplus value, monetary changes do affect the relative distribution of the working day between the values of labor power and surplus value. Marx considers a rise in price levels resulting from the discovery of richer deposits of gold or the legal depreciation of currency. If wages do not rise proportionately to the price-level increase to compensate for the increase in the value of necessities, "the price of labor power would sink below the value of labor power" (VPP, 102). Marx writes, "All history proves that wherever such depreciation of money occurs, the capitalists are on the alert to seize this opportunity for defrauding the workman" (VPP, 105).

(c) SURPLUS VALUE AND CAPITAL DEPRECIATION

Prolongation of the working day provides for more rapid utilization of constant capital. This increased speed of capital absorption into the production process reduces the cost of capital depreciation and thereby affects the magnitude of surplus value. Marx analyzes three forms of capital depreciation: (1) *circulatory,* the direct physical consumption of capital in the production process; (2) *nonuse,* capital "idleness"; [5] and (3) *moral,*[6] loss of exchange value, "either by machinery of the same sort being produced cheaper than it, or by better machines entering into competition with it" (C. I, 442). Circulatory depreciation varies directly with the length of the working day while nonuse and moral depreciation vary inversely to it.

If the working day were lengthened, the machinery employed would be depreciated in a shorter period of time. This reduces the penalty of moral depreciation, i.e., of operating less efficient machines if new and more productive machines become available (C. I, 631). Moral depreciation, d_m is measured by

$$d_m = c_1 - c_2 \qquad (3.2)$$

where c_1 represents the value of the machine at the beginning of the process and c_2 the value of the new machine introduced during the production period. To cut down the possibility of this moral depreciation, relay systems of alternate shifts to provide for continuous production are introduced (C. I, 282).

(4) MARXIAN THEORY OF INNOVATION

(a) SOCIAL AND INDIVIDUAL VALUES

The exchange value of any commodity on the market is determined by the socially necessary labor time embodied in its production (see

5. Nonuse depreciation is thus defined by Marx: "Constant capital . . . only exists to absorb labor. . . . While they fail to do this, their mere existence causes a relative loss to the capitalist, for they represent during the time they lie fallow, a useless advance of capital. And this loss becomes positive and absolute as soon as the intermission of their employment necessitates additional outlay at the recommencement of work" (C. I, 282).

6. "Moral depreciation" equals "technological obsolescence." The word "moral" in this odd usage has become embedded in Marxian terminology. Marx's translator would perhaps have served his meaning better by translating the original German by "social" or "cultural."

Chap. 2, sec. 3). Marx calls this exchange value *real* or *social* (C. I, 348). Any capitalist operating under "normal" conditions with an outlay of constant (c) and variable (v) capital can realize from production a normal profit (s) (C. III, 398). Under normal conditions the individual commodity value produced, C_i, coincides with the commodity's social value, C_s, which can be expressed as

$$C_s = C_i \qquad (3.3)$$

In cases where capitalists operate with less than normal efficiency or under conditions less favorable than normal, the individual commodity value, C_i, would be higher, i.e., it would embody a greater quantity of labor than that value which can be realized on the market, C_s (C. III, 210). In this case,

$$C_i > C_s$$

The capitalist's profit or surplus value, in this instance, would be less than normal; it would be the quantity determined by

$$S_i = C_s - (c_i + v_i) \qquad (3.4)$$

The stability of the market exchange value depends upon the stability of demand and supply conditions (see Chap. 2, sec. 8). If the demand for the commodity contracts, then the social value falls, and capitalists who were formerly realizing normal profits receive a diminished surplus. Marx writes:

If the market cannot stomach the whole quantity at the normal price . . . this proves that too great a portion of the total labor of the community has been expended. . . . The effect is the same as if each individual . . . had expended more labor-time upon his particular product than is socially necessary [C. I, 120].

Where capitalists can produce a commodity under conditions more favorable than normal or where demand for the commodity increases, profit realized would be greater than normal. The increase in profit, over and above normal, Marx calls *extra surplus value* or *surplus profit* (S_e). Here, less labor is expended than is considered socially necessary,

$$C_s > C_i$$

Therefore,

$$S_e = C_s - C_i \qquad (3.5)$$

The total profit of capitalists operating under such favorable conditions, therefore, is [7]

$$S = S_n + S_e \tag{3.6}$$

(b) EFFECT OF INNOVATION ON PROFIT

Innovation in the Marxian system is defined to mean the institution of a "new method" of commodity production.[8] The Marxian innovation appears in three forms, viz., labor-saving, characterized by increasing organic composition of capital; capital-saving, characterized by decreasing organic composition of capital; and neutral innovations, which have no effect on capital composition.[9] The labor-saving innovations are the most common in the Marxian system and form the basis of the Marxian dynamic model. The economic effects of all Marxian innovations, however, are identical—the reduction of labor time required to produce a given quantity of commodities. Innovating profit thus results:

$$C_e > C_i$$

7. Marx assumes (C. III, 752) that commodity exchange value is equal to price of production:

$$C_1 = P_1$$

Now

$$P_1 = K_1 + p'k \tag{2.7}$$

Assume $k_1 = 100$, and $p' = 15\%$, therefore $P_1 = 115$. Assume, conditions more favorable than normal, $k_2 = 90$; therefore

$$P_2 = k_2 + p'k_2$$
$$103\frac{1}{2} = 90 + 15\% \, (90)$$

Since

$$S = S_n + S_e$$

therefore,

$$S = 15\% \, (90) + (115 - 103\frac{1}{2})$$
$$= 13.5 + 11.5$$
$$= 25$$

8. Nowhere does Marx explicitly employ the concept of "innovation," although "change in technique," "new method," "invention," and "technological applications of science" are used interchangeably.

9. Actually, all techniques of production that give rise to surplus profit in the Marxian system are labor-saving—by definition—since all value is measured in terms of labor content. Distinction between "labor-saving" and "capital-saving" methods can be made in this analysis only by distinguishing the labor savings in variable and constant capital. If an innovation provides for a reduction of labor materialized in constant capital, then it is called capital-saving. If the labor-saving is concentrated in the variable component, it is labor-saving. If the innovation results in a reduction of both constant and variable, i.e., the constant-variable ratio remains constant, the innovation is neutral. These concepts, it must be noted, are *not* Marxian, but are employed none the less to classify the innovation which Marx refers to in his major works (see C. III, 751).

Therefore,

$$S_e = C_s - C_i \qquad (3.5)$$

$(C_s - C_i)$ is greater than zero only under conditions of less than perfect competition. If the market were perfectly competitive, instantaneous adjustment of real or social commodity value to the lowered individual commodity value would result, with the consequent elimination of extra surplus value. Marx writes that when machinery is first introduced into the industry, it maintains a "sort of monopoly" where profits are "exceptional" (C. I, 444). Innovating profit is thus dependent upon the existence of temporary monopoloid market structures. Market-price movements, from C_s to C_i, depend upon two variables: (1) the effect of the innovator's increased supply upon the demand and supply conditions in the commodity market, and (2) the ability and rapidity of other capitalists to imitate the innovator. Marx describes the behavior of the innovator thus:

If he can for example produce a whole yard of linen in the same labor time in which his competitors weave half a yard, how will this capitalist operate?

He could continue to sell half a yard of linen at the old market price; this would, however, be no means of driving his opponents from the field and of enlarging his own sales. But in the same measure in which his production has expanded, his *need to sell also increased*. The more powerful and costly means of production that he has called into life *enable* him, indeed, to sell his commodities more cheaply, they *compel* him, however, *to sell more commodities,* to conquer a much *larger* market for his commodities; consequently our capitalist will sell his half yard of linen more cheaply than his competitors.

The capitalist will not, however, sell a whole yard as cheaply as his competitors sell half a yard, although the production of the whole yard does not cost him more than the half yard costs the others. Otherwise he would not gain anything extra but only get back the cost of production by the exchange . . . ; he attains the object he wishes to attain, if he puts the price of the goods only a small percentage lower than that of his competitors. He drives them from the field, then wrests from them at least part of their sales by underselling them [WLC, 44–45].

The eventual adoption of the innovation by the capitalist's competitors, with the resulting increase in commodity supply on the market, erases the innovator's monopoly profit and reduces the market price to a lower commodity social value (C. III, 755). Marx writes:

As soon as the new mode of production begins to expand, and thereby to furnish tangible proof that these commodities can actually be produced more cheaply, the capitalists working under the old methods of production must sell their products below their full prices of production, because the value of these commodities has fallen, because the labor time required by these capitalists for the production of these commodities is longer than the social average. In one word—this appears as the effect of competition—*these capitalists are compelled to introduce the new method of production* under which the proportion of the variable to the constant capital has been reduced [C. III, 311; italics added].

(c) THE INNOVATOR

The innovator, as an individual, is considered as a "built-in mechanism" in the Marxian model. He is the logical resultant of the capitalist system and as such commands little attention in his capacity as the creator of new methods. The innovations introduced into the economy are described by Marx as products of such obscure entities as "modern industry," "technology," "science," "progress of industry," and "gifts of history." Marx makes one exception to his evasion of the "innovating character" of the capitalist:

This circumstance, that a man without wealth, but with energy, solidity, ability and business sense may become a capitalist . . . is very much admired by the apologists of the capitalist system, and the commercial value of each individual is pretty accurately estimated under the capitalist mode of production. Although this circumstance continually brings an unwelcome number of new soldiers of fortune into the field and into competition with the already existing individual capitalists, it also secures the supremacy of capital itself, expands its basis, and *enables it to recruit ever new forces for itself out of the lower layers of society.* In a similar way . . . the Catholic Church in the Middle Ages formed its hierarchy out of the best brains of the people without regard to estate, birth, or wealth; [this] was one of the principal means of fortifying priest rule and suppressing the laity. *The more a ruling class is able to assimilate the most prominent men of a ruled class, the more solid and dangerous is its rule* [C. III, 705–6; italics added].

The application of an innovation in an industry, Marx states, produces cumulative effects, both internal and external to the industry. Considering the cumulative internal process of innovations, Marx writes:

When machinery is first introduced into an industry, new methods of producing it more cheaply follow blow upon blow, and so do improvements, that not only affect individual parts and details of the machine, but its entire build [C. I, 442].[10]

The original innovator is thus forced to innovate again: "The same game begins again. More division of labor, more machinery, enlarged scale of exploitation of machinery and division of labor. And again competition brings the same counteraction against this result" (WLC, 45). Innovation in a specific process of production, Marx states, because of industrial interdependence in the capitalist system, compels the introduction of innovations in complementary industries so that the increased product resulting from the innovation can be absorbed in the product market and the increased factor requirements needed for the enlarged scale of production will be forthcoming. Marx writes:

The revolution in cotton spinning calls forth the invention of the gin, for separating the seeds from the cotton fibre; it was only by means of this invention, that the production of cotton became possible on the enormous scale at the present required. But more especially, the revolution in the modes of production of industry and agriculture *made necessary* a revolution in the general conditions of the social process of production, i.e., in the means of communication and of transport [C. I, 419; italics added].

(5) CONCLUSION

Profit, or surplus value, in the Marxian system is derived solely from the process of production. Profit formation is divided into two major classifications, absolute and relative, the distinction being based upon the source of labor exploitation, i.e., upon the prolongation of the working day or the increase in labor productiveness. The formation of relative surplus value is the more significant factor in the Marxian system. This is particularly interesting since the development of relative surplus value is primarily contingent upon the increasing mechanization of production, i.e., constant capital. Yet Marx insists that all surplus

10. Marx quotes C. Babbage, *On the Economy of Machinery* (1832), "It has been estimated, roughly, that the first individual of a newly-invented machine will cost about five times as much as the construction of the second" (C. I, 442 n.). Marx himself writes, "The far greater cost of operating an establishment based on a new invention as compared to later establishments arising out of the ruins of the first one, as it were. This is carried to such an extent that the first leaders in a new enterprise are generally bankrupted, and only those who later buy the buildings, machinery, etc., cheaper, make money out of it. It is, therefore, generally the most worthless and miserable sort of money-capitalists who draw the greatest benefits out of the universal labor of the human mind and its co-operative application in society" (C. III, 124).

is derived from the variable component. The Marxian innovation is the critical variable in Marx's dynamic model. The innovation is incorporated into profit analysis as a special case of surplus profit.

The analysis undertaken in this chapter is fundamental to an understanding of the predictions developed in Part II. The development of the prediction on the falling rate of profit is almost exclusively dependent upon the material examined here. Other chapters, particularly Chapter 9, section 1, on international market expansion; Chapter 10, sections 2 and 3, on the industrial cycle; Chapter 11, section 2, on the misery of the proletariat; and Chapter 12, section 2, on the prophecies of communism, explicitly refer to the analysis of profit here expounded.

4

Interest

THE PURPOSE OF THIS BRIEF CHAPTER is to construct the Marxian theory of interest. In the analysis of interest and interest-rate determination, the institutions of banking and credit are examined and incorporated into the Marxian economic system. The emergence of the money-capitalist class and its relation to the industrial capitalist are also considered. The chapter concludes with an exposition of Marx's capitalization principle and its relevance to money-capital formation and interest-rate determination.

(1) DEFINITION OF INTEREST

The payment made to the money capitalist by the industrial capitalist for the use of the former's money in the production process is called *interest*. Marx writes:

That part of the profit, which he [the industrial capitalist] pays to the owner [money capitalist], is called interest. It is merely another name, a special term, for a certain part of the profit, which capital in process of its function has to give up to its owner, instead of keeping it in its own pockets [C. III, 398].

Interest (i) thus emerges in the Marxian system with the separation of the ownership of the production process from the ownership of the monetary funds required to finance the process. Where both forms of ownership are consolidated in one individual or group of individuals acting as a unit, then interest, in the Marxian sense, does not appear. "If," Marx writes, "all capital were in the hands of the industrial-capitalist, there would be no interest and no rate of interest" (C. III, 443).

Where separation of ownership exists, the institution of money-borrowing and lending develops. The borrowers, who are owners of production processes, Marx calls *industrial capitalists*. Moneylenders, or owners of monetary funds, Marx calls *money capitalists* (C. III, 412). The commodity borrowed and loaned is defined as *money capital*. The distinction made here between money and money capital is of salient importance; while they may possess identical physical properties, they differ functionally. Only money capital has the unique property of possessing dual use values, viz., universal equivalence in commodity exchange and serviceability to the production process (C. III, 399). Thus, when money capitalists advance funds, they advance not money per se but capital (C. III, 410).

Interest, Marx notes, is not a price of money capital. "To call interest the price of capital," he claims, "is to use at the outset an irrational expression" (C. III, 417). The concept of price signified the expression of value in money terms. Money capital is essentially a sum of money, and consequently any value of money capital is, by definition, its own price:

It [money capital] is the use-value, which the money assumes by being capable of being invested as capital and performing the functions of capital, so that it can create a definite surplus-value, the average profit . . . during its process, in addition to pre- serving its original magnitude of value [C. III, 413].

None the less, interest payments do express, Marx argues, the self- expansion of money capital and thus *appear* as a price which the lender received for it (C. III, 418). The return on money capital is divorced, in the Marxian system, from any implication of productiveness; it is "not the expression, not the consequence or result, of a definite series of economic processes, but the outcome of a specific legal agreement between buyer and seller" (C. III, 410).

The existence of the money capitalist depends exclusively upon the existence of the industrial capitalist. An individual possessing money has the choice of investing his money as money capital, i.e., in interest-bearing property, or investing it as industrial capital, i.e., productively (C. III, 443). If the individual invests it productively, he assumes the role of industrial capitalist, and the return on his money capital is defined as profit. If, however, he chooses to invest his funds as money capital per se, he must find industrial capitalists who are willing to borrow the funds to invest productively. *It is only from the produc- tion process that profits emerge, and it is only from profits that interest can be paid.* Marx writes:

The idea of a conversion of the total capital of society into money-capital without the existence of people, who shall buy and utilize the means of production, which form the total capital with the exception of [a] relatively small portion existing in the shape of money, is sheer nonsense. It implies the additional nonsense, that capital could yield interest on the basis of capitalist production without performing any productive function, in other words, without producing any surplus-value, of which interest would be but a part; that the capitalist mode of production could run its course without any capitalist production [C. III, 444].

The symbolic representation of exchange developed in Chapter 2, section 4, can be expanded to incorporate the separation of monetary ownership from the process itself. In the accompanying diagram M_a

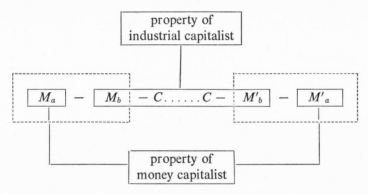

represents the value of money advanced by the money capitalists, M_b the money capital in the hands of the owner of the production process, M'_b the money equivalent of the commodity, and M'_a the quantity of money returned to the money capitalist who advanced the funds.

The analysis of interest lies outside the sphere of production. "It is our assumption," Marx writes, "that this entire transaction takes place between two kinds of capitalists, the money-capitalist and the industrial or the merchant capitalist" (C. III, 416). The contract between borrower and lender is thus represented in $M_a - M_b$ and in $M'_b - M'_a$ (the dotted boxes). The magnitude of interest is determined by $(M'_a - M_a)$, while industrial profit, the net return to the industrial capitalist, is consequently reduced by that value, i.e., from $(M'_b - M_b)$ to $[(M'_b - M'_a) - M_b]$.

Marx quotes from the *Economist:* "The relation between the amount paid for the use of some capital and this capital itself expresses the rate of interest, measured in money" (C. III, 421). The rate of interest, i', can be symbolized by

$$i' = \frac{M'_a - M_a}{M_a} \tag{4.1}$$

(2) DETERMINATION OF THE MAGNITUDE OF INTEREST

The magnitude of interest payments depends primarily upon two factors: (1) the prevailing rate of profit in the economy and (2) the relative strength of the demand for and supply of loanable funds in the money market (C. III, 419). The maximum limit to interest payment on a specific money loan to an industrial capitalist is the surplus value that results from the productive employment of the money capital. Interest would coincide, in this case, with profit (C. III, 437). At this maximum, industrial capitalists receive zero net profits. The minimum limit to interest payments, Marx states, is indefinable, that is, it may approach any depth, e.g., zero. In this extreme case the industrial capitalist would realize all surplus value created. Interest payments in the capitalist economy, therefore, fluctuate between the two limits

$$s \geqslant i \geqslant 0 \tag{4.2}$$

The relationship between the money capitalists and industrial capitalists is therefore antagonistic; an increase in the return to one class, *ceteris paribus,* is achieved only at the expense of the other; whereas, in relation to the laborer, from whom the surplus is exploited, the interests of both the money and industrial capitalists appear to agree. An increase in the degree of exploitation, assuming the profit-interest ratio constant, augments both interest payments to the money capitalists and profits to the industrial capitalists.

Unlike the determination of profits, which result from "general laws" operating within the production process, the determination of interest, Marx writes, is founded upon a quite different and less profound basis— the conditions of demand and supply of loanable funds (C. III, 431). The prevailing interest rate depends, therefore, solely upon the bargaining strengths of the borrowers and lenders of loanable funds. When supply of money capital is short relative to demand, interest rates are high; and, the converse, when supply is relatively large, interest rates are low. In this respect, determination of interest rates is similar to the determination of market prices of commodities. Those factors which influence the quantity of loanable funds determine, therefore, the magnitude of interest rates.

The supply of loanable funds on the money market, Marx states, is conditioned by (1) the size of the money-capitalist class, (2) the development of the credit and banking systems, (3) the savings of the community, (4) the international flow of precious metals, and (5) the customs and legal traditions of the society.

The allocation of funds by money-owners between productive and money investments is an important determinant of interest rates. Assuming the demand for money capital to be constant,[1] the larger the class of money capitalists, the greater will be the supply of funds on the loanable-funds market. Under competitive market conditions, interest rates vary inversely with supply.[2] Marx analyzes the development of the money-capitalist class; quoting from Ramsay's *Essay on the Distribution of Wealth,* he writes:

As a people progresses in the development of wealth, there arises and grows more and more a class of people, who find themselves possessed of funds through the labors of their ancestors, and who can live on the mere interest on them. . . . In old and rich countries . . . that portion of the national capital, whose owners do not care to invest it themselves, makes up a larger proportion of the total productive capital of society than in newly settled and poor countries [C. III, 425].

The development of the banking and credit institutions in the Marxian system is coincident with the development of the capitalist mode of production. The banking system, through the process of deposit aggregation, becomes itself a "money capitalist" for the industrial class, making available on the money market a greater supply of loanable funds. Marx says:

With the development of the bank system, and particularly as soon as they pay interest on deposits, the money savings and the temporarily unemployed money of *all classes* are deposited with them. Small amounts, each by itself incapable of acting in the capacity of money-capital, are combined into large masses and thus form money power . . . ; since they are cashiers of the industrial-capitalists, there is concentrated into their hands the money-capital, which every producer and merchant must have as a reserve fund, or which he receives in payment. These funds are thus converted into loanable capital. In this way the reserve fund of the commercial world, being concentrated into a common treasury, is reduced to its necessary minimum, and a portion of the

1. It is interesting to note that in analyzing the demand and supply conditions on the loanable-funds market, Marx continuously discounted the forces on the demand side. Fluctuation in the interest rate is made almost exclusively a function of changing supply. A comparison can be made with Marx's treatment of production and market capacities in Chapter 10. Here, too, emphasis is placed on the supply outrunning the market capacity.

2. "So long as the scale of production remains the same, this expansion leads only to an abundance of the loanable money-capital compared to the productive. Hence the rate of interest is low" (C. III, 573).

money-capital, which would otherwise slumber as a reserve fund, is loaned and serves as interest-bearing capital [C. III, 473; italics added].

The credit system facilitates the conversion of commodity capital to money capital through the procedure of discounting bills of exchange, i.e., by obtaining loans on the security of commodities:

Commodities are not sold for money, but for a written promise to pay for them at a certain date. We may comprise all these promises to pay for brevity's sake under the general category of bills of exchange. Such bills of exchange in their turn circulate as means of payment until the day on which they fall due; and they form commercial money in the strict meaning of the term. . . . Just as these mutual advances of producers . . . form the real foundation of credit, so their instrument of circulation, the bill of exchange, forms the basis of credit money proper [C. III, 469–70].

Interest rates, Marx writes, depend upon the ease at which these bills of exchange can be discounted by the banking system (C. III, 511).[3] The ability to obtain such credit, Marx states, is subject to the prevailing and expected economic conditions and banking legislation (C. III, 708). While the short-run changes in economic conditions may alter credit policy, the overriding development of the institution and its effect on the money supply, Marx argues, lead to a general depression of interest rates:

The development of the credit system, and with it the continually growing control of the industrialists and merchants over the money savings of all classes of society by the co-operation of bankers, and the progressive concentration of these savings into such volumes as will enable them to serve as money-capital, must also depress the rate of interest somewhat [C. III, 425].

International movement of precious metals, Marx states, influences the magnitude of banking reserves, which in turn affects the level of interest rates:

If this export of precious metals assumes a larger scope and lasts longer, then the English bank reserve is touched, and the English money market, with the Bank of England at the head, must take precautionary measures. These consist mainly, as we have already seen, in the raising of the rate of interest. When the drain of gold is considerable, the money market is always difficult, that is, the

3. In discussing precapitalist conditions and the historical evolution of the money economies, Marx refers to the development of commercial credit and the level of interest rates (C. III, 707, 709).

demand for loan capital in the form of money exceeds the supply by far, and the raising of the rate of interest follows quite naturally from this; the rate of discount fixed by the Bank of England corresponds to this condition and asserts itself on the market. However, there are cases, where the drain of metal is due to other than the ordinary combinations of business (for instance, to loans of foreign states, investment of capital in foreign countries, etc.), when the London money market in that respect does not justify such an effective raise of the rate of interest; in that case the Bank of England must first make money "scarce" by heavy loans in the "open market" and thus create artificially a condition, which justifies a raise of the rate of interest, or renders it necessary; a maneuver, which becomes from year to year more difficult for it [C. III, 674–75].

Factors quite unrelated to the demand and supply conditions, such as custom and legal tradition, Marx writes, "have as much to do with the determination of the average rate of interest as competition itself" (C. III, 427). While Marx was not particularly concerned with interest-rate differentials in various investment fields, the factor of risk as an element of interest is suggested. Contrasting the investment of the "do-nothing" landlords with the usurer, Marx writes, "Only the usurer would at least risk his own capital in the operation" (C. III, 733). Again, in contrast with "other investments": "Since landed property is considered in all old countries as a particularly noble form of property, and its purchase also an eminently safe investment of capital, the rate of interest at which groundrent is bought is generally lower than that of other investments" (C. III, 731).

(3) PRINCIPLE OF CAPITALIZATION

In the analysis of industrial-credit formation, Marx distinguishes between the creation of capital funds and the conversion of capital funds from one form to another. In the legitimate banking operation of discounting bills of exchange, no capital value is created. All that takes place, Marx asserts, is a transfer of commodity capital to the money-capital form:

The ordinary business man discounts, in order to anticipate the money-form of his capital and thereby to keep his process of reproduction in flow; not in order to expand his business or secure additional capital, but in order to balance the credit which he gives by the credit which he takes. And if he wants to expand his business on credit, the discounting of bills will do him little good, because it is merely the transformation of capital, which he has already in his hands, from one form into another; he will rather take up a direct loan for a long time [C. III, 503].

Capital is created through the discounting process, however, when the banking system extends credit on nonexistent commodity capital, that is, on fraudulent bills of exchange. This form of creation Marx defines as *fictitious capital* (C. III, 481–88).

"The forming of a fictitious capital is called capitalizing" (C. III, 548). *Certificates of indebtedness*, which command an annual fixed income for indefinite periods of time, have market values which are determined by the magnitude of the prevailing rate of interest and the fixed periodic income. Thus

$$CV = y/i' \tag{4.3}$$

where CV represents the capital value of the certificate of indebtedness, y the fixed income per period, and i' the interest rate. For example,

If the annual income is 100 pounds sterling and the rate of interest 5%, then these 100 pounds sterling would represent the annual interest on 2,000 pounds sterling, and these 2,000 pounds sterling are regarded as the capital-value of the legal title of ownership upon these 100 pounds sterling annually [C. III, 548].

These interest-bearing certificates, mainly in the form of government securities, i.e., bonds and treasury notes, compose, in varying degrees, an element of banking capital (C. III, 545). When there exists a surplus of money capital, which would tend to lower the interest rate, a creation of government demand for money capital, by issuance of securities, exerts an upward pressure on the interest rate. Marx quotes from *The Currency Question Reviewed:*

In England, a steady accumulation of additional wealth takes place, which has a tendency to assume ultimately the form of money. But next to the desire to acquire money, the most insistent desire is that of disposing of it by some kind of investment bringing interest or profit. . . . *For a long series of years the national debt was the great means of absorbing the superfluous wealth of England* [C. III, 489; italics added].

To a large extent, government securities compose this fictitious capital (C. III, 546).

Marx recognized yet another form of fictitious capital, viz., the increase in the capital value of certificates of indebtedness that arises from an increase in the rate of return to a particular enterprise, i.e., a

5–10 per cent return on an investment of 100 pounds sterling of stock. Assuming the rate of interest constant at 5 per cent, the capital value of the stock would increase from 100 to 200 pounds sterling, which, Marx claims, represents a creation of 100 pounds sterling of fictitious capital.

(4) CONCLUSION

Interest, in the Marxian system, is a derivative of surplus. Its magnitude depends essentially upon the magnitude of the surplus and the market forces for loanable funds. The determination of interest (or the interest rate) in the Marxian analysis is almost exclusively a study of the supply conditions in the loanable-funds market. Interest and the interest recipients (money capitalists), however, play a subordinate role in the Marxian system. Marx's analysis of the capitalist economy is primarily an analysis of commodity production. Since the determination of the interest rate and the relation between the money and industrial capitalists occur outside the framework of commodity production, their influence upon the development of the capitalist system is almost totally discounted. None the less, as a derivative of surplus, interest does affect the share of profit which the industrial capitalists receive, and, in this respect, fluctuations in the interest rate will affect the return to the latter class. Since, as we shall see, commodity production is dependent upon the maintenance of a return to industrial capitalists above a specific minimum, interest rates may be said to influence the growth of the capitalist economy.

The analysis undertaken in this chapter is fundamental to an understanding of the predictions developed in Part II, specifically those in Chapter 8, section 1, dealing with the effect of interest rates on profit rates; Chapter 10, sections 2, 3, and 5, dealing with the effect of credit on the industrial cycle; Chapter 11, section 2b, dealing with the industrial reserve army; and Chapter 12, section 2, dealing with the institution of a communist society.

5

Rent

THIS CHAPTER considers Marx's theory of rent. An examination of the theory includes an explicit definition of rent, an exposition of its source, and an analysis of the variables which determine its magnitude. Marx divides rent into three classifications: (1) differential rent I, resulting from extensive land cultivation; (2) differential rent II, resulting from intensive land cultivation; and (3) absolute rent, the return to the monopoly of land. Each classification is examined; the assumptions and variables, in each case, are made explicit. The chapter concludes with an analysis of land-price determination.

(1) DEFINITION OF AGRICULTURAL PRODUCTION AND GROUND RENT

"Landed property," Marx says, "is conditioned on the monopolization of certain portions of the globe by private persons, for the purpose of making these portions the exclusive spheres of their private will and keeping all others away from it" (C. III, 722).

The capitalist mode of production in agriculture is analogous to the capitalist mode of production in manufacturing, Marx points out, the latter producing yarn, coats, etc., while the former mode is defined by the production of principal plant crops (C. III, 721). Both spheres portray the fundamental characteristic of capitalist production, i.e., the dissociation of the original producer from possession of his means of production; in manufacturing the laborer is dissociated from his tools and machinery, in agriculture, the tillers from the ownership of land (C. III, 721).

Agricultural production in the capitalist economy entails the interaction of three social classes: (1) the actual *tillers* of the soil, who are

56

wage-earners employed by the capitalists; (2) the *capitalist-farmer,* who produces agricultural products merely as a special field of exploitation for his capital; and (3) the *landowner,* the owner of the soil exploited by the capitalist-farmer. "Here, then," Marx writes, "we have all three classes together, which constitute the framework of modern society" (C. III, 725).

Marx defines the return to landlords for the use of property as *ground rent:*

This renting capitalist pays to the land owner, the owner of the soil exploited by him, a sum of money at definite periods fixed by contract, for instance annually (just as the borrower of money-capital pays a fixed interest), for the permission to invest his capital in this particular sphere of production. This sum of money is called *groundrent,* no matter whether it is paid for agricultural soil, building lots, mines, fishing grounds, forests, etc. [C. III, 725].

The problem of what constitutes "soil" arises. What appears as qualitative gradations in soil (land material) may be merely the manifestations of quantitative differences of fixed capital (land capital) applied to the soil by either the capitalist-farmer or landowner. These investments are categorized by Marx into (1) *transient,* such as chemical applications to land and fertilization, and (2) *permanent,* such as drainage canals, irrigation works, leveling, and farm buildings (C. III, 725). The returns on these investments constitute additional revenue for the landowner and *appear* as rent.

The landowner's acquisition of this revenue stems from the terms of land tenure which are formalized in the contract between the landlord and the capitalist-farmer. During the life of the contract, Marx states, the returns from soil-improvement schemes made during the period of the contract are the legal property of the capitalist-farmer. As soon as the time stipulated by the contract expires, however, "the improvements embodied in the soil become the property of the land owner as an inseparable part of the land" (C. III, 726). Consequently, in a subsequent contract between the landowner and the capitalist-farmer (the same or another), the landowner leases an improved soil (material soil plus land capital), which commands a higher ground rent, i.e., the former ground rent plus the interest on the land capital incorporated in the soil.[1] These circumstances, Marx states, explain the landowners'

1. The absorption of the interest of land capital by the landowner is most obvious in the case of permanent investment in buildings. Marx writes, "In agriculture proper this process does not yet appear quite so plainly as when land is used for building lots. The overwhelming part of the land used in England for

desire for short-term and the capitalist-farmers' desire for long-term leases (C. III, 789). These additions to the revenue of the landowner Marx calls *foreign ingredients* in ground rent (C. III, 732). Aside from the return on land capital, deductions from the capitalist-farmer's profit and the tiller's wages constitute additional elements of the foreign ingredient.

While Marx draws the analogy between the capitalist-farmer and the capitalist operating in manufacture, distinctions are none the less noted, i.e., risk and social position. In general, the lower return to the capitalist-farmer is compensated for by the relative security of his investment and the social prestige attached to the landed classes. A number of small capitalists, Marx writes, are "compelled to be satisfied" with less than average profits by the circumstances of tradition, education, training, and competition (C. III, 734).

(2) THE FORMATION OF GROUND RENT

The determination of ground rent, like the determination of innovating profits, depends upon the difference between social and individual value (or price) in a particular sphere of production. This difference, we have seen, depends upon the introduction of a new technique into a production process which reduces the cost of production below that considered socially necessary (see Chap. 3, sec. 4a). In the formation of ground rent, the "technique" is explicitly defined. The "individual cost" of commodity production falls below its "social cost" by the employment of a *natural force* for a *labor-consuming* factor of production.[2]

Marx illustrates the development of ground rent by contrasting two production techniques in the same sphere, one employing steam as motive power, the other a waterfall. The value of a commodity produced with the waterfall is less than the commodity value produced with steam power because of the smaller quantities of labor materialized in the former's constant capital equipment (C. III, 751). It also costs less

---

building purposes, but not sold as a freehold, is rented by the landowners for 99 years, or for a shorter time if possible. After the lapse of this time, the buildings fall into the hands of the land owner together with the land" (C. III, 728).

2. "A natural power, the motive power of water, which is found ready at hand in nature and which is not itself a product of labor has no value, it need not be paid by an equivalent, it costs nothing. It is a natural agency of production, which is not produced by labor" (C. III, 753).

variable capital, Marx adds, because the water wheel, in contrast to steam power, need not be attended (C. III, 752). While the commodity produced with water power costs less, it none the less is sold at the market price (social value) and consequently realizes a surplus profit or extra surplus value. Thus:

$$S_e = C_s - C_i \qquad (3.5)$$

The difference between the stability of surplus profits resulting from labor-saving techniques other than natural power and the stability of surplus profits resulting from applications of natural power depends upon the degree to which the techniques become widespread throughout their respective production processes. Where duplication of the technique is possible, the social value of the commodity falls to its lower individual value, and the surplus profits consequently disappear.[3] Wherever duplication is effectively eliminated, surplus profits persist. Such is the case, Marx claims, when capitalists use water power. "The increased productive power of his labor is not due either to his capital or his labor. . . . It is a *monopolized* natural power which . . . is only at the command of those who can avail themselves of particular pieces of the globe and its opportunities" (C. III, 755). Duplication of water power is impossible. The difference between the individual and social values in that sphere is consequently maintained.

Possession of the nonduplicatable power is the property claim to the surplus profits.[4] Here Marx makes the transition from surplus profit to ground rent. Monopoly conditions are characteristic of the agricultural sphere (C. III, 756). The surplus profit resulting from the employment of the waterfall falls as ground rent into the hands of the owner of the land upon which the waterfall is located (C. III, 757). Marx generalizes from the waterfall illustration:

This groundrent . . . is due to the greater relative fertility of definite individual capitals invested in a certain sphere of production, as compared with investments of capital, which are excluded from these exceptional and natural conditions favoring the productivity [C. III, 757].

3. The employment of a natural power in a production process does not automatically result in surplus profits. It is only in cases where the natural power cannot be imitated that the surplus arises. Thus, if all firms in the production sphere had the waterfall available for use as motive power, the commodity value of the individual firm's production would fall, but the market price would fall as well, without surplus profits emerging (C. III, 754).

4. "Hence private property in land does not create that portion of value, which is transformed into surplus-profit, but it merely enables the landowner, who has possession of the waterfall, to coax this surplus-profit out of the pocket of the industrial capitalist into his own" (C. III, 758).

Thus,

$$S_e = GR \qquad (5.1)$$

This ground rent (GR) Marx defines as *differential rent*, i.e., the difference between the market price and the individual cost in a production process:

$$GR = P_1 - P_2 \qquad (5.2)$$

In equation (5.2) GR is the dependent variable, and prices, fixed by technical factors, are the independent variables. Thus Marx writes that differential rent is not a part of price but is actually determined by it (C. III, 757).

(3) DETERMINATION OF DIFFERENTIAL GROUND RENT

(a) DIFFERENTIAL RENT I

Differential ground rent depends upon the quantitative differences in products resulting from cultivation of equal areas of land with equal quantities of land capital (C. III, 760). These production inequalities emerge from variations in (1) *natural soil fertility* and (2) *soil location* (C. III, 761). Fertility and location, Marx points out, are not independent variables. In the analysis of fertility he draws the distinction between natural and actual fertility. The former is a function of (a) climatic conditions and (b) chemical composition of topsoil; the latter includes natural fertility and (c) transient and/or permanent land capital already invested in the soil which provides "artificially created improvement in the composition of the soil" (C. III, 763). The location factor, Marx writes, is a function of the economy's communication and transportation systems (C. III, 762). The order in which land is brought under cultivation depends upon the relative importance of fertility and location. In a situation where lands are equidistant from the market, those with greater fertility will be cultivated first. In cases where distance from the markets varies with different lands, the simple priority of superior land no longer holds. Determination of priorities in land cultivation must include the differences in transportation costs as well as differences in land productivity. Less fertile lands will be brought under cultivation first if the transportation costs on the more fertile areas are greater than the value difference in fertility.

To illustrate the derivation of simple differential rent, Marx makes the following assumptions:

1. The agricultural production sphere consists of 4 acres, A, B, C, and D, of increasing degrees of fertility.
2. Equal quantities of land capital are applied to the areas, i.e., 50 shillings per acre.
3. Average rate of profit in the economy is 20 per cent.
4. Commodities produced on the cultivated areas are sold at the market price of 60 shillings per quarter of wheat, which is the price determined by the price of production on the worst soil cultivated.
5. A sellers' market for land exists between the landowners and the capitalist-farmers.
6. Competition in the product market exists.

These assumptions are incorporated in Table 4.

Table 4

Class of Soil	Products Qts.	Products Sh.	Capital Advanced	Profit Qts.	Profit Sh.	Rent Qts.	Rent Sh.
A	1	60	50	⅙	10		
B	2	120	50	1⅙	70	1	60
C	3	180	50	2⅙	130	2	120
D	4	240	50	3⅙	190	3	180
Total	10	600				6	360

Source: C. III, 764.

The productive capacity of the agricultural sphere in Table 4 is 10 quarters of wheat. The fertility differences in the areas are measured from the most to the least fertile, from soil D to soil A. The quantity of wheat produced on the least fertile area, A, is 1 quarter. The total capital invested on A is 50 shillings. Therefore

$$P_a = k_a + k_a p' \qquad (2.7)$$
$$60 = 50 + 20\% \text{ of } 50$$

The *cost of production* on A establishes the market price of a quarter of wheat. The quantity of wheat produced on soil B is two quarters. The cost of production on B, however, like that on A, is equal to 60 shillings, since $k_a = k_b$. The value of the total product on soil B is equal to the number of quarters of wheat produced multiplied by the price of production, i.e., $2 \times 60 = 120$ shillings, as shown in column 3 of Table 4. The total profit received from cultivation on B is thus equal to the total revenue, 120 shillings, minus the capital cost or outlay of 50 shillings, that is, 70 shillings, as shown in column 6 of Table 4. Since the average profit on 50-shilling land capital is 10 shillings, the surplus profit or differential ground rent on soil B is $70 - 10$, or 60 shillings, as shown in column 8 of Table 4. Measured in real terms, the total product on B is 2 quarters of wheat, the total profit is 1⅙, and the ground rent is 1⅙ − ⅙, or 1 quarter of wheat.

Following the analysis through on areas C and D, with the assumed total products of 3 and 4 quarters of wheat respectively, ground rent on the most fertile soil, D, would be 190 − 10, or 180 shillings, and ground rent on C would be 130 − 10, or 120 shillings. The total differential rent resulting in the sphere would equal the summation of the individual ground rent of B, C, and D, or 360 shillings, which is equal to 6 quarters of wheat (C. III, 764).

The succession of land cultivation which gives rise to simple differential rent may, Marx writes, *descend* from D to A, from the most to the least fertile areas, or *ascend* from A to D, that is, from the least to the most fertile lands:

This does away with the primitive misconception of differential rent still found among men like West, Malthus, Ricardo, to the effect that it necessarily required a progress toward worse and worse soil, or an ever decreasing productivity of agriculture. It rather may exist when a better soil takes the lowest position formerly occupied by the worst soil; it may be accompanied with a progressive improvement of agriculture. Its premise is merely the inequality of the different kinds of soil [C. III, 772].

In examining the emergence of rent through the descending order, Marx assumes the initial demand for wheat to be 4 quarters. Production will thus take place on soil D with the price of production of 15 shillings per quarter of wheat. If the demand for wheat increases so that production on soil D no longer is sufficient, the market price will rise above its market value to the point where agricultural production on soil C becomes profitable, that is, yields 20 per cent on its capital outlay. The minimum price required to bring C into cultivation will be 20 shillings per quarter. At the price of 20 shillings, differential rent emerges on area D. As more wheat is demanded, the market price rises until B is under cultivation, and the price of production of wheat increases from 20 to 30 shillings. Money rent (MR) on soil D increases from 20 to 60 shillings, and a rent of 30 shillings emerges on C, which was formerly no-rent soil. With the incorporation of soil A into cultivation, the market price increases to 60 shillings, money rent on D increases to 180, on C to 120, and emerges on B at 60 shillings. A remains no-rent land under these conditions.

Consider the cultivation of land in ascending order, from least to most fertile. An initial condition is made, i.e., the demand for wheat is 1 quarter, which is satisfied by production on soil A at its cost of production of 60 shillings. As demand increases, price tends to rise, and soil B is brought under cultivation. Because of the superior fertility of soil B, providing 2 quarters of wheat on a capital outlay of 50 shillings, the price falls to 60 shillings and affords soil B a differential ground rent of 60 shillings. Assuming, as Marx does, that demand continuously increases, more areas are brought into cultivation, i.e., soils C and D, with the consequent development of differential rents on soils B, C, and D which correspond to those produced in the descending analysis. The basic difference in the descending and ascending approach to ground rent is the initial condition of production. In the case of inferior lands, commodity prices remain constant; on superior lands, prices rise with increasing demand.

The magnitude of differential rent thus depends upon the character of the production and demand functions in the economy, namely, (1) the number of soils taken under cultivation, (2) the productivity differential between the soils, and (3) demand conditions. Ground rent increases with increasing differentials.

General land improvements affect the various soils differently, consequently altering their relative productivity differentials (C. III, 768). In all cases the market price is assumed constant. The effect of such improvements on total and individual soil ground rents depends upon the distribution of the productive increases among the soils. Marx cites three distribution possibilities: (1) proportional increase in the productivity per soil; (2) a greater productive increase in the more fertile soils, i.e., soils C and D; and (3) a greater productive increase in the less fertile areas, i.e., soils B and A. In the first case both total and individual rents would increase; in the second, differential rent would increase, particularly in the superior soils; and in the final case rent on superior soils would fall as the differential between the better and the worst lands narrowed (C. III, 769).

Marx also considers the effect of extension of cultivation on differential ground rent. As in the analysis of general land improvement, the effect of expansion depends upon the relative importance each particular soil plays in the expansion scheme. Here, too, three possibilities are analyzed. In the first possibility—the proportional expansion of cultivation on all soils—differential ground rent increases in the same ratio as the lands cultivated, that is, as each area under cultivation doubles, the total ground rent doubles. This case is illustrated in the comparative Tables 5 and 6.

While total cultivated lands increased from four acres (Table 5) to eight acres (Table 6), both ground (*GR*) and money (*MR*) rents increased from 6 quarters and 18 pounds sterling to 12 quarters and 36

Table 5

Class of Soil	Acres	Cost of Product	Product	Rent in Grain	Rent in Money
A	1	3 £	1 qr.	0	0
B	1	3 £	2 qrs.	1 qr.	3 £
C	1	3 £	3 qrs.	2 qrs.	6 £
D	1	3 £	4 qrs.	3 qrs.	9 £
Total	4		10 qrs.	6 qrs.	18 £

Source: C. III, 774.

Table 6

Class of Soil	Acres	Cost of Product	Product	Rent in Grain	Rent in Money
A	2	6 £	2 qrs.	0	0
B	2	6 £	4 qrs.	2 qrs.	6 £
C	2	6 £	6 qrs.	4 qrs.	12 £
D	2	6 £	8 qrs.	6 qrs.	18 £
Total	8		20 qrs.	12 qrs.	36 £

Source: C. III, 775.

pounds sterling. The average money rent per cultivated acre remained constant, however, at 4½ pounds sterling per acre. In the second possibility considered by Marx, where concentration of expanded cultivation is made on the less fertile lands, money rents per acre decline. This is demonstrated by comparing Tables 5 and 7, where MR per acre falls from 4½ pounds sterling to 3½ pounds sterling, i.e., 42/12.

Table 7

Class of Soil	Acres	Cost of Product Per Acre	Total	Product	Rent in Grain	Rent in Money
A	4	3 £	12 £	4 qrs.	0	0
B	4	3 £	12 £	8 qrs.	4 qrs.	12 £
C	2	3 £	6 £	6 qrs.	4 qrs.	12 £
D	2	3 £	6 £	8 qrs.	8 qrs.	18 £
Total	12		36 £	26 qrs.	14 qrs.	42 £

Source: C. III, 775.

In the remaining possibility considered by Marx—where the concentration of expanded cultivation fell to the more fertile areas—money rents per acre increased from 4½ to 6 pounds sterling. This is illustrated in Table 8. Differential ground rent thus depends not only upon the productivity differential between the various soils but upon the relative weights the particular soils bear in relation to the total agricultural product.

Table 8

Class of Soil	Acres	Cost of Product Per Acre	Total	Product	Rent in Grain	Rent in Money
A	1	3 £	3 £	1 qr.	0	0
B	2	3 £	6 £	4 qrs.	2 qrs.	6 £
C	5	3 £	15 £	15 qrs.	10 qrs.	30 £
D	4	3 £	12 £	16 qrs.	12 qrs.	36 £
Total	12		36 £	36 qrs.	24 qrs.	72 £

Source: C. III, 775.

(b) DIFFERENTIAL RENT II

Differential rent arises, Marx points out, not only from land-capital investments applied to unequally productive areas but also from capital investments concentrated on one specific soil. The former Marx calls *extensive,* the latter *intensive* land-capital investments (C. III, 790). The emergence of differential ground rent from intensive applications of land capital is, in essence, identical to the extensive formulation described in the descending succession of land cultivation. Marx writes:

If the same capital of 10 pounds sterling . . . invested in the shape of separate capitals of 2½ pounds sterling by different tenants in one acre of each of the soils A, B, C, and D, were invested successively in one and the same acre D, so that its first investment yielded 4 quarters, the second 3 quarters, the third 2 quarters, and the fourth 1 quarter (or vice versa), then the price of the 1 quarter, which is furnished by the least productive capital, namely the price of 3 pounds sterling, would not pay any differential rent, but would determine the price of production, so long as the supply of wheat with a price of production of 3 pounds sterling would be needed. . . . It is evident . . . that differential rent No. II is but a different expression of differential rent I, but that it coincides with it in substance [C. III, 792].

In analyzing the effects of intensive land-capital investment on differential ground rent, particularly money rents (*MR*), Marx assumes price flexibility. As more capital is applied to the agricultural sphere, total productivity, and therefore the supply of agricultural commodities, increases. The increasing supply, Marx claims, in a competitive commodity market tends to reduce the market price. The reduction in price depends upon the extent to which agricultural demand keeps pace with the increasing supply. The effect on money rents depends upon the relative changes in price and productivity. Money rent is by definition equated to the product of ground rent (GR) and the price of grain (P), i.e.,

$$MR = GR \times P \tag{5.3}$$

Assume that additional capital is invested in a specific area without affecting the magnitude of money rents. In that case,

$$MR_1 = GR_1 \times P_1 = MR_2 = GR_2 \times P_2 \tag{5.4}$$

or,

$$\frac{P_1}{P_2} = \frac{GR_2}{GR_1} \tag{5.5}$$

If, however,

$$\frac{P_1}{P_2} > \frac{GR_2}{GR_1} \tag{5.5a}$$

MR declines. On the other hand, if

$$\frac{P_1}{P_2} < \frac{GR_2}{GR_1} \tag{5.5b}$$

MR increases.[5]

Marx's exposition of differential ground rent covers the various possibilities of fluctuating prices and productivities, i.e., the combinations of falling, increasing, and constant prices with falling, increasing, and constant productivity per capital investment allocated among the cultivated areas in varying concentrations on superior and inferior soils. The various possibilities, which Marx calls *variants,* are employed principally for classificatory purposes. Variant II, falling prices and productivity per capital, characterizes the European agricultural situation:

Our second case, Variant II (falling prices and falling productivity of the additional investment of capital) became the rule for Europe. This accounts for the woes of the landlords from Scotland to Italy, and from Southern France to Eastern Prussia. Fortunately all prairie lands have not been taken under cultiva-

5. "If the increase of productivity by means of additional capital should produce different results upon different soils, it would cause a change in their differential rents. At any rate we have demonstrated, that the rent per acre, for instance with a double capital, may not only be doubled but more than doubled, while the price of production is falling in consequence of an increased rate of productivity of the additional capitals (as soon as productivity grows at a greater rate than the advance of capital). But it may also fall, if the price of production should fall much lower as a result of a more rapid increase of productivity upon the soil A" (C. III, 826).

tion. There are enough of them left to ruin all the great landlords of Europe and the small ones into the bargain [C. III, 842].

The distinction between intensive and extensive applications of land capital is purely analytical in the Marxian system. In either case, total differential ground rent results from the differences between prices and products of the areas under cultivation and the least fertile capital investment. However, where intensive cultivation of land occurs, *ground rent per acre* is higher than in the extensive case:

Consequently, if we had two countries, in which the prices of production are identical, the differences in the various kinds of soil the same, and the same amount of capital invested, but in such a way that the investment is made in the form of successive outlays upon a limited area in one country, whereas in the other country it is made more in the shape of co-ordinated outlays upon a wider area, then the rent per acre, and with it, the price of land, would be higher in the first and lower in the second country, although the mass of rent would be the same in both countries. The difference in the size of the rent could not be explained in such a case out of the natural fertility of the various kinds of soil, nor out of the quantity of employed labor, but solely out of the different ways in which the capital is invested [C. III, 809].

(4) DETERMINATION OF ABSOLUTE RENT

While differential rent is determined by price and is not price-determining, *absolute rent* in the Marxian system is a determinant of price. Absolute rent therefore constitutes an important qualification upon the Marxian theory of rent developed above. Recall that, in the analysis of differential rent, the rent evolved from the price differential between the least productive and any other investment of capital. Thus,

$$P_b - P_a = d \tag{5.6}$$

where P_b is the price of the commodity, determined by the least productive soil, P_a is the cost of production on a more fertile area, and d is the resulting differential rent. The modification of agricultural price determination to include a constant, absolute rent r does not affect the magnitude of differential rent d (C. III, 868). Thus,

$$(P_b + r) - (P_a + r) = d \tag{5.7}$$

The emergence of absolute rent in the Marxian system is dependent upon the institution of private property (C. III, 871). Those in possession of land, Marx claims, are able to exact a charge for the use of their property. This charge, which must be paid, is passed on to the agricultural consumer in terms of higher market prices, i.e., $P + r$. The determination of r depends upon the existence of three specific conditions in the agricultural sector of the economy: (1) a lower-than-social organic composition of capital; (2) cultivated areas held in the hands of landlords; and (3) market rigidities.

In the analysis of price formation, the commodity price differed from its value by the difference between the individual commodity surplus value and the average profit (Chap. 2, sec. 5b). Commodities were sold at their market price—cost plus average profit—because of the competitive product and factor market structures. The existence of absolute rent in the agricultural sphere emerges with a modification of the competitive factor market structure. Intersphere competition among capitals is eliminated with the institution of private ownership of land. The migration of capital into the agricultural sphere would occur in the absence of private ownership of land, since surplus value in agriculture is greater than the average profit in the economy. Marx says:

> This fact could be explained . . . from the earlier and more rapid development of the mechanical sciences, and especially by their application, compared to the later and partly quite recent development of chemistry, geology and physiology, and particularly their application to agriculture [C. III, 882].

Because this migration is effectively curtailed by the monopoly of property (C. III, 886), Marx writes:

> If capital meets some foreign power, which it cannot overcome . . . then it is evident that the excess of the value of commodities in such spheres of production over their prices of production would give rise to a surplus profit, which could be converted into rent and made independent as such compared to profit. Such a foreign power is private ownership of land . . . ; such a power is the landlord in his relation to the capitalist [C. III, 884–85].

The maximum limit to r is therefore established by the difference between the surplus value received by an investment in the agricultural sphere and the average profit received by a quantitatively equal investment in a nonagricultural sphere of production (C. III, 888). Thus:

$$r = s - p \tag{5.8}$$

Marx defines the price of agricultural commodities as *monopoly price* (C. III, 885, 887). While the maximum limit of r is determined by the difference between the surplus value and average profit, the prevailing *r* is conditioned by (1) the quantity of additional investment of capital made upon *old* lands, which will increase the differential rent at the expense of *r*, (2) the competition between landlords (C. III, 789–90), and (3) the wants and solvency of the consumers (C. III, 80–87). Thus, Marx writes,

Although the private ownership of land may drive the price of the products of the soil above their prices of production, it does not depend upon this ownership, but upon the *general condition of the market,* to what extent the market price shall exceed the price of production and approach the value, and to what extent the surplus-value created in agriculture over and above the given average profit shall either be converted into rent or enter into the general equalization of the surplus-value to an average profit [C. III, 887; italics added].

(5) THE PRICE OF LAND

Because the value of a commodity depends upon its labor content, the value or price of land material is theoretically zero (Chap. 2, sec. 1). While the concept "price of land" is an irrational expression in terms of Marxian definitions, it nevertheless represents a real economic relation (C. III, 720). Like interest on capital bonds, ground rent, in the Marxian system, can be capitalized. The capitalized value of such rent *appears,* in the capitalist economy, as a real price of land. Marx employs the capitalization principle to compute the purchase price of land:

$$CV = y/i' \tag{4.3}$$

Given the interest rate i' and the fixed annual return (GR) or y, the CV, the computed value of land, can be determined. Thus,

If a capitalist buys land yielding a rent of 200 pounds sterling annually and pays 4,000 pounds sterling for it, then he draws the average interest of 5% on his capital of 4,000 pounds sterling, just as though he had invested this capital in interest-bearing papers or loaned it directly at 5% interest.

It follows, then, that the price of land may rise or fall inversely as the rate of interest rises or falls, if we assume that groundrent is a constant magnitude. If the ordinary rate of interest should fall from 5% to 4%, then the annual groundrent of 200 pounds sterling would represent the annual self-expansion of a capital of

5,000 pounds sterling instead of 4,000 pounds sterling [C. III, 730–31].

(6) CONCLUSION

Rent, in the Marxian system, is both price-determined and price-determining. Differential rents are the product of the inequalities in land fertility and distance to market. Absolute rent is derived from the difference between the social organic composition of capital and the capital composition in agriculture. In both cases rents are the property of the landowner. It is interesting to note that in the analysis of differential rents Marx assumes that the cost of production on the least fertile soil determines the market price. This may appear as an inconsistency in his price theory (see Chap. 2, sec. 5b), but the seeming inconsistency becomes resolved with the introduction of land monopoly into the analysis. Any surplus earned over the average profit (determined in the nonagricultural spheres) becomes the property not of the capitalists but of the landowners. Under these conditions the averaging-out process of the total agricultural surplus among capitalists is effectively eliminated.

Marx's analysis of absolute rent requires the additional assumption that all uncultivated lands cannot yield a surplus as large as the average profit. Otherwise it would certainly pay the landowner to lease the land, since rent would be greater than zero. It should be noted, however, that the above assumption is *implied* in the assumption that the least fertile soil determines price, an assumption which Marx employs in the analysis of differential rent. One further point must be made concerning Marx's treatment of differential rent. The emergence of rent in the ascension from the least to the most productive soils occurs, Marx states, if the demand for the commodity increases to bring soil B under cultivation. Why the superior soils C and D are not cultivated before B is not explained. Indeed, why soil A is first cultivated with three soils of superior quality available is left to the reader's imagination. But unless this can be explained, differential rent, arising in this manner, is meaningless.

The analysis of rent presented in this chapter forms the basis upon which predictions developed in Book II of this study are made. In particular, see Chapter 8, section 1, dealing with the effect of rent on the rate of profit; Chapter 9, section 2, dealing with the polarization of production under capitalism; Chapter 11, section 3, dealing with the class struggle; and Chapter 12, section 2b, dealing with the prophecies on production under communism.

6

Capital circulation

THIS CHAPTER and the next gather together the essential theoretical contributions Marx makes in Volume II of *Capital*. In this chapter the theory of capital circulation is developed. It forms an integral part of Marx's general theory of commodity valuation, particularly the determination of aggregate surplus value, and his theory of economic dynamics. In capital-circulation theory, Marx introduces a time variable to distinguish between capital advanced for production and capital actually employed in the production process. The functional linkage between these two capitals is the capital-turnover time. The discussion begins with an analysis of Marx's concept of capital circulation, then explores the nature of capital turnover in circulation, and finally relates these to the production of surplus value.

(1) THE CIRCULATION OF CAPITAL

The structures of exchange developed in Chapters 2 and 4 are expanded and incorporated into Marx's capital-circulation analysis. Recall that, in the development of these structures,

$$M - C \ldots C' - M'$$
$$M_a - M_b - C \ldots C' - M'_b - M'_a$$

Marx sought to explain the expansion of value in the production process (Chap. 2, sec. 4) and the integration of monetary institutions, i.e., the banking and credit systems, into the capitalist system (Chap. 4, sec. 1). The purpose of the structural elaboration of exchange, shown in the diagram, is to facilitate the analyses of capital circulation, commodity distribution, and their effects on the formation of surplus value. The expanded exchange structure makes explicit the various *forms* that

71

capital takes in circulation. By *capital circulation* Marx means the repeated movements of capital through the spheres of production and circulation.[1] Four distinct forms [2] of capital in circulation are defined:

1. *Money capital* $(M$ and $M + m)$: Capital in possession of the industrial capitalist before and after actual production.
2. *Commodity capital* $(C^l_{pm}$ and $C + c)$: [3] The productive factors and finished products of capitalist production.
3. *Productive capital* (P): Commodity capital in the process of being transformed from its factor to product form.

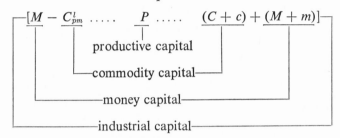

4. *Industrial capital:* The generalized form of money capital, commodity capital, and productive capital, as distinct from money capital in the hands of money capitalists. In continuous production, Marx states, industrial capital flows in sequence: from money capital to commodity capital, to productive capital, to commodity capital, to money capital.

The exchange structure can be divided for analytical purposes into two parts: (1) the *period of production,* embracing the production process (P); and (2) the *periods of circulation,* $[M - C^l_{pm}]$ and $[(C + c) - (M + m)]$, which compose four distinct markets: M—C^l, the labor market; M—C_{pm}, the capital-goods market; C—M, the commodity market for the original commodity value; and c—m, the commodity market for surplus production. Only in the periods of circulation is the relationship between the industrial and merchant capitalists expressed. Marx writes:

1. The terms capital circulation, capital rotation, capital movement, and capital flow are used interchangeably by Marx.
2. "Money capital, commodity-capital, productive capital are not, therefore, terms indicating independent classes of capital, nor are their functions processes of independent and separate branches of industry. They are here used only to indicate special functions of industrial capital, assumed by it *seriatim*" (C. II, 59–60).
3. The C_{pm} notation is, of course, Marx's. It is constructed to identify the capital in circulation with the commodity-capital form, specifically, the factor form where the employment of labor is indicated by l, the employment of means of production by pm.

The quantity of commodities produced by capitalist production depends on the scale of production and on the continual necessity for expansion following from this production. It does not depend on a predestined circle of supply and demand, nor on certain wants to be supplied. Production on a large scale can have no other buyer, apart from other industrial capitalists, than the wholesale merchant. Within certain limits, the process of reproduction may take place on the same or on an increased scale, although the commodities taken out of it may not have gone into individual or productive consumption [C. II, 86].

Continuous production depends upon continuous sale. Capital rotation thus depends upon the coincidence of market and productive capacities. Where factor shortages arise in the $M—C_{pm}$ markets, money capital lies idle. This Marx defines as a *hoard* (C. II, 60). Where the capacity of the market fails to absorb the total quantity of commodities produced, commodity capital accumulates, constituting, in the Marxian system, a *glut* (C. II, 60). The occurrence of either glut or hoard obstructs the normal rotation or circulation of capital.

Rotation of capital is described by Marx as "progressive" or "simple," depending upon the destination of the monetized value of the surplus commodity, *m*. The rotation is called *simple reproduction* when the surplus money capital, *m,* is removed from the industrial sphere as income spent by capitalists on consumption. In simple reproduction the magnitude of industrial capital in circulation remains constant (C. II, 76). Accumulation of *progressive reproduction* is defined by the inclusion of some fraction of the surplus, *m,* into industrial capital (C. II, 89). Incorporation of surplus into industrial capital, however, is regulated by a minimum capital requirement for production which is functionally related to the existing state of technology:

Since the proportions of the expansion of the productive process are not arbitrary, but determined by technical conditions, the produced surplus-value, though intended for capitalization, frequently does not attain a size sufficient for its function as additional capital, for its entrance into the cycle of circulating capital-value, until several cycles have been repeated so that it must be accumulated until that time [C. II, 89].

The Marxian system is thus characterized by discontinuous production functions. These production discontinuities form the basis for Marxian *latent capital;* its magnitude at any time is determined by the difference between the surplus accumulated and the minimum requirement for its incorporation into production (C. II, 89).

(2) CAPITAL TURNOVER

Commodity value, we have seen, depends upon embodied labor time, or what Marx calls *time of production.* The *total period of production, t,* however, through which industrial capital moves, includes not only time of production, t_p, but also *time of circulation, t_c.* In other words, it refers to that time within which a particular commodity is produced and sold so that its monetized value can be re-employed as money capital–capital to reproduce the commodity. Thus:

$$t = t_p + t_c \qquad (6.1)$$

(a) TIME OF CIRCULATION: t_c

Though time-consuming, industrial capital in the time-of-circulation phase of reproduction is not productive capital and therefore produces no surplus value (C. II, 147). The surplus value that an industrial capital can produce in any given time depends upon the allocation of this time between production and circulation in the total period of production. Marx writes:

The expansion and contraction of the time of circulation are, therefore, a check on the contraction and expansion of the time of production or of the volume which a given capital can assume for its productive function. To the extent that the metamorphoses of circulation of a certain capital are reduced, to the extent that the time of circulation approaches zero, its productivity and increment of surplus value will increase. . . . In short, the time of circulation of a certain capital limits its time of production and the process of creating surplus-value. And this limitation is proportional to the duration of the time of circulation. Seeing that this time may increase or decrease in different ratios, it may limit the time of production in various degrees [C. II, 142].

Expressed symbolically,

$$s = f(t_p/t_c) \qquad (6.2)$$

Marx defines *expenses of circulation, k_c,* as the costs incurred by the merchant capitalist during the time of circulation. The expenditure of capital resources in circulation, although considered part of the total cost of surplus creation, "does not create value any more than the work done in a civil process increases the value of the object of contention" (C. II, 148). Marx continues:

He [the merchant] expends his labor-power and labor-time in the operations C − M and M − C. And he makes his living that way, just as another does by spinning or by making pills. He performs a necessary function, because the process of reproduction itself includes an unproductive function. He works as well as any other man, but intrinsically his labor creates neither products nor values. He belongs himself to the unproductive expense of production [C. II, 149–50].

The concept of cost price, developed in Chapter 2, reflects both production and circulation costs:

$$k = k_p + k_c \qquad (6.3)$$
$$P = p'(k_p + k_c) \qquad (6.4)$$

Not all circulation costs, however, can be transferred to commodity valuation. Marx lists the following expenses of circulation: (1) *genuine,* the costs of buying and selling and bookkeeping, (2) *storage,* the cost of factor and product inventory, and (3) *transportation,* the cost of moving commodities to the market (C. II, 147–72). Of the three expenses, only those of storage and transportation are added to price, i.e., k_c. The expenses incurred in buying and selling commodities, whether performed by the capitalist or merchant, do not constitute any addition to commodity value (C. II, 151). Bookkeeping costs, Marx writes, "constitute a deduction from the time available for productive consumption and from the materials which are used in the actual process of production and are embodied in the creation of products and values" (C. II, 152). Both marketing and bookkeeping expenses, however, are relatively fixed; and once the capitalist mode of production is established, they vary inversely, as a percentage of total costs, with the organic composition of capital. Marx examines the storage expenses. To provide for continuous commodity production, factor inventories, particularly in raw materials, must be accumulated and maintained. Additional expenses in constant capital, associated with the inventory stock, i.e., buildings, stores, and warehouses, as well as outlay of variable capital to operate the storage facilities, are included in storage expenses. Protection against stock perishability, Marx writes, requires still additional outlays of variable and constant capital (C. II, 157). At the other end of the production process, inventory in commodity stocks is considered essential to the normal rotation of industrial capital. Commodity supply, Marx writes, must be larger than the "average sale or the average extent of demand" (C. II, 168). The costs of storage, both in factor and commodity inventory, Marx writes, vary directly with the development of capitalist production and inversely to the number and size of the suppliers and the development of transportation facilities (C. II, 162).

Although the expenses of transportation are not value-creating, they constitute an element of price:

Quantities of products are not increased by transportation, neither is the eventual alteration of their natural qualities, with a few exceptions, the result of premeditated action, but an inevitable evil. But the use-value of things has no existence except in consumption, and this may necessitate a change of place on the part of the product, in other words, it may require the additional process of production of the transportation industry. The productive capital invested in this industry adds value to the transported products, partly by transferring value from the means of transportation, partly by adding value through the labor-power used in transportation. This last-named addition of value consists, as it does in all capitalist production, of a reproduction of wages and of surplus-value [C. II, 170].

The magnitude of this cost, Marx writes, varies inversely with the development of the transportation industry and directly with the distance traveled (C. II, 171).

(b) TIME OF PRODUCTION: t_p

Marx defines the time of production as the *working period:*

If we speak of a working day, we mean the length of working time during which the laborer must daily spend his labor-power, must work day by day. But if we speak of a working period, then we mean a number of consecutive working days required in a certain branch of production for the completion of the finished product. In this case, the product of every working day is but a partial one, being elaborated from day to day and receiving its complete form only at the end of a longer or shorter period of labor, when it is at last a finished use-value [C. II, 262].

The material requirements for the working period or time of production include the advancement of wages, paid weekly to the laborers for the period, sufficient stocks of raw materials, and the necessary capital equipment (C. II, 264). Prolongation of the working period reduces the number of capital turnovers per year as does the time of circulation (C. II, 264). The time of production of a specific outlay of capital is a variable depending upon the employment of machinery in production, the development of extensive cooperation in production, the development of a credit system, the development of markets, and the development of transportation facilities. Marx thus writes that

the shortening of the working period is thus mostly accompanied by an increase in the capital advanced for this shortened time, so that the amount of capital advanced increases to the extent that the time for which the advance is made decreases [C. II, 268].

Symbolically, this is

$$t_p = f(1/K_o) \qquad (6.5)$$

Advanced capital thus becomes, in the Marxian system, a substitute for time. The time of circulation consists of time spent in commodity marketing and varies with changing market conditions (C. II, 285, 364). Improvements in transportation, however, while cutting time in established markets, may prolong the time of circulation by introducing new and more distant markets into the analysis (C. II, 287).

(c) TIME OF CAPITAL TURNOVER: t

The total period of production is the summation of the time of circulation and the time of production. Marx defines the total period of production as the *time of turnover* (t) (C. II, 176). Turnover time measures the complete rotation of a given quantity of industrial capital. Marx selects a year as the temporal unit in the analysis of capital turnover:

Just as the working day is the natural unit for the function of labor-power, so the year is the natural unit for the periods of turn-over of rotating capital. The natural basis of this unit is found in the fact that the most important crops of the temperate zone, which is the mother country of capitalist production, are annual products [C. II, 176].

The number of turnovers a specific industrial capital can make in a unit of time, i.e., one year, is measured by

$$n = 1/t \qquad (6.6)$$

where n represents the number of turnovers of a particular capital and t is the time of turnover, measured as a fraction of a year, of the given industrial capital.

In considering the rotation of a specific quantity of industrial capital, Marx distinguishes between *circulating capital, cK_o,* the capital trans-formed from factor to product, i.e., capital used up in production, and *fixed capital, fK_o,* the capital remaining in the factor state during the time of turnover or the production and sale of the commodity (C. II, 178–80). While it is true that in the long run all capital is circulating, this distinction between fixed and circulating is relevant to a specific capital-turnover period (C. II, 190). The relationship between the quantity of capital *advanced* annually in producing, K_o, and the quantity of capital *employed* annually in production, K_e depends upon the extent to which the capital advance is in the form of fixed or circulating capital. Thus:

$$\frac{K_e}{K_o} = f\left(\frac{cK_o}{fK_o}\right) \qquad (6.7)$$

Capital employed in production varies with the number of capital turnovers per year:

$$K_e = n(cK_o) \tag{6.8}$$

Compare equations (6.6) and (6.8). If the total capital advanced produced a set of commodities which were sold at the end of a year's production, then $K_e = cK_o = K_o$. Capitalist production, Marx states, is not characterized by this coincidence (C. II, 209).

(3) CAPITAL TURNOVER AND SURPLUS VALUE

Annual production of both commodity value and surplus value is measured by the *employment* of variable capital (C. II, 346). Recall that $K_e = n(cK_o)$. The employment of capital and the annual mass of surplus value, S, vary directly, therefore, with the number of times capital rotates or turns over in a year. The proportion of the total quantity of surplus value produced during one year to the value of the advanced variable capital is what Marx calls *annual rate of surplus value*, S' (C. II, 338). The annual surplus value is measured by the rate of surplus value, the variable capital advanced, and the number of capital turnovers. This is expressed in the following notation:

$$S = sn \tag{6.9}$$

The annual rate of surplus value is written (C. II, 350):

$$S' = s'n \tag{6.10}$$

Marx illustrates the above relationships by comparing two capitals, A and B, of equal quantity but varying composition (C. II, 354). Consider the case of capital A, where (1) the variable capital advanced = 500 pounds sterling, (2) the constant capital = zero, (3) the rate of surplus value = 100 per cent, and (4) the capital turnover = 10. In the first cycle of capital rotation, a surplus value of 500 pounds sterling is created. Important, however, is the fact that the variable capital advanced in wages during the production process assumes a commodity form which is monetized and reconverted into money capital at the termination of the first turnover period. Assuming continuous production, the money capital becomes, in the second period, variable capital for the re-employment of laborers. The 500 pounds sterling advanced as variable capital has therefore functioned as 1,000 pounds sterling of variable capital. In other words, the 500 pounds advanced became, in two periods, 1,000 pounds employed and created a surplus value of 1,000 pounds sterling. At the end of the year, therefore, the 500 pounds sterling advanced as variable capital has served in the production process as 5,000 pounds sterling of variable capital or annual labor subsistence and has produced a surplus value of 5,000 pounds sterling. The annual rate of surplus value, in this case, would be $s'n$ or 1,000 per cent.

In contrast to capital A, Marx examines capital B. Here the annual product and the surplus created at the end of a year's production is 5,000 pounds sterling, as in capital A, but the period of production in capital B is assumed equal to one year. Capital turnover in B therefore is 1, i.e., $K_e = K_o$. Because the product does not mature until the end of the year, annual subsistence *must be advanced* to maintain continuous production, i.e., the variable capital advanced must be 5,000 pounds sterling in capital B. The advanced variable capital serves as variable capital only for the time in which it is actually employed, not for the time in which it is held available without being employed (C. II, 343). The annual rate of surplus value in capital B is thus $s'n$, or 100 per cent. The difference in the capital turnovers of A and B thus accounts for the difference in their respective annual rates of surplus value.

(4) CONCLUSION

The reproduction of industrial capital in the Marxian system is contingent upon the total period of production, i.e., time of production plus time of circulation. With the development of the capitalist mode of production, particularly the expansion of the transportation industries, both circulation and production times are reduced. Annual capital turnovers, measuring the number of times industrial capital is reproduced, therefore increase. The annual production of surplus value, which is related directly to the number of capital turnovers, is consequently augmented. In the examination of the expenses of circulation, Marx distinguishes between production costs, i.e., expenses of transportation and storage, and selling costs, i.e., costs of buying and selling. While the former costs are included in commodity valuation, the latter cost is omitted. The merchant capitalist, an unproductive agent in the economy, is directly associated with the buying and selling function of circulation. Although simple and progressive reproduction are defined in this chapter, the analysis of the reproduction models is left to the following chapter, which deals with capital accumulation.

The exposition undertaken in this chapter is fundamental to an understanding of the predictions analyzed in Part II, in particular Chapter 8, sections 4 and 5, dealing with the effect of capital turnover on the rate of profit and innovations; Chapter 9, section 1, dealing with the development of the world market; and, to a much greater extent, Chapter 10, dealing with Marx's predictions concerning the industrial cycle.

7

Capital accumulation

THE PURPOSE OF THIS CHAPTER is to analyze the capital-accumulation model which Marx incorporates into his economic system. Chief attention is given to making explicit the assumptions of the model and examining the properties of capital growth which evolve from it. The analysis of capital accumulation is preceded by an examination of Marx's simple-reproduction model, which he claims is the first approximation to the study of capital formation in the capitalist economy. The chapter concludes with an exposition of capital concentration and centralization and their relation to capital accumulation.

(1) SIMPLE REPRODUCTION

The rate of economic growth, in the Marxian system, is determined by the magnitude and disposition of economic surplus. Since the surplus in the Marxian model constitutes the property of the capitalist class, economic growth depends primarily upon the capitalists' behavior in relation to the disposal of this surplus. The assumptions Marx makes concerning such behavior are therefore salient to the development of a capital-accumulation model. Conversion of surplus into capital is defined by Marx as accumulation (C. I, 634). On the other hand, complete disposal of the capitalists' surplus through purchase of consumer goods is defined by Marx as *simple reproduction* (C. I, 621).

In the analysis of simple reproduction, which Marx treats as a first approximation to the study of capital accumulation, the economy is divided into two major producing industries: *Department I,* producing capital goods, and *Department II,* producing consumer goods (C. II, 457). In each department the capital structure is composed of varying constant and variable proportions. Social capital, or the total capital

81

outlay in the economy (K), is defined as the summation of the capital outlay in the two industries or departments:

$$K = (K)_1 + (K)_2 = (c + v)_1 + (c + v)_2 \qquad (7.1)$$

Total production in the economy (C) is therefore equal to the commodities produced during the period by both departments:

$$C = C_1 + C_2 = (c_1 + v_1 + s_1) + (c_2 + v_2 + s_2) \qquad (7.2)$$

The difference between total annual product and the cost of production is the annual surplus (S):

$$S = C - K = (s_1 + s_2) \qquad (7.3)$$

The Marxian simple-reproduction model can be illustrated in a simplified input-output table,[1] as in Table 9. Construction of the table

Table 9

		Output of the Departments		
		Dept. I	Dept. II	Total
Inputs	Dept. I	c_1	$(v_1 + s_1)$	$c_1 + v_1 + s_1$
of the	Dept. II	c_2	$(v_2 + s_2)$	$c_2 + v_2 + s_2$
Depts.	Total	$(c_1 + c_2)$	$(v_1 + s_1) + (v_2 + s_2)$	C

implies the following assumptions: (1) constant relative market prices; (2) constancy of capital compositions in both departments; (3) equality in the rates of profit; (4) capitalists' surplus in both departments is spent on commodities of Department II; (5) constant size of the working class, which implies that wages must be greater than or equal to subsistence; and (6) gross investment $(c_1 + c_2)$ is equal to real depreciation, so that the capital stock of the economy is maintained. $(c_1 + c_2)$ measures the total value of capital goods produced by Department I, while $(v_1 + s_1) + (v_2 + s_2)$ measures the total value of consumption goods produced by Department II. In the process of commodity exchange, *interdepartmental transactions* include (1) the purchases of capital goods (c_2) from Department I by capitalists of Department II and (2) the purchases of consumer goods from Department II by capitalists and laborers of Department I. *Intradepartmental transactions* include (1) the purchases of consumer goods by laborers and capitalists

1. In correspondence with Engels, Marx attempted to set out a rough draft of the input-output relations by constructing a *Tableau économique* for his model. Thus, in the first paragraph of his letter to Engels, Marx writes: "If you find it possible in this heat, look with some care at the enclosed *Tableau économique* which I substitute for Quesnay's Table, and tell me of any objections you may have to it. It embraces the whole process of reproduction" (MEC, 153).

of Department II (C. II, 460–64). Marx illustrates the simple-reproduction model with a numerical example:

Department I consists of: $4000c + 1000v + 1000s = 6000C$
Department II consists of: $2000c + 500v + 500s = 3000C$
Annual product $= \overline{9000C}$

To finance subsistence of capitalists and laborers of Department I, capital goods are sold to Department II. Capital requirements of Department II are $2000c$. In the exchange, Department II trades 2000 units of consumer goods for 2000 units of capital-replacement goods. The 4000 of the 6000 capital goods remaining in Department I are used in that department to maintain its capital stock, i.e., $4000c$. The 1000 of the 3000 consumer goods occurring in Department II are used by that department to provide subsistence for its own laborers and capitalists. Therefore, at the end of the period the capital compositions of both departments are maintained, and reproduction again produces 9000 total annual product.

The stability of the system is defined by the equation of interdepartmental sale and purchase:

$$c_2 = v_1 + s_1 \qquad (7.4)$$

This equation, Marx states, is not inevitable. There is nothing inherent within the system to produce the coincidence. The equation is quite "accidental," depending upon the utility functions of the social classes (C. II, 578). Marx was quite definite concerning the possibilities of simple reproduction in the real world. He writes:

The premise of simple reproduction, that $I(v + s)$ is equal to IIc, is irreconcilable with capitalist production, although this does not exclude the possibility that a certain year in an industrial cycle of 10 or 11 years may not show a smaller total production than the preceding year, so that there would have not been even a simple reproduction, compared to the preceding year. Indeed, considering the natural growth of population per year, simple reproduction could take place only in so far as a correspondingly larger number of unproductive servants would partake of the 1500 representing the aggregate surplus-product [C. II, 608].

The remaining equations of intradepartmental transactions, assuming constant technology, follow from the interdepartmental-transaction equation.[2]

2. Marx introduces into the simple-reproduction analysis a qualitative division within Department II, viz., production of (1) necessary consumer goods and (2) luxury goods, the latter consumed only by the capitalist class and composing a definite percentage of their total consumption. This division, however, has no effect on this model (C. II, 467).

(2) ACCUMULATION
OF CAPITAL

Accumulation (a) emerges with the allocation of surplus to capital:

$$a = g(s) \tag{7.5}$$

The behavior of the industrial capitalist in the Marxian system is here developed. Recall that, in the theory of profit, Marx discounted the reward-for-service and abstinence theories of profit. The capitalist, Marx claims, is merely "personified capital" (C. I, 648). Elsewhere he says:

Accumulate, accumulate! That is Moses and the prophets. . . . Therefore, save, save, i.e., reconvert the greatest possible portion of surplus-value, or surplus product into capital! Accumulation for accumulation's sake, *production for production's sake:* by this formula classical economy expressed the historical mission of the bourgeoisie, and did not for a single instant deceive itself over the birth-throes of wealth [C. I, 652; italics added].

That accumulation should take place at the expense of consumption, is, as a general assumption, an illusion contradicting the nature of capitalist production. For it takes for granted that the aim and compelling motive of capitalist production is consumption, instead of the gain of surplus-value and its capitalization, in other words, accumulation [C. II, 588].

The capitalist economy is therefore defined by accumulation, the product of the unique behavior of the capitalist. Transformation of the simple-reproduction model into expanded or progressive reproduction necessitates a modification of some basic assumptions outlined in the simple-reproduction model. The properties of the Marxian growth model are:

1. Relative prices are constant.
2. Profit rates in each department are constant.
3. All surplus is held by capitalists.
4. A given percentage of the surplus in Department I is converted into capital, i.e., $a = gs_1$, where g represents the specific percentage.
5. A labor supply to complement capital formation exists.
6. The state of technology is constant.
7. The form of the surplus already comprises the material elements of new capital.

8. The net investment is sufficient to expand the scale of production, i.e., over the minimum requirement necessary for production.

Given the value of g, Marx writes: ". . . accumulation resolves itself into the reproduction of capital on a progressively increasing scale. The circle in which simple reproduction moves, alters its form, and, to use Sismondi's expression, changes into a spiral" (C. I, 636–37).

The expansion of capital can be expressed in the generalized form:

$$K_t = K(1 + p'g)^{t} \tag{7.6}$$

where K_t is the amount of capital in time period t, K_o is the original capital, p' is the rate of profit, and g is the proportion of surplus converted into net investment. The technique of capital accumulation in the "two-department model" is analyzed by Marx. Accumulation is defined by the model by which Marx traces the process of departmental transactions which provide for the spiral ascension of capital formation in the following sequence:

1. Transaction between $[v_1 + s_1 - a \ (= gs_1)]$ and c_2 where $(v_1 + s_1 - a)$ represents the total consumption of capitalists and laborers in Department I.
2. a is decomposed into the organic elements of capital for Department I, i.e., $(ac_1 + av_1)$.
3. To provide for av_1, transaction occurs between av_1 (capital goods) and s_2 (consumer goods), where $(s_2 = av_1)$.
4. c_2 has, in the course of the above interdepartmental transactions, increased to $[c_2 + \Delta c_2 \ (= av_1)]$ and, in order to maintain the capital composition in Department II, v_2 is necessary to offset the increased c_2 and is furnished from s_2.

The new capital structure is presented in the following form:

Department I $(c_1 + \Delta c_1) + (v_1 + \Delta v_1) + s_1 - (\Delta c_1 + \Delta v_1)$
Department II $(c_2 + \Delta c_2) + (v_2 + \Delta v_2) + s_2 - (\Delta c_2 + \Delta v_2)$

The following period of production $(t + 1)$ is characterized by:

Department I $(c_1 + \Delta c_1) + (v_1 + \Delta v_1) + (s_1 + \Delta s_1)$
Department II $(c_2 + \Delta c_2) + (v_2 + \Delta v_2) + (s_2 + \Delta s_2)$

3. $K_1 = K_o + p'K_o g$
$= K_o(1 + p'g)$
$K_2 = K_1 + pK_1 g$
$= K_1(1 + p'g)$
$= K_o(1 + p'g)^2$
$K_t = K_o(1 + p'g)^t$

It should be noted here that nowhere in Marx's writings is this equation stated. It merely follows from the assumptions of the Marxian capital accumulation model.

Marx sets up numerical examples to illustrate the accumulation process. He assumes values for the two departments as follows:

$$\text{Department I} \quad 4000c + 1000v + 1000s = 6000C$$
$$\text{Department II} \quad 1500c + 750v + 750s = 3000C$$
$$\text{Annual product} \qquad\qquad\qquad\qquad\quad = \overline{9000C}$$

He postulates the following values:

1. The rate of exploitation is 100 per cent.
2. The rate of profit is 20 per cent for Department I and 33⅓ per cent for Department II.
3. The organic composition of capital in Department I is 80 per cent; in Department II it is 66⅔ per cent.
4. The rate of accumulation in Department I is 50 per cent.

The process, following the sequence outlined above, is as follows:

1. Accumulation in Department I is $500a_1$ ($= \frac{1}{2}s_1$) and takes the form $400c_1 + 100v_1$.
2. c_1 therefore increases from $4000c_1$ to $4400c_1$.
3. Department I now prefers to exchange the value of $1100v_1 + 500s_1$ of capital goods for the equivalent value of consumer goods. But Department II requires only $1500c_2$ for replacement. To satisfy Department I, the exchange of the additional $100v_1$ must be made from $100s_2$; this reduces capitalists' consumption in Department II from 750 to 650.
4. With the transfer of $100v_1$ to Department II, increasing c_2 from $1500c_2$ to $1600c_2$, an increase in v_2, proportionate to the organic composition of capital in Department II, of $50v_2$ is made. The outlay for $50v_2$ comes also from s_2, an intradepartmental transaction, which further reduces s_2 from 650 to 600.

After this first round, the capital structures appear as follows:

$$\text{Department I} \quad 4400c + 1100v + 500s$$
$$\text{Department II} \quad 1600c + 800v + 600s$$

The capital values $(c_1 + v_1)$ $(c_2 + v_2)$ have increased from 7250 to 7900, a net increase of 650. Production in the following period is increased to:

$$\text{Department I} \quad 4400c + 1100v + 1100s = 6600C$$
$$\text{Department II} \quad 1600c + 800v + 800s = 3200C$$
$$\text{Annual product} \qquad\qquad\qquad\qquad\quad = \overline{9800C}$$

Following the same procedure through for period $(t + 2)$:

$$\text{Department I} \quad 4840c + 1210v + 1210s = 7260C$$
$$\text{Department II} \quad 1760c + 880v + 880s = 3520C$$
$$\text{Annual product} \qquad\qquad\qquad\qquad\quad = \overline{10780C}$$

Following the accumulation process through with constant g and $s_1 > 0$, the system becomes explosive. The rate of accumulation in the Marxian model is the independent variable (C. I, 679). The material means for accumulation are drawn, Marx explains, from the surpluses of Departments I and II, the former determined by g, the latter by the consumer goods necessary to complement the increase in constant-capital formation. Since the net investment is provided by surplus, the surplus consumed by the capitalists $[s(c)_1 + s(c)_2]$ must be less than that surplus produced by the process $(s_1 + s_2)$. In comparing capitalists' consumption in the simple-reproduction and accumulation models, Marx argues that, while consumption in the simple-reproduction model coincides with its surplus production, in time a point is reached beyond which the surplus consumed by capitalists in accumulation surpasses the consumption of capitalists in simple reproduction, given the same capital investment.[4] Marx writes:

At the historical dawn of capitalist production—and every capitalist upstart has personally to go through this historical stage—avarice, and desire to get rich, are the ruling passions. But the progress of capitalist production not only creates a world of delights; it lays open, in speculation and the credit system, a thousand sources of sudden enrichment. When a certain stage of development has been reached, a conventional degree of prodigality, which is also an exhibition of wealth, and consequently a source of credit, becomes a business necessity to the "unfortunate" capitalist [C. I, 650–51].

The magnitude of the surplus consumed in any period of time depends upon (1) the rate of accumulation and (2) the organic compositions of capital in both departments. Thus:

4. When numerical values for the two departments are:

Department I	$4000c + 1000v + 1000s = 6000C$	
Department II	$1500c + 750v + 750s = 3000C$	
Annual product	$= \overline{9000C}$	

the surplus produced in time period t is 750. In simple reproduction, therefore, capitalist consumption in Department II would be 750. Under conditions of accumulation, however, $s(c)_2$ would be 600. Following the analysis through for the successive years, $s(c)_2$ takes the following growth pattern: 560, 616, 679, 749, and 771. Compared to simple reproduction after the fifth production period, capitalists' consumption under conditions of accumulation surpass that in simple reproduction.

Considering Department I, under conditions of simple reproduction capitalist consumption $s(c)_1$ would be 1000. Under conditions of accumulation it would take the following series: 500, 550, 605, 665, 732, 805, 974, 1071. Thus after the eighth production period, consumption under accumulation becomes greater than under simple reproduction.

$$s(c)_2 = s_2 - ([v_1 + s_1(1 - g) - c_2] + av_1/c_1 + v_1$$
$$+ v_2/c_2[v_1 + s_1(1 - g) - c_2] + [(v_2/c_2)(av_1/c_1 + v_1)]) \qquad (7.7)$$
$$s(c)_1 = s_1(1 - g) \qquad (7.8)$$

In the simple case where $v_1 + s_1(1 - g) = c_2$, the above equations may be reduced to

$$s(c)_2 = s_2 - [(av_1/c_1 + v_1) + (v_2/c_2)(av_1/c_1 + v_1)]$$
$$= s_2 - [(1 + v_2/c_2)(av_1/c_1 + v_1)] \qquad (7.9)$$
$$s(c)_1 = s_1(1 - g)$$

It is this simplification that characterizes the Marxian examples in Volume II of *Capital.*

Since capital formation in any time period is the conversion of surplus to capital in that period, the magnitude of investment or capital accumulation can be expressed by

$$K_t = ([v_1 + s_1(1 - g) - c_2] + [av_1/c_1 + v_1] + [v_2/c_2][v_1 + s_1(1 - g) - c_2]$$
$$+ [v_2/c_2(av_1/c_1 + v_1)] + s_1[1 - g])_t \qquad (7.10)$$

or, in the simplified case,

$$K_t = [(1 + v_2/c_2)(av_1/c_1 + v_1) + s_1(1 - g)]_t \qquad (7.11)$$

(3) CONCENTRATION, CENTRALIZATION, AND INCREASING TECHNOLOGY

Capital *concentration* is defined by Marx as growing accumulation in the hands of individual capitalists (C. I, 685). This concentration, Marx states, not only compounds individual holdings but creates new independent capitals through division of property by family inheritance. This division of social capital into separate holdings is counteracted, however, by a second force acting on capital stock holdings which Marx calls *centralization* (C. I, 687). The two "levers of centralization," Marx writes, are competition and the availability of credit. The larger capitals, he argues, in the struggle for markets cut out the lesser capitals through price reductions, made possible by the expanding scales of production. Credit discrimination facilitates the further weeding-out of the smaller capitals by making funds more readily available to well-established and larger productive organizations (C. I, 650, 687).

Capital accumulation is linked in the model with increasing organic compositions of capital. Marx writes:

The continual re-transformation of surplus-value into capital now appears in the shape of the increasing magnitude of the capital that enters into the process of production. This in turn is the basis of an extended scale of production, of the methods for raising the productive power of labor that accompany it, and of accelerated production of surplus-value. If, therefore, a certain degree of accumulation of capital appears as a condition of the specifically capitalist mode of production, the latter causes conversely an accelerated accumulation of capital. With the accumulation of capital, therefore, the specifically capitalistic mode of production develops, and with the capitalist mode of production the accumulation of capital [C. I, 684–85].

While the basis for increasing technology is made possible through capital accumulation, no causal relationship is established by Marx. The association of capital accumulation and increasing organic compositions of capital must be considered simply as another assumption which Marx introduces into the model. Recall, however, that the expansion of capital, $K_t = K_o(1 + p'g)^t$, is based upon the assumption of constant state of technology. This assumption is violated, however, when concentration and centralization of capital are introduced into the analysis. Centralization implies increasing organic compositions of capital. The rate of profit, however, is inversely related to the organic composition of capital. Therefore, when technology develops, the rate of profit (p') in equation (7.6) falls. The value of K_t therefore becomes indeterminate. Marx, however, refers to increasing compositions as increasing labor productivity (C. I, 684). To assume that $s = f(c/c + v)$ is, however, inconsistent with the assumption of constant rate of exploitation.

The Marxian models of accumulation may be classified into two distinct categories: (1) accumulation with constant technology and rate of accumulation, in which case the model is explosive, and (2) accumulation with changing technology and rates of accumulation, in which case the rate of economic growth depends upon the relative rates of technology and accumulation.

(4) CONCLUSION

Marx's expositions of simple reproduction and capital accumulation, it should be noted, are expressed solely in value terminology. Had Marx transformed value into price notations in this context, the simple-reproduction model he developed could no longer generate the equilibrium situation which he presumed followed from the model. The selection of value instead of price also damages his capital-accumulation model. In developing the model on economic growth, Marx distinguishes between capital-goods and consumer-goods industries, i.e.,

Departments I and II. He assumes that they are characterized by different organic compositions of capital. It follows, therefore, that the rates of profit in the two departments must differ. Yet this violates the assumption that Marx introduces in the second approximation to price theory (Chap. 2, sec. 4b), that in the capitalist system the rate of profit in all industries is equal. Although Marx states that accumulation in the capitalist economy increases at an increasing rate, no conclusions concerning the growth rate of capital can be made from his model if the rate of profit is permitted to fall. The incorporation of increasing technology into the model, however, by definition implies a fall in the rate of profit.

The exposition undertaken in this chapter is fundamental to an analysis of the predictions analyzed in Part II, in particular Chapter 10, which deals with an analysis of the predictions related to the cyclical behavior of the capitalist economy, and Chapter 11, section 2, dealing with the expansion of the industrial reserve army.

Part II: Marxian predictions

8

The falling rate of profit
and the developing modes
of production

MARX'S THEORY of economic growth is also a theory of economic decay. The *Communist Manifesto*, published while Marx was still gathering material for *Capital*, foretells the theme of his major work, namely, that the capitalist system will sow the seeds of its own destruction. The completion of *Capital* provided the theoretical underpinnings for the *Manifesto*'s forecast.

From the economic theories set down in *Capital*, a number of predictions emerge which detail the inevitability of capitalism's ultimate degeneration. The present chapter concerns itself principally with two such predictions: the inevitability of incessant technological change and the inevitability of declining rates of profit. In the development of these primary predictions, twenty-four other related prophecies are examined. These are listed at the end of the chapter.

(1) INCREASING ORGANIC COMPOSITIONS OF CAPITAL

In most of Marx's writings, but particularly in the pages of the *Communist Manifesto* and the three volumes of *Capital,* Marx prophesies continuous technological change of production under capitalism. For example,

The bourgeoisie cannot exist without constantly revolutionizing the instruments of production, and thereby the relations of production, and with them the whole relations of society [CM, 13].

. . . in no other system of production is improvement so continuous, and the composition of the capital so constantly changing as in the factory system [C. I, 491].

As soon as the new mode of production begins to expand, and thereby to furnish the tangible proof that these commodities can

93

actually be produced more cheaply, the capitalists working under the old methods of production must sell their product below their full prices of production, because the value of these commodities has fallen, because the labor time required by these capitalists for the production of these commodities is no longer than the social average. In one word—this appears as the effect of competition— *these capitalists are compelled to introduce the new method of production* under which the proportion of the variable to the constant capital has been reduced [C. III, 311; italics added].

Consider simple reproduction, expanded reproduction without technological change, and expanded reproduction with technological change as alternative systems that might represent Marx's capitalism. First, the simple-reproduction model must be ruled out. It violates an important characteristic that Marx ascribes to the capitalist, namely a passion for accumulation (see Chap. 7, sec. 2). Second, expanded reproduction without technological change also fails to satisfy Marx's exemplar of the capitalist. Although accumulation occurs in this model, it is employed merely to multiply existing techniques, so that expected rates of profit remain unchanged. This violates still another salient characteristic of the capitalist, namely, the pursuit of *higher* rates of profit. To pursue these higher rates, capitalists must, on pain of extinction, innovate. Hence, the third alternative. The innovating process under capitalism is self-generating. The superprofits that incite capitalists to innovate are wiped out by the intense competition among those who adopt the innovation. Their only recourse is to innovate further.

Although capitalism is marked by continuous innovations, not all systems characterized by innovation are capitalist. Marx, for example, foresees technological change occurring even more rapidly under socialism and communism than under capitalism. The creativity associated with the innovation is attributed not to the capitalist but to the general environment which produces the science. In Marx's view the capitalist merely exploits the innovation as a technique for pursuing higher rates of profit.

(2) THE LAW OF FALLING PROFITS

(a) THE STATEMENT

Marx measures the rate of profit, p', by the net return on the capital advanced for commodity production and sale (see Chap. 2, sec. 5); thus, $p' = s/c + v$. Marx's forecast of declining rates of profit applies ultimately to all enterprises and consequently to all industries, as well as to the general rate prevailing in the economy. It would be difficult to overstate the importance Marx attaches to this forecast. In a letter to Engels, he writes:

I am getting some nice developments. For instance, I have thrown over the whole doctrine of profits as it has existed up to now. . . . *The tendency of the rate of profit to fall as society progresses.* This [idea] already follows from what was developed in Book I, on the *change in the composition of capital with the development of the social productive forces.* This is one of the greatest triumphs over the great *pons asini* [stumbling block] of all previous economics [MEC, 102, 244].

Or in *Capital,* after deriving this prediction, or as Marx calls it, this law of capitalism, he comments:

Simple as this law appears from the foregoing statements, all of political economy has so far tried in vain to discover it, as we shall see later on. The economists saw the problem and cudgeled their brains in tortuous attempts to interpret it. Since the law is of great importance for capitalist production, it may be said to be that mystery whose solution has been the goal of the entire political economy since Adam Smith [C. III, 249–50].

The primary determinants of the rate of profit are the rate of surplus value, s/v, and the organic composition of capital, $c/c + v$. The capitalist's pursuit of higher rates of profit and the forces of competition compel him to adopt ever increasing organic compositions of capital. As these compositions increase, the rate of surplus value remaining constant, the rate of profit will fall. The mechanics of the law are simple.

Consider an industry characterized by the production process

$$10c + 10v + 10s = 30C$$

with a constant rate of surplus value. The rate of profit forthcoming from such a process is 50 per cent. Suppose now that an innovation is introduced. The organic composition of the innovated process increases from, say, 50 to 80 per cent. Since commodities produced by the process are valued at the socially necessary labor time which, for the industry, is $30C$, the innovated production process would then *appear* to the capitalist as

$$12c + 3v + 15s = 30C$$

Since the rate of surplus value is constant, $12s$ of the $15s$ must represent superprofits. The rate of profit accruing to the innovated process therefore is 100 per cent. Competition, however, forces the other capitalists in the industry to adopt the new process, with the result that the socially necessary labor time decreases from $30C$ to $18C$ and the value of the commodities established by the innovating process becomes

$$12c + 3v + 3s = 18C$$

The rate of profit thus decreases to 20 per cent. This demonstrates the law of declining rates of profit.

Marx's illustration of the law (C. III, 247) is described in five sequential processes that are characterized by increasing organic compositions of capital. Assuming that the rate of surplus value is 100 per cent, if

1. $c =$ 50, and $v = 100$, then $p' = 100/150$ or $66\frac{2}{3}\%$
2. $c = 100$, and $v = 100$, then $p' = 100/200$ or 50%
3. $c = 200$, and $v = 100$, then $p' = 100/300$ or $33\frac{1}{3}\%$
4. $c = 300$, and $v = 100$, then $p' = 100/400$ or 25%
5. $c = 400$, and $v = 100$, then $p' = 100/500$ or 20%

The organic composition of capital is the independent variable. Because the compositions increase from $33\frac{1}{3}$ to 80 per cent, the rate of profit declines from $66\frac{2}{3}$ to 20 per cent.

(b) VARIABILITY IN s/v

Had Marx left the statement in this simple form, criticism would be as obvious as it is elementary. The rate of surplus value is not constant as the organic composition of capital increases because the rate of surplus value is functionally dependent upon the organic composition of capital. A change in the latter must induce a change in the former. This Marx recognized. Although the assumption of a constant rate of surplus value is made in the first volume and through parts of the second and third volumes of *Capital,* its importance to the derivation of Marx's profit-rate prediction is purely expository. Marx was interested in underscoring the principle determinant of the rate of profit, namely, the organic composition of capital, and for this reason de-emphasized all other considerations. The rate of profit will decline, he predicts, whatever the rate of surplus value.

Marx now relaxes the assumption of constant rates of surplus value. The rate of surplus value, he asserts, varies directly with the productiveness of labor (see Chap. 3, sec. 6). The more productive the laborer, the smaller is that portion of the working day that must be devoted to his subsistence. The greater, therefore, will be the absolute surplus and, consequently, the rate of surplus value. Although capital cannot create value, Marx insists, it can affect the distribution of the workday, permitting greater allocations to surplus. The higher the organic composition of capital, the more productive the laborer, and the greater is the rate of surplus value. "Modern industry," Marx writes, "raises the productiveness of labor to an extraordinary degree" (C. I, 422). Repeated references to this relationship appear in *Capital* (e.g., C. III, 178, 257, 261, 269, 290).

If Marx permitted surplus value to vary without restraint, then little could be said concerning the fate of the rate of profit. It is obvious that an infinite increase in surplus value will raise the rate of profit infinitely, whatever the organic composition of capital. This Marx realized. His prophecy concerning the declining rate of profit necessitates some sort of upper limit to surplus value. Marx constructs such a limit:

To the extent that the development of the productive power reduces the paid portion of the employed labor, it raises the surplus value by raising its rate; but to the extent that it reduces the total mass of labor employed by a certain capital, it reduces the factor of numbers with which the rate of surplus value is multiplied in order to calculate its mass [C. III, 290].

Marx illustrates:

Two laborers, each working twelve hours daily, cannot produce the same mass of surplus value as 24 laborers, each working only 2 hours, even if they could live on air and did not have to work for themselves at all [*ibid.*].

And so Marx concludes:

In this respect, then, the compensation in the reduction of the number of laborers by means of an intensification of exploitation has certain impassable limits. It may for this reason, check the fall of the rate of profit, but it cannot prevent it entirely [*ibid.*].

Herein lies the major defect in Marx's derivation of the profit-rate prediction. Marx *measures* surplus value, as he does all forms of value, in terms of labor hours. Using this measurement, he cannot fully incorporate into profit-rate determination the variations in productivity that result from different capital compositions. Although elsewhere Marx draws attention to the import of such variations upon the rate of surplus value, its incorporation into profit-rate analysis becomes confusing and incomplete. Had Marx properly considered productivity, his rate-of-profit prediction would have had to be qualified.

(c) CRITIQUE OF THE LAW

Recall Marx's proof of the upper limit to surplus value: "Two laborers each working 12 hours daily cannot produce the same mass of surplus value as 24 laborers each working 2 hours daily." Incorporating productivity considerations into Marx's demonstration of the upper limit substantially alters the conclusions.

Assume in the second case, of the 24 men each working 2 hours daily, that:

1. Output is 84u. The unit u measures real output.
2. Constant capital is 24u.
3. The organic composition of capital is 100 per cent (24u/24u) since the variable cost is zero.
4. The price of a unit of constant capital is 1u.

The capital-labor ratio is 24 units for 24 laborers, or 1 unit per laborer. The production function can be represented by

$$c + v + s = C$$
$$24u + 0 + s = 84u$$
$$s = 60u$$

The surplus remaining after the variable and constant capital costs are met is, therefore, 60u. The rate of surplus value, a purely derived value, s/v, is 60u/0 or infinite. The rate of profit is 60u/24u or 250 per cent. Of critical importance here is the recognition that the relationship between surplus value and the rate of profit is wholly dependent upon the rate of productivity.

Compare this second case to the first case in his illustration, where only 2 laborers are employed. Assume that:

1. Output is 96u.
2. Constant capital is 24u.
3. The organic composition of capital is 100 per cent.
4. The price of a unit of constant capital is 1u.

The capital-labor ratio in this case is 24 units for 2 laborers, or 12 units per laborer. This marks a 12-fold increase in capital per man. The production process can be represented by

$$c + v + s = C$$
$$24u + 0 + s = 96u$$
$$s = 72u$$

The rate of profit under these conditions is 72u/24u or 300 per cent.

Contrary to Marx's assertion, the rate of profit increases as the number of laborers declines. So, too, does total output. Further, there is no reason to suppose why 2 laborers, each with 12 units of capital, cannot produce a greater output than 24 laborers, each working with only 1 unit. And since Marx does not conceive of a productivity restraint to production—indeed, he forecasts the opposite [1]—no upper limit to the mass of surplus value can be derived. The rate of profit, therefore, need not decline.

This same productivity analysis can be applied to Marx's earlier illustration of the declining-rate-of-profit prediction. Recall Marx's value formulation of the five sequential processes. Consider the first two processes:

$$50c + 100v + 100s = 250, \quad p' = 66\tfrac{2}{3}\%$$
$$100c + 100v + 100s = 300, \quad p' = 50\%$$

These can be rewritten in real terms as

$$c + v + s = C$$
$$1u + 2u + s = 5u$$
$$s = 2u$$

and

$$c + v + s = C$$
$$2u + 2u + s = 6u$$
$$s = 2u$$

In the first production process, the surplus value remaining after the variable and constant costs have been met is $2u$. The rate of surplus value, *a derived value,* must be $2u/2u$ or 100 per cent. The corresponding rate of profit is $2u/3u$ or $66\tfrac{2}{3}$ per cent. In the second process, designed to be consistent with Marx's value formulation, the organic composition of capital is 50 per cent, or an increase of $16\tfrac{2}{3}$ per cent over the composition of the first process. The laborers now work with twice the capital equipment. Total output recorded is $6u$, up $1u$ from the first process. The rate of surplus value is constant at 100 per cent; the rate of profit decreases from $66\tfrac{2}{3}$ to 50 per cent.

The critical question is: Why does Marx here assume that a 100 per cent increase in the capital used per man increases the output by only 20 per cent? There exists no relationship in his model that links specific changes in organic compositions of capital to changes in productivity. It is interesting to note, however, that in all the examples cited by Marx which deal with increasing organic compositions of capital the assigned increases in the productiveness of labor never suffice to maintain the rate

1. Marx writes: "Here the capitalist mode of production falls into another contradiction. Its historical mission is the ruthless development in geometrical progression of the productivity of human labor" (C. III, 308).

of profit.[2] *But this is convenience, not necessity.*

If, in the above productivity interpretation of the Marxian law, output increases to $7u$ instead of to Marx's assumed $6u$, the surplus value derived from the process would increase from 100 to 150 per cent. The corresponding rate of profit, under this condition, would increase from 66⅔ to 75 per cent. Marx's prophecy concerning the declining rate of profit thus becomes merely a possibility; upon its probability Marx sheds little light.

(d) THE LAW OF THE TENDENCY

While Marx states the law as an inevitability, he does acknowledge the possibility that temporary increases in the rate of profit may occur. It is in this sense that Marx speaks of the law as a tendency; the prediction is modified to become the *law of the falling tendency of the rate of profit.* There are counteracting forces, he asserts, that tend to check the decline in the rate of profit. In the long run, however, they only hasten it (C. III, 274).

Marx lists six counteracting forces which tend to affect the rate of profit.

(i) INCREASED INTENSITY OF EXPLOITATION

Marx points to the possibility of increasing the rate of surplus value without changing the organic composition of capital. Increases in production efficiency and in the utilization of machinery, e.g., accelerated depreciation, affect the intensity of the labor power employed so that more surplus value can be produced by a given labor power (see Chap. 3, sec. 3). The prolongation of the working day is another technique used by capitalists to increase the surplus value. To the extent that

2. Consider another of Marx's illustrations (C. III, 255). Here he shows that while the rate of profit declines, the absolute profit may still increase.

$$\text{(a)} \quad 4c + 2v + 2s = 8$$
$$\text{(b)} \quad 15c + 3v + 3s = 21$$

Note that the capital-labor ratio increases by 300 per cent. Profits increase from $2s$ to $3s$, or by 50 per cent. If the productiveness of labor were to increase 250 per cent, then total output would be 30. Under this condition, process (b) in real terms would be

$$\text{(b')} \quad 15c + 3v + s = 30$$
$$s = 12$$

Comparing process (a) to (b'), the rate of surplus value must increase by 400 per cent, and the rate of profit, instead of decreasing as Marx assumed it must, increases to 66⅔ per cent. While there is no logical explanation for assuming that productivity increases as rapidly as the capital-labor ratio, neither can Marx provide a logical explanation for assuming that 3 laborers, each with 5 units of capital, can only produce a commodity valued at 21.

capitalists are successful in intensifying exploitation by these means, the rate of profit will increase.

(ii) DEPRESSION OF WAGES BELOW THEIR VALUE

Capitalists purchase labor power with wages. That wages could be less than the value of labor power is, Marx states, an empirical fact. And to the extent of this wage-value differential, surplus value is augmented. Such a condition, however, is only temporary, for, were it to continue, starvation would reduce the labor supply and restore wages to their value. What may persist, however, is the fall in the value of labor power itself.

(iii) CHEAPENING OF THE ELEMENTS OF CONSTANT CAPITAL

Marx distinguishes between physical and value formulations of the organic composition of capital. He writes: "The same development, which increases the mass of the constant capital relatively over that of the variable, reduces the value of its elements as a result of the increased productivity of labor" (C. III, 276–77). In exceptional cases, he notes, the mass of the elements of constant capital may increase while its value remains the same or even falls. In those cases where it falls, the rate of profit will increase.

This is perhaps the most interesting of Marx's discussion of the counteracting forces. Here Marx correctly interprets the implications of productivity increases for the rate of profit. But why he considers this counteracting force to *temporarily* check the decline in the rate of profit is not at all clear.

(iv) RELATIVE OVERPOPULATION

Marx predicts that capitalist production will become more extensive and more luxurious (MEP, 120). This he attributes to the development of relative surplus populations. As the compositions of capital increase, the laborers that are displaced by the new technology join the ranks of the relative surplus population.[3] This growing supply of labor provides

3. Marx apparently uses the terms relative surplus population and absolute surplus population interchangeably. In so doing he ignores the question of labor reabsorption and consequently the possibility that there may exist reduced labor input per process with full employment in the economy. On these grounds his consideration of relative overpopulation as a counteracting force to the declining rate of profit breaks down. The confusion of relative and absolute surplus of population is treated in detail in Chap. 11, sec. 1.

the basis for the production of luxury commodities. Since luxury production is characterized by relatively low organic compositions of capital, the average rate of profit rises (C. III, 297).

Here, too, Marx fails to explain why the counteracting force is merely temporary in its effects. Recall from his growth theory that capitalists' consumption increases at an increasing rate (Chap. 7, sec. 2). This suggests unlimited possibilities for luxury production. This counteracting force must be questioned on still another ground. Since capitalists seek the highest rate of profit, they would naturally move into luxury production without waiting upon relative surplus populations.

(v) FOREIGN TRADE

International trade and international capital movements tend to raise the rate of profit. Extensions of the commodity market to areas characterized by lower capital compositions permit capitalists to sell commodities at prices higher than domestic values so that profit rates accruing from foreign trade are above, and therefore tend to raise, the general rate of profit. Also, capital investments in processes of lower organic compositions of capital yield higher rates of profit.

(vi) INCREASES IN STOCK CAPITAL

The development of joint-stock companies appears to counteract the decline in the general rate of profit. Here Marx distinguishes between the appearance and the reality. These companies appear to counteract the decline because their returns, although lower than the average, are not defined as profit and therefore are excluded from profit-rate evaluation. Since Marx foresees capitalist development taking the form of joint-stock companies, the recorded rate of profit will appear to decline less rapidly than it actually does.

These counteracting forces check, retard, and weaken the absolute enforcement of the law; but what they cannot do is suspend it (C. III, 275). And so Marx concludes: "The law therefore shows itself only as a tendency, whose effects become clearly marked only under certain conditions and in the course of long periods" (C. III, 280). The analysis here suggests that if any of the counteracting forces persist, then the law may become suspended indefinitely or be "permanently temporarily" checked. Marx's law of the tendency, under such a condition, loses any meaning. To illustrate by analogy, it would be meaningless to claim that there exists a law of rising prices because, on the demand side, demanders compete among themselves and this tends to increase price.

So, too, with Marx's prediction concerning the tendency for the rate of profit to fall.

The argument here is not that the rate of profit will not decline. What is shown here is that specific parameter values must be assumed in the profit-rate equations before such a decline will occur. Whatever else Marx does, he does not prove that the specific values required for the falling-rate-of-profit prediction can be derived from his model.

(e) FACTORS INFLUENCING THE TENDENCY

The Marxian theories of price, rent, capital circulation, and capital accumulation provide further insight into the effect expanding modes of production have upon the rate of profit. Certain economic relationships are strengthened, others are weakened, by the constantly changing values of the variables in Marx's system. For example, the value compositions of the capital structures are so modified. These modifications bear upon the rate of profit. These are not temporary influences but tend to persist as long as the economy develops. Consider the influence on the rate of profit of (i) changing values of variable and constant capital, (ii) changing values of capital turnover, (iii) changing values of merchant's capital, and (iv) changing distributions of profit.

(i) CHANGING VALUES OF VARIABLE AND CONSTANT CAPITAL

The quantitative changes in the organic composition of capital which characterize the expanding capitalist economy produce, as well, qualitative changes in its variables, i.e., constant and variable capital. These qualitative changes affect (*a*) the values of labor power, (*b*) the values of capital depreciation, and (*c*) the values of raw materials.

(*a*) *Changing value of labor power.* Skill and exertion of manual labor are, Marx states, inversely related to the complexity of machinery. The transition from manufacture to machinery, i.e., the application of higher capital compositions, introduced two distinct qualitative changes in the mode of production: (1) the use of the machine and (2) the replacement of human motive power by mechanical and water power. Prior to the advent of machinery, the quantity of commodities produced in a given time depended upon the proficiency of the laborer operating the tool. The application of the machine to production, however, meant that the number of tools that could be placed in operation at any one time was no longer restricted to the laborers' "bodily organs" (C. I, 408). The substitution of mechanical and water power for human power, Marx writes, was the necessary complement to the development of the machine and emancipated the productiveness of the machine from the restrictions of human strength (C. I, 412). In brief, the contrast between the role of the laborer before and after the advent of machinery is striking. Before, all production was regulated by the dexterity and strength of the laborer. He handled the tool directly and applied his own power in production. With machinery, not only is the motive power independent of the laborer but also the number of tools or operations employed in the process in a given time. Marx writes:

Owing to the extensive use of machinery and to division of labor, the work of the proletarians has lost all individual character, and consequently, all charm for the workman. *He becomes an appendage of the machine,* and it is only the most simple, most monotonous, and most easily acquired knack that is required of him [CM, 18; italics added].

In manufacture the workmen are parts of a living mechanism. In the factory we have a lifeless mechanism independent of the workman, who becomes its mere living appendage. . . . The special skill of each individual insignificant factory operative vanishes as an infinitesimal quantity before the science. . . . The technical subordination of the workman to the uniform motion of the instruments of labor . . . is elaborated into a complete system in the factory [C. I, 461–63].

It is upon the basis of these qualitative changes in the laborer that Marx derives the following predictions:

1. With the advancement of machinery, there develops the tendency to equalize and reduce to one and the same level every kind of work that has to be done by the minders of the machines (C. I, 459).
2. With increasing simplicity of operation, greater labor mobility results (C. I, 459).
3. The greater the application of modern industry, the more is the labor of men superseded by that of women and children (C. I, 431–32).
4. Modern industry will tear away from the family the sentimental veil and reduce it to a mere money relation.[4]

4. The family, a purely social relationship between man and wife, parents and children, must relate to the mode of production. Quoting from *German Ideology,* "With savages each family has of course its own cave or hut like the separate family tent of the nomads. This separate domestic economy is made only the more necessary by the further development of private property. . . . The setting-up of a communal domestic economy presupposes the development of machinery, of the use of natural forces and of many other productive forces, e.g., of water-supplies, of gas-lighting, steam-heating, etc., the removal of the antagonism of town and country. . . . *That the abolition of individual economy is inseparable from the abolition of the family is self-evident"* (GI, 17–18, italics added; cf. C. I, 513; LTA, 24; CM, 32).

5. Modern industry revolutionizes educational institutions, forcing the predominance of technical and vocational training (C. I, 534).

Realization of these predictions leads directly to the more general prediction that, *as modern industry develops, the value of labor power declines.*

Recall that the value of labor power is determined by the real subsistence of the family unit or the real costs of reproducing the laboring class (Chap. 2, sec. 3). Reproduction of the labor power in manufacture included the costs of apprenticeship which then were essential to produce the requisite quality of labor. Also physical force and skill were essential in manufacture, so that the male member of the family was, by circumstance, the sole provider for the family unit. The value of the individual labor power thus included the costs of maintaining the entire family. With the advent of machinery, the value of subsistence undergoes radical change. Expenses of apprenticeship are reduced or at times eliminated. Inclusion of women and children in the labor force permits more than one provider for the family unit, e.g., four family members. In this case the individual value of labor power, based on family subsistence, would be reduced by 75 per cent (C. I, 431). The rate of surplus value increases to 700 per cent. Thus, quite apart from the effect quantitative changes in the organic composition of capital have upon the productiveness of labor and consequently upon the rate of profit, qualitative changes in the labor component of the capital composition increase relative surplus value and hence the rate of profit. *And this tendency to increase should persist as long as industry expands.*

(*b*) *Changing values of capital depreciation.* Recall from Chapter 3 Marx's analysis of moral depreciation, d_m, or capital obsolescence. As new technology is introduced into the economy, the value of the existing technique is depreciated according to the constant-capital value differential between the two techniques. Thus:

$$d_m = c_1 - c_2 \tag{3.2}$$

This obsolescence is incorporated into the profit-rate equation as an additional capital charge on production:

$$p' = \frac{s}{c + v + d_m}$$

By this charge, the rate of profit is reduced.

The more rapidly technology is introduced into the economy, the greater will be the disparity between new and prevailing techniques, and, consequently, the more rapidly will the profit rate decline. Further, capital obsolescence is related not only to the *rate* at which the technology is introduced but also to the *level* of technology. As the compositions increase, obsolescence tends to increase as well. To this extent the rate of profit is further depressed.

Capitalists, aware of the import of obsolescence on profit rates, try to avoid such costs by speeding up the utilization of the constant capital. Thus the introduction of relay or shift systems in production are, Marx states, inevitable. Too, capitalists seek to prolong the working day, for this prolongation not only increases the surplus value through greater exploitation of the laborer but also cuts moral depreciation. Marx predicts: "Hence that remarkable phenomenon in the history of Modern Industry, that machinery sweeps away every moral and natural restriction on the length of the working day" (C. I, 445).

(*c*) *Changing prices of raw materials.* The raw-material component of commodity values increases with increasing organic compositions of capital (C. I, 682). This relative value change directly affects the rate of profit:

If the price of raw material falls by the amount d, then . . . $s/c + v$ becomes $s/c + v - d$, in other words, the rate of profit rises. On the other hand, if the price of raw materials rises, then $s/c + v$ becomes $s/c + v + d$, in other words, the rate of profit falls [C. III, 126–27].

The supply of raw materials, dependent upon natural conditions, is relatively fixed in the short run. As demand for raw materials increases with expanding production capacities, raw-material prices also increase (see Chap. 2, sec. 7). The rate of profit, therefore, falls. In time the general application of higher capital compositions affects all industries and alters all supply conditions. The innovations in inter- and intracontinental transportation, the application of scientific techniques to raw-material production, the discovery of new and richer raw-material resources, the conversion of the colonies to primarily raw-material suppliers are all factors which tend, over the long run, to increase the total availability of raw materials. Their prices therefore will tend to decline, and by this tendency the general rate of profit increases. Hence, like changes in the value of labor power and the prolongation of the working day, changes in the prices of raw materials may be a continuing force that tends to raise the rate of profit.

(ii) CHANGING VALUES OF CAPITAL TURNOVER

In relating rates of profit to changing organic compositions of capital, Marx distinguishes between the general and the annual rate:

We cannot compute the rate of profit on any output of commodities we choose,—e.g., a weekly output—but that $sv/c + v$ here represents the surplus value produced *during the year* to the capital *advanced* during the year (i.e., as distinct from the capital *turned over*). The formula $sv/c + v$ stands here, therefore, for the *annual* rate of profit. We next examine how variations in the *turnover* of capital . . . modify the *rate of profit* while *the rate of surplus value remains the same* [MEC, 242].

Recall the development of Marx's theory of capital circulation (see Chap. 6, sec. 3). A complete rotation or reproduction of a given quantity of industrial capital is defined as a turnover, t. The number of turnovers per year is measured by

$$n = 1/t \tag{6.6}$$

Capital turnover, n, relates the value of the capital advanced during the year, K_o, to the value of the capital actually employed during the year, K_e:

$$K_e = cK$$

The surplus value created during the year depends not upon the value of the capital advanced but upon the value of the capital actually employed. The more a specific capital is turned over within a year, the greater will be the annual surplus value, and consequently the higher is the annual rate of profit measured on the value of the capital advanced. Marx explains:

Now let us select a capital A composed of $80c + 20v = 100K$. Let this have a rate of surplus value of 100%, and let it be turned over twice per year.

The annual product then is $160c + 40v + 40s$. But for the purpose of ascertaining the rate of profit we do not calculate the $40s$ on the turned over capital of 200. We calculate it on the advanced capital of 100, and we obtain thus a rate of profit of 40%.

Now let us compare this with a capital B composed of $160c + 40v = 200K$, which has the same rate of surplus value, 100%, but which is turned over only once a year.

The annual product of this capital is the same as that of A, namely $160c + 40v + 40s$. But the $40s$ in this case are to be calculated on an advance of capital amounting to 200, so that the rate of profit of B is only 20% or one-half of that of A [C. III, 87].

Marx records the general relationship between increasing organic compositions of capital and capital turnover. Consider the following elaboration of Marx's illustration (C. II, 210). The following assumptions are made:

1. $K_o = 100,000$
2. $c = 80,000$
3. $v = 20,000$
4. Depreciation of $c = 10$ per cent, so that every year 8,000 of the 80,000c appears as the constant capital used in production.
5. $n = 5$, so that the constant capital per turnover per year is $\frac{1}{5}$ of 8,000 or 1,600.
6. $s/v = 100$ per cent.

The annual structure of production would take the form:

$$
\begin{array}{llll}
\text{First} & t: & 1600c + & 20000v + & 20000s \\
\text{Second} & t: & 1600c + & 20000v + & 20000s \\
\text{Third} & t: & 1600c + & 20000v + & 20000s \\
\text{Fourth} & t: & 1600c + & 20000v + & 20000s \\
\text{Fifth} & t: & \overline{1600c +} & \overline{20000v +} & \overline{20000s} \\
\text{Annual} & & 8000c + & 100000v + & 100000s
\end{array}
$$

The total capital advanced is $80,000c + 20,000v$ or $100,000K_o$. The total capital employed during the year, however, is $80,000c + 100,000v$ or 108,000. The total annual surplus value is $100,000s$. The annual rate of profit, calculated on the capital outlay, is $100,000s/80,000c + 20,000v$, or 100 per cent.

Let us now assume that $10,000c$ is added to the production process so that the organic composition of capital increases from $80,000/80,000 + 20,000$ to $90,000/90,000 + 20,000$. Further, assume that the number of turnovers increases from 5 to 6. In this case the constant capital per turnover would be $\frac{1}{6}$ of 10 per cent of 90,000c or 1,500c. The structure of production under these circumstances would take the form:

$$
\begin{array}{llll}
\text{First} & t: & 1500c + & 20000v + & 20000s \\
\text{Second} & t: & 1500c + & 20000v + & 20000s \\
\text{Third} & t: & 1500c + & 20000v + & 20000s \\
\text{Fourth} & t: & 1500c + & 20000v + & 20000s \\
\text{Fifth} & t: & 1500c + & 20000v + & 20000s \\
\text{Sixth} & t: & \overline{1500c +} & \overline{20000v +} & \overline{20000s} \\
\text{Annual} & & 9000c + & 120000v + & 120000s
\end{array}
$$

The total capital outlay in this second case of higher capital composition is 110,000. The total capital employed is $9,000c + 120,000v$ or 129,-000. The total annual surplus value is 120,000. The annual rate of profit, therefore, is $120,000/110,000$ or 109 per cent. In other words, though the total capital outlay increased and the rate of surplus value remained constant, the annual rate of profit increased from 100 to 109 per cent. This increase is attributed to the increase in the number of capital turnovers per year.

Nowhere in the Marxian analysis is the relationship between capital turnover and capital outlay explicitly established. If, in the above illustration, the number of turnovers increased from 5 to 5.5, the rate of profit would have remained the same. At any increase below 5.5, the rate of profit would have declined.

Certain predictions, derived from Marx's model of capitalism, suggest continuing increases in the number of capital turnovers per year:

> The circumstances which augment the product of the individual working day, such as cooperation, division of labor, employment of machinery, shorten at the same time the working period of connected acts of production. Thus machinery shortens the building time of houses, bridges, etc.; a mowing and threshing machine, etc. shorten the working period required to transform the ripe grain into a finished product. Improved ship-building reduces by increased speed the time of turnover of capital invested in navigation [C. II, 267].

Marx predicts: "The day is not far distant when, by a combination of railways and steam vessels, the distance between England and India, measured by time, will be shortened to eight days, and when that once fabulous country will thus be actually annexed to the Western world" (OB, 387).[5] In addition to its effect on capital turnover, improved transportation permits a reduction in the stock of inventories, the non-surplus-producing cost in capital outlay. On this account as well, profit rates should increase (C. II, 291). It is only in the agricultural sphere that restrictions on increasing annual capital turnovers with increasing capital compositions emerge. This argument, however, is based on climatic or natural factors (C. II, 268).

Marx further prophesies that the institution of the factory system and the increased mobility of labor will produce geographical reallocations of population from which will emerge urban industrial centers:

> The bourgeoisie has subjected the country to the rule of the towns. It has created enormous cities, has greatly increased the urban population as compared with the rural. . . . The bourgeoisie keeps more and more doing away with the scattered state of the population [CM, 15]. The application of modern science to production clears the land of its inhabitants, but it concentrates people in manufacturing towns [OB, 375].

5. In Marx's day the journey took four months (C. II, 288).

The aggregation of population into urban areas increases the density of the market (C. I, 387). The time of circulation and hence the total period of production are thereby reduced. The number of capital turnovers increases, and this tends to raise the annual rate of profit.

(iii) CHANGING VALUES OF MERCHANT'S CAPITAL

As the capitalist system develops, the costs and time associated with the marketing of commodities become divorced from the actual production organization. These are undertaken exclusively by the merchant. This transfer of marketing functions from the industrial capitalist to the merchant, Marx asserts, results in higher annual rates of profit:

If . . . a capital of $720c + 180v + 180s$, assisted by a merchant's capital of 100, leaves a profit of 162 or 18% for the industrial capitalist, or, in other words, implies a deduction of 18, then the additional capital required without the assistance of this independent merchant's capital would probably be 200, and the total advance to be made by the industrial capitalist would be 1,100 instead of 900, which, with a surplus of 180, would mean a rate of profit of only $16\frac{4}{11}\%$ [C. III, 343].

The specialization of the marketing functions permits economies of scale that could not otherwise be realized, e.g., one merchant handling the production of more than one capitalist, the economizing on inventories and inventory facilities, and the lowering of unit transportation costs (see Chap. 6, sec. 4). Of this specialization, Marx writes:

To the extent that it helps to expand the market and promotes the division of labor between capitals, thereby enabling capital to work on a larger scale, its function enhances the productivity of the industrial capital and the accumulation of this capital. Inasmuch as it may shorten the time of circulation, it raises the ratio of surplus value to the advanced capital, that is, the rate of profit [C. III, 330].

(iv) CHANGING DISTRIBUTIONS OF PROFIT

A redistribution of profit among industrial capitalists, merchants, money capitalists, and landowners affects the rate of capital accumulation and consequently the rate of change in the general rate of profit. Although Marx's law of the falling rate of profit assures that ultimate decline in the rates of return to all surplus-receiving classes, the rate at which they each decline may differ. If the rate of interest and the rate of return to land fall more rapidly than the general rate of profit, that rate of profit accruing to the industrial capitalist may, for some periods of capitalist development, actually increase, remain constant, or at least decline less rapidly than the general rate. Marx was aware of such rate differentiations. Also, he stressed that the rate of capital accumulation depends primarily upon the return to the industrial capitalist. Consider his predictions concerning the returns to capital and land.

(*a*) *Marx's prediction concerning declining interest rates.* The rate of interest, we have seen, depends primarily upon the prevailing rate of profit in the economy and the relative strengths of the demand for and the supply of loanable funds in the money market (Chap. 4, sec. 2). The rate of profit sets the upper bound. And since Marx forecasts declining profit rates, he can predict that "the fall in the interest on money is a necessary consequence and result of industrial capitalism" (EPM, 127).

Marx's analysis of the loanable-funds market seems to suggest that additional forces are operating to depress the interest rate. His discussion relates almost entirely to the supply side of the market. For example, he says that

the rate of profit has a tendency to fall in the course of social progress, and . . . the rate of interest has the same tendency, so far as it is regulated by the rate of profit . . . ; furthermore, the rate of interest has a tendency to fall in consequence of the growth of loanable capital [C. III, 731].

Marx quotes Ramsay's *Essay on the Distribution of Wealth:*

Let us assume that capital were never borrowed for any other but productive investments, it is nevertheless possible that the rate of interest may vary without any change in the rate of gross profits. For, as a people progresses in the development of wealth, there arises and grows more and more a class of people, who find themselves possessed of funds through the labors of their ancestors, and who can live on the mere interest on them. Many, having actively participated in business in their youth and prime, retire, in order to live quietly in their old age on the interest of the sums accumulated by them. *These two classes have a tendency to increase with the growing wealth of the country* [C. III, 424–25; italics added].

Elsewhere, and much earlier, Marx had set down what may seem to be a contradictory forecast. In *Economic and Philosophic Manuscripts of 1844,* Marx develops the thesis that ultimately all forms of property are transformed to industrial capital.

The extravagant *rentier*'s means therefore dwindle day by day in inverse proportion to the increasing possibilities and pitfalls of pleasure. Consequently, he must either consume his capital himself, thus ruining himself, or must become an industrial capitalist. [EPM, 127].

The contradiction disappears if the above quote is considered as a long-run forecast so that the *rentier* class will first increase in size and then ultimately dissolve.

Marx attributes no general law to the determination of interest rates. There is no "natural" rate of interest. It is "as much a purely empirical fact belonging to the realm of accident as the division of the share of common profit of some corporative business among different shareholders by percentages" (C. III, 428).

The decline in the rate of interest is more dramatically marked when comparison is made between capitalism and earlier economic systems. Marx writes of India, for instance,

where the ryot manages his farm as an independent producer, whose production, strictly so called is not yet under the complete sway of capital, although the usurer may not only rob him of his entire surplus-labor by means of interest, but also curtail his wages, to use a capitalist term. For the interest of such stages comprises all of the profit . . . instead of merely expressing an aliquot part of the produced surplus-value, or profit, as it does in countries with a developed capitalist production [C. III, 252].

(*b*) *Marx's prediction concerning declining rents.* Recall that ground rent is composed of two elements: differential and absolute rent (Chap. 5, secs. 3, 4). Factors determining the magnitude of absolute rent are the monopolization of land and the assumed lower organic composition of capital in the agricultural industries (Chap. 5, sec. 2). This lower composition, Marx claims, results primarily from the skewed distribution of innovations between agricultural and nonagricultural industries:

This fact could be explained, aside from all other economic circumstances which are of paramount importance, from the earlier and more rapid development of mechanical sciences, and especially by their application, compared to the later and partly quite recent development of chemistry, geology and physiology, and particularly their application to agriculture. For the rest it is an indubitable and long known fact that also the progress of agriculture expresses itself steadily in a relative increase of the constant over the variable capital [C. III, 882].

Marx suggests the narrowing of the organic composition of capital gap with the new applications of science to agricultural industries (MEC, 132). The suggestion takes the form of a prediction:

How far the difference goes, or whether it exists at all, depends upon the relative development of agriculture as compared to industry. In the nature of the case, *this difference must decrease with the progress of agriculture,* unless the proportion in which the variable capital decreases as compared to the constant, is still greater in the industrial than in the agricultural capital [C. III, 897; italics added].

The qualification in the last quotation does not affect the prediction. For Marx elsewhere asserts that growth in agriculture surpasses that in the industrial sphere:

In the sphere of agriculture, modern industry has a more revolutionary effect than elsewhere. . . . The irrational, old fashioned methods of agriculture are replaced by scientific ones. Capitalist production completely tears asunder the old bond of union which held together agriculture and manufacture in their infancy [C. I, 554; cf. C. I, 553].

The existence of differential rent, on the other hand, depends upon the varying productivities of land-capital investments. Whether *total* productivity of land increases or decreases is irrelevant. What is important is the distribution of land capital among varying qualities of soils (see Chap. 5, sec. 4). If the product per unit of land capital between the best and worst soils decreases as more capital is invested in agriculture, differential rent declines. The development of the capitalist system, particularly the applications of the fertile foreign areas to the agricultural market, Marx predicts, diminishes the productivity differential of land-capital investments and hence differential ground rent. As he says:

The transoceanic steamboats and the railroads of North and South America and India enabled very peculiar masses of land to enter into competition upon the European grain markets. There were on the one hand the North American prairies, the Argentine pampas, steppes, made fertile for the plow by nature itself, virgin soil, which offered rich harvest for years to come even with a primitive cultivation and without any fertilization. Then there were the lands of the Russian and Indian communes. . . . A portion of the soil of Europe fell definitely out of the competition for the raising of grain, *the rents fell everywhere.* . . . This accounts for the woes of the landlords from Scotland to Italy, and from Southern France to Eastern Prussia. Fortunately all prairie lands have not been taken under cultivation. *There are enough of them left to ruin all the great landlords of Europe and the small ones into the bargain* [C. III, 842–43; italics added].

Thus in agriculture, as in money capital, there is a tendency for the rates of return to decline.

The consequences of such a decline are felt initially by the smaller landowners. As in industry, so too in landed property does Marx forecast concentration in the hands of the few:

In general the relationship of the large and small landed property is like that of the big and small capital. But in addition, there are special circumstances which lead inevitably to the accumulation of large landed property and to the absorption of small property by it [EPM, 58].

Marx projects the analysis further. He predicts that, in time, even the largest of the landowners will be displaced by the capitalist process. The landlord class, therefore, will ultimately become extinct (EPM, 60).

(3) CONCLUSION

Marx's forecast of falling rates of profit is dependent upon increasing organic compositions of capital. Marx prophesies such increases in the compositions on the basis of the general nature of the capitalists. Their unceasing quest for higher rates of profit will be temporarily satisfied only by innovating. Although Marx's demonstration of his profit-rate prediction was based on the assumption of a constant rate of surplus value, the variability of the rate, he argued, cannot invalidate the prediction.

The critical defect in Marx's derivation of the prediction was his failure to incorporate into profit-rate determination the effect of productivity changes resulting from the higher capital compositions. Had he done so, Marx would have had to qualify the prediction. The rate of surplus value, it was shown, is a derived variable. Its value depends upon the productivity of the production process. Without making explicit the relationship between the rate of surplus value and the capital composition, no law concerning movements in the rate of profit can be formulated. Marx's analysis, however, does reveal some important tendencies that operate on the rate of profit.

An examination of Marx's theories of price, profit, interest, rent, capital circulation, and capital accumulation points to other factors that tend to influence the rate of profit. They include (1) changing values of variable and constant capital, (2) changing values of capital turnover, (3) changing values of merchant's capital, and (4) changing distributions of profit. In our discussion of the first factor, the absolute and relative surplus value and therefore the rate of profit were shown to increase with falling values of labor power, with prolongation of the working day, and with changes in the price of raw materials. In discussion of the second factor, the number of capital turnovers per year was shown to increase with higher organic compositions of capital so that the annual rate of profit also tended to increase. The third factor showed the effect of specialization in merchandising upon capital turnovers. Here, the costs of circulation decrease with the development of the merchant class so that more capital turnovers per year result and hence higher rates of profit. In discussion of the fourth factor, it was shown that although the general rate of profit may decline, the rates of return to the money capitalist and landowner fall at a greater rate than the average so that the rate of profit accruing to the industrial capitalist may, at the same time, increase. This distinction between the general and the industrial rate of profit bears upon the rate of capital accumulation and therefore upon the rate at which the rate of profit declines.

In sum, no definite statement concerning movements in the rate of profit can be deduced from the Marxian system. If certain parameter values are assumed, then the rate of profit will fall. If, however, different sets of parameter values are selected, the rate of profit will increase. Since Marx provides no insight into the estimation of future parameter values, the prediction concerning the falling rate of profit is logically untenable.

PREDICTIONS

The various predictions introduced in this chapter may be categorized into primary, secondary, and specific. The primary relate to the general determinants of the capitalist system. Secondary predictions include those directly related to the primary. Specific predictions refer to definite dates, names, or events.

PRIMARY PREDICTIONS

1. Capitalists cannot exist without constantly revolutionizing their instruments of production.
2. The general rate of profit will decline.

SECONDARY PREDICTIONS RELATED TO PRIMARY PREDICTION NO. 2

3. The productivity of labor will expand in geometrical progression
4. The value of labor power will decline.

5. Labor will be equalized and reduced to the commonest skill.
6. Labor mobility will increase.
7. The labor of men will be superseded by that of women and children.
8. Modern industry will tear away from the family the sentimental veil and reduce it to a mere money relation.
9. Modern industry revolutionizes educational institutions, forcing the predominance of technical and vocational training.
10. The value of moral capital depreciation will increase.
11. The working day will be prolonged.
12. The price of raw materials will decline.
13. The number of capital turnovers will increase.
14. Geographical redistributions of population will result in the aggregation of laborers into urban centers.
15. The marketing function will separate from the actual production process.
16. The distribution of profit among profit-receiving classes will change.
17. The rate of interest will decline.
18. The rate of return to landowners will decline.
19. The gap between the organic compositions of capital in agricultural and nonagricultural industries will narrow.
20. Capitalist production will become more luxurious.
21. The *rentier* class will increase with the growing wealth of the country.
22. The *rentier* class will ultimately disappear.
23. Large landed properties will absorb the smaller landed properties.
24. The landowning class will ultimately disappear.

TWO SPECIFIC PREDICTIONS

25. There is enough uncultivated land in the underdeveloped areas to ruin the large and small landowners of Europe.
26. With the development of the railway and steam power, the distance between England and India will be shortened to eight days and India will be annexed to the Western world.

9

Internationalization of the capitalist mode of production and the creation of the world market

MARX PREDICTED the ultimate internationalization of capitalism. In the *Communist Manifesto,* as elsewhere,[1] he set down the course for capitalist development:

The need of a constantly expanding market for its products chases the bourgeoisie over the whole surface of the globe. It must nestle everywhere, settle everywhere, establish connections everywhere. . . . The bourgeoisie, by the rapid improvement in all means of production, by the immensely facilitated means of communication, draws all, even the most barbarian, nations into [capitalist] civilization [CM, 14–15].

In this context Marx also foresaw the emergence of an international division of labor. This set the basis for a corollary forecast, viz., the polarization of the world into industrial and raw-material-supplying economies. On this matter Marx was specific. He predicted which economies would eventually attain industrial stature and which, on the other hand, would be destined to subservience as raw-material suppliers. His commentaries on the fate of American capitalism included predictions concerning economic and military conflict that antedated the Civil War by fifteen years. The subject of protective tariffs and their relation to the development of capitalist economies also came under Marx's prophetic pen.

Essentially, this chapter draws together all prophecies Marx made with respect to the spread of the capitalist system throughout the globe. The chapter is divided into three sections, each of which pertains to a primary prediction concerning international capitalism. The secondary and specific predictions are discussed within these sections. Finally, all predictions relating to international capitalism are listed at the end of the chapter.

1. C. III, 392; MEC, 117; WLC, 44–47.

(1) DEVELOPMENT OF THE WORLD MARKET

Marx developed his prediction concerning the conversion and unification of all national economies to international capitalism by extending his profit-rate analysis to the international market. He directed his analysis specifically to the development of international capital movements and international commodity exchange.

(a) MARX'S PREDICTION CONCERNING THE DEVELOPMENT OF INTERNATIONAL CAPITAL MOVEMENTS

Recall that in the exposition of profit-rate determination, Marx distinguished between specific and average rates of profit (Chap. 2, sec. 5). The former referred to the rate yielded by each production process; the latter defined the arithmetic mean of the specific rates. Also, individual capitalists were remunerated—whatever the specific rates yielded by their own processes—according to the average rate prevailing in the economy. Marx explained:

Capital withdraws from spheres with low rates of profit and invades others which yield a higher rate. By means of this incessant emigration and immigration . . . it brings about such a proportion of supply to demand that the average profit in the various spheres of production becomes the same [C. III, 230].

Variations in specific rates of profit reflected variations in specific organic compositions of capital, e.g., techniques of lower than average composition yielded higher than average rates of profit.

Marx applied this simple analysis of profit-rate determination to the international market. Some national economies, he noted, are characterized by relatively primitive means of production. The average rates of profit forthcoming from production in these areas, he argued, are, by virtue of their low average organic compositions of capital, generally higher than the average rates of profit accruing in the relatively technically advanced economies. Since capitalists constantly strive to attain the highest possible return on investment, capital exportation from developed to less developed economies seemed assured (C. III, 279). Also, continuing pressures to innovate in capitalist economies tend to depress the average rates of profit, thus reinforcing the conditions for capital emigration to backward areas. Theoretically, this capital migration should continue until the average organic compositions of capital in all national economies are the same, that is, until the initially backward economies have transformed their production processes by introduction of the most advanced capitalist technology. It is partially in this sense that Marx envisaged the drawing-together of "even the most barbarian nations into [capitalist] civilization."

Furthermore, technological changes in production alter the relative component values of the organic composition of capital, e.g., values of plant, equipment, labor, raw material, etc. These value changes, he showed, also bear upon the capital-migration prophecy. Marx argued that, because of the unique condition associated with raw-material production, i.e., dependence upon nature, raw-material prices generally fall less rapidly than other factor prices, reflecting the different rates of productivity change (C. III, 140). The profit-rate differential between the raw-material-using and raw-material-producing economies increases. The incentive to export capital is thereby enhanced.

(b) MARX'S PREDICTION CONCERNING THE DEVELOPMENT OF INTERNATIONAL COMMODITY EXCHANGE

In the analysis of prices of production, Marx set down the inverse relation between changing organic compositions of capital and changing commodity values and prices (see Chap. 2, sec. 5). Technical superiority of production, measured by the application of the highest organic composition of capital available, would consequently afford to any enterprise or group of enterprises a price advantage in the competitive commodity market.

Characteristically, enterprises of European origin were technically superior to their counterparts in the colonial areas. Further, market prices prevailing in the colonial areas were determined primarily by the commodity values derived from indigenous production. Surplus profits, therefore, could be made by any enterprise producing in the advanced and marketing in the colonial areas (C. III, 278). Under these conditions, rates of profit accruing from international trade would be greater than corresponding rates derived from production and sale within the national market. Principally on the basis of this observation, Marx forecast the development of international commodity exchange.

In comparing Marx's predictions concerning international capital movements and international commodity exchange, the question of constancy in the rate of surplus value emerges. For if Marx assumes the rate of surplus value constant, then his capital-migration prophecy is sound; but the derivation of international commodity exchange is faulty since the assumed higher productivity associated with production in technically advanced economies implies variability in the rate of surplus value. If, on the other hand, the rate is assumed to vary, then the capital-migration prophecy, based strictly on the rate-of-profit differential, breaks down. Marx must state that the capital exported to the colonial areas for higher profits is concentrated solely in producing commodities in which the colonies command a productive advantage over the advanced economies due to natural and climatic factors, e.g., raw materials. This analysis is pursued in the following section.

Marx, however, recognized an important qualification to the technical-superiority rule. He was aware that costs of transportation, necessarily affixed to exportables, may offset the price advantages accruing to enterprises utilizing superior technology. His world-trade forecast, therefore, rested not only upon lower production costs in the advanced economies but also upon demonstration that techniques of transportation, too, were being constantly revolutionized to facilitate the development of foreign trade. This Marx confidently predicted would occur; for example, he said, ". . . the cheapness of the articles produced by machinery, and the improved means of transport and communication furnish the weapons for conquering foreign markets" (C. I, 493).

The institution of credit also contributed to the development of international commodity trade. Credit availability, Marx had shown, facilitated the centralization of capital—a requisite for investments in transportation and communication (C. II, 287). "The world would still be without railroads," Marx said, "if it had been obliged to wait until accumulation should have enabled a few individual capitalists to undertake the construction of a railroad" (C. I, 688).

Other considerations derived from Marx's general theory of capitalist development lead to the international-commodity-exchange prophecy. Only capitalists, Marx explained, engage in productive accumulation. Such accumulation, he argued, did not impede consumption spending (see Chap. 7, sec. 2). Not only did consumption increase concurrently with accumulation, but qualitative changes in consumption also occurred, incorporating, by increasing degrees, luxuries originating in foreign countries (C. I, 651–52). Such luxuries, he predicted, were not only desired for personal satisfaction but became, under expanding capitalism, a business necessity:

When a certain stage of development has been reached, a conventional degree of prodigality, which is also an exhibition of wealth, and consequently a source of credit, becomes a business necessity to the "unfortunate" capitalist. Luxury enters into the capital's expense of representation [C. I, 651].

Marx's discussion concerning capitalists' consumption habits with respect to international trade is summarized in the *Communist Manifesto:* "In place of the old wants, satisfied by the production of the country, we find new wants, requiring for their satisfaction the products of distant lands and climes" (CM, 14).

Marx also argued the inevitability of international commodity exchange on the ground that, while advancements in technology augmented productive capacity seemingly without limit, they provided no complementary expansion in market capacity (C. IV, 403). Commodity demand must therefore be sought in foreign markets (C. III, 302). The Opium War, Marx wrote, was merely a British excuse to force manufactures upon the Chinese market (MOC, 52). England's domination of the Indian market had the same paternity (OB, 381). Commenting on the Eastern Question, Marx prophesied:

The supreme necessity of never-ceasing expansion of trade— this factum which spectre like haunts modern England . . . this inflexible necessity has caused the interior of Asia to be attacked from two sides by English trade; from the Indus and from the Black Sea; and although we know very little of the exports of Russia to that part of the world, we may safely conclude from the increase of British exports to that quarter that the Russian trade in that direction must have sensibly fallen off. . . . The importance of this fact with regard to any future solution to the Eastern Question, and to the part which both England and Russia may take in it, is evident. *They are, and must always be, antagonists in the East* [EQ, 16].

But creation of world commodity trade provided merely temporary relief from, not a cure for, the inherent maladies of the capitalist system. The world market, Marx explained, had finite limits. In correspondence with Engels, Marx predicted that the final development of the world market would be completed with the colonization of California and Australia and the opening-up of China and Japan (MEC, 117–18). He further predicted:

The attention of our readers has often been called to the unparalleled growth of British manufactures since 1850. . . . Notwithstanding California and Australia, notwithstanding the immense and unprecedented emigration, there must ever without any particular accident in due time arrive a moment when the extension of the market is unable to keep pace with the extension of British manufactures [MOC, 4].

Thus Marx set down his forecast concerning the development of the international market. The migration of capital to underdeveloped areas, promoted by the quest for higher rates of profit, will convert the backward areas to advanced forms of capitalist technology. The development of international commodity exchange, a product of the increasing demands for foreign luxuries, and the inability of the national markets to absorb the products of advanced technology, as well as the unceasing quest for the highest rate of profit, will unify the various national economies into one all-embracing market.

(2) PRODUCTION POLARIZATION OF THE WORLD'S ECONOMIES

The development of the international factor and commodity markets permitted the extension of division of labor to international dimensions which, Marx prophesied, would establish a geographically segregated pattern for factor and commodity production. He wrote:

A new and international division of labor, a division suited to the requirements of the chief centers of modern industry springs up, and converts one part of the globe, into a chiefly agricultural field of production, for supplying the other part, which remains a chiefly industrial field [C. I, 493].

Cost and price advantages accruing to enterprises employing relatively higher organic compositions of capital effectively eliminate all competitors from the international market. Thus Marx wrote of the classical free-trade doctrine: "Whenever we look closely into the nature of British free trade, monopoly is pretty generally found to lie at the bottom of its 'freedom' " (MOC, 59).

In the extreme case of polarization, England should dominate the international industrial market while the rest of the world catered to England's raw-material needs. In outlining one of his many economic tracts, Marx entitled one section "The Commercial Subjugation and Exploitation of the Bourgeois Classes of the Various European Nations by the Despot of the World—England" (WLC, 16). This section, however, was never written. Marx generally included in the classification of industrial nations the economies of Western Europe (including Russia) and the northern states of America. Nowhere, however, does he account for this particular selection. A logical criterion—the prevailing state of industrial achievement—must be ruled out, for, in correspondence with P. V. Annenkov, Marx wrote: "As for the European nations, they were driven to adopt machinery owing to English competition, both in their home markets and on the world market" (MEC, 10). Why England's technical superiority could not be maintained or how the other European economies were going to overcome their initial industrial disadvantages, or, on the other hand, why all economies could not also adopt machinery owing to English competition are questions Marx did not explore.

Russia's status as a viable international industrial competitor was explicitly acknowledged by Marx. England's monopoly on silk and tea, he predicted, would be seriously challenged as soon as Russia completed her system of railroads (MOC, 35). Germany was also included in the industrial entente even though Marx had once written of the German economic system: "The ancient manufactures of Germany had been destroyed by the introduction of steam, and the rapidly extending supremacy of English manufactures" (RCR, 5). Interesting, too, was Marx's inclusion of the United States as an industrial power. Marx predicted that the United States would "exploit its tremendous industrial resources with the energy and on the scale that must shortly break the industrial monopoly of Western Europe, and especially of England (CM, 103).[2]

The rest of the world, Marx predicted, would serve the industrial powers merely as factor-supply bases. International competitive market forces would destroy whatever industry might exist there. Marx's prediction concerning the fate of the Indian industrial economy provides the classic example. He wrote:

By ruining handicraft production in other countries, machinery forcibly converts them into fields for the supply of its raw material. In this way East India was compelled to produce cotton, wool, hemp, jute, and indigo for Great Britain [C. I, 493].

Marx noted this pattern of industrial destruction in Asia Minor, where low-priced imports of English manufactured goods were "rapidly superseding the domestic industry of the Asiatic harems" (EQ, 15). The subjugation of Ireland to England, he wrote, began when free trade was instituted, which consequently destroyed all industrial life in Ireland (MEC, 229). The destiny of Ireland, he predicted, is "that of an English sheep walk and cattle pasture" (C. I, 782). Australia, he argued, was in a similar manner converted into a British colony for

2. Still earlier, in a letter to Danielson dated April, 1879, Marx wrote: "The United States has at present overtaken England in the rapidity of economical progress" (MEC, 360). And in 1859 Marx referred to the United States as "the most modern of bourgeois societies" (CPE, 299).

growing the raw materials needed by England, especially wool (C. I, 493). In China, foreign industrial despotism forced industries out of existence. He wrote:

This introduction of foreign manufactures has had a similar effect on the native industry to that which it formerly had on Asia Minor, Persia and India. In China the spinners and weavers have suffered greatly under this foreign competition, and the community has become unsettled in proportion [MOC, 3].

The southern states of America emerged as a leading producer of raw cotton in response to the resource requirements of the expanding English textile industry (C. I, 483).

The competitive ax, however, cuts both ways. Recall Marx's prediction concerning the fate of English agriculture. While the competitive international market insured English supremacy in industrial production, this same market imperiled the position of English agriculture. Thus Marx predicted the elimination of the English landed aristocracy (Chap. 8, sec. 4).

Colonial capitalist development requires a sufficiently skilled labor force to complement the introduction of capitalist technology. These skills, Marx predicted, would be forthcoming. The education of native labor and the immigration of surplus population from Europe would, he predicted, provide the basis for the transition to capitalism. Concerning India, Marx wrote: "From the Indian natives, reluctantly and sparingly educated at Calcutta, under English superintendence, a fresh class is springing up, endowed with the requirements for government and imbued with European science" (OB, 387). Canadian, American, and Australian labor needs are primarily satisfied by the inflow there of European surplus population, a product of continuous labor-saving changes in European production (C. I, 493).

The effects of the internationalization of the capitalist mode of production transcend the economic sphere. Basic structural changes in the political and social orders of the various economies undergoing transformation to capitalism also occur. In the *Future Results of the British Rule in India,* Marx predicted the inevitable social reconstruction of India:

England has to fulfill a double mission in India: one destructive, the other regenerating—the annihilation of old Asiatic society, and the laying [of] the material foundations of Western society in Asia [OB, 386].

I know that the English millocracy intend to endow India with railways with the exclusive view of extracting at diminished expenses the cotton and other raw materials for their manufactures. But when you have once introduced machinery into the locomotion of a country, which possesses iron and coals, you are unable to withhold it from its fabrication. You cannot maintain a net of railways over an immense country without all those industrial processes necessary to meet all the immediate and current wants of railway locomotion, and out of which there must grow the application of machinery to those branches of industry not immediately connected with railways. The railway system will therefore become, in India, truly the forerunner of modern industry. . . . Modern industry, resulting from the railway system, will dissolve the hereditary divisions of labor, upon which rest the Indian castes, those decisive impediments to Indian progress and Indian power [OB, 389–90].

The effects of the international market, Marx predicted, would be widespread in Japan:

If the foreign trade, forced upon Japan by Europeans, should lead to the substitution of money rents for rents in kind, it will be all up with the exemplary agriculture of that country. The narrow economical conditions under which that agriculture is carried on, will be swept away [C. I, 158].

Examination of the Austrian economy revealed a similar pattern of economic and social transformation (RCR, 37).

Marx's predictions concerning the development of the United States prior to and during the Civil War is interesting on three counts; he predicted (1) the inevitability of the Civil War; (2) that the North would defeat the South; and (3) that the defeat of the South would destroy the economy of North America. These prophecies conflict sharply with his prediction that America would develop into a great industrial power.

Marx based the inevitability of civil war primarily on the nature of southern cotton production:

The cultivation of the Southern export articles, cotton, tobacco, sugar, etc., carried on by slaves, is only remunerative as long as it is conducted with a large gang of slaves, on a mass scale and wide expanses of a naturally fertile soil, that requires only simple labor. Intensive cultivation, which depends less on fertility of the soil than on investment of capital, intelligence and energy of labor, is contrary to the nature of slavery. Hence the rapid transformation of states like Maryland and Virginia, which formerly employed slaves on the production of export articles, into states which raised slaves in order to export these slaves into the deep South. Even in South Carolina, where the slaves form four-sevenths of the population, the cultivation of cotton has for years been almost completely stationary in consequence of the exhaustion of the soil. . . . As soon as this point is reached, *the acquisition of new Territories becomes necessary* in order that one section of the slaveholders may equip new fertile landed estates with slaves and in order that by this means a new market for slave-raising, therefore for the sale of slaves, may be created for the section left behind it. It is, for example, indubitable that without the acquisition of Louisiana, Missouri, and Arkansas by the United States, slavery in Virginia and Maryland would long ago have been wiped out [CWUS, 67].

Economic development of the South depended upon territorial expansion. It is here that conflict arises. The necessity to expand geographically meets with resistance from an expanding northern population of free labor (CWUS, 226). "The Kansas Affair" of 1856 exemplified this struggle, Marx wrote, and the formation of the Republican party was a direct result of southern expansion (CWUS, 66). Predicting the inevitability of civil war, Marx wrote:

The present struggle between the South and the North is, therefore, nothing but a struggle between two social systems, between the system of slavery and the system of free labor. The struggle has broken out because the two systems can no longer live peacefully side by side on the North American continent. It can only be ended by a victory of one system or the other [CWUS, 81].

While the detailed outline of the inevitability of civil war was developed by Marx just prior to the outbreak of conflict, he predicted as early as 1844, in an article entitled *Moralizing Criticism,* that the "slavery system . . . will lead to the most terrible collisions in the southern states of republican North America" (SE, 145).

Early in the conflict Marx confidently predicted victory for the North. His prediction was based primarily on noneconomic considerations, e.g., superior numbers and quality of soldiery (CWUS, 225). Defeat of the South implied the destruction of the slave system. Yet, writing to P. V. Annenkov fourteen years before the conflict, Marx had predicted:

Direct slavery is as much the pivot of our industrialism today as machinery, credit, etc. *Without slavery no cotton, no modern industry.* Slavery has given their value to the colonies; the colonies have created world trade; world trade is the necessary condition of large scale machine industry. Before the traffic of Negroes began, the colonies only supplied the old world with very few products and made no visible change in the face of the earth.

Slavery is thus an economic category of the highest importance. *Without slavery, North America, the most progressive country, would be transformed into a patriarchal land.* You have only to wipe North America off the map of the nations and you get anarchy, the total decay of trade and modern civilization. But to let slavery disappear is to wipe North America off the map of the nations [MEC, 14].

No reconciliation is made between this prediction and the prophecy that America will join the ranks of the industrial nations.

(3) TARIFF PROTECTION IN COLONIAL ECONOMIES

Transition from international free trade to national protection—in effect, a movement reversing the trend toward production polarization of world economies—is at times suggested by Marx. He predicted the inevitability of protectionist policies arising in some colonial economies in an effort to create or recreate industrial production, but his references to such policies are too sparse to be treated as an integral part of the Marxian system of economic development. None the less, it is interesting to note that after predicting the destruction of Irish industry Marx further predicted: "Once the Irish are independent, necessity will turn them into protectionists, as it did Canada, Australia, etc." (MEC, 230).[3] Marx neither elaborated on "necessity" nor presented any analysis on the Canadian and Australian policies. Only in a letter to Engels, written five years earlier, did he make a passing comment on Australian and North American protectionist policies. Here he predicted the end of English domination and pointed to colonial protectionist policies as hastening the inevitable (CWUS, 237). Elsewhere Marx wrote: Now England preaches free trade, and the colonies find protection against England better suited to their interests (CWUS, 150).

In his "Discourse on Free Trade," Marx defines the protectionist system as a "means of establishing among a people the great capitalist industry . . . ; the protective system furthers the development of free competition within the interior of a country" (CWUS, 25). This policy is taking effect in Germany, he continued, with the rise of the bourgeoisie.

3. Marx also foretold the independence of Ireland: "I used to think the separation of Ireland from England impossible. I now think it is inevitable" (MEC, 228).

(4) CONCLUSION

The transition from national capitalism to international capitalism follows directly upon the emergence of the international market. Expanding production and transportation capacities, increasing demands for raw material and foreign commodities, the falling rate of profit, the existence of surplus populations, and credit institutions all generate the conditions which make market expansion not only feasible but imperative. The development of the international market produces structural changes in the political and social as well as the economic spheres in both the technically advanced and less developed economies. The domination of all economies by international competition destroys the industrial production in the colonial areas, converting them to raw-material supply bases for the advanced economies. International polarization of production evolves. Concurrently with the economic transition to capitalist modes of production, the newly developed bourgeoisie may pursue policies of national economic protection. In these cases, the trend toward production polarization may be reversed. Thus Marx describes the fate of world economies.

PREDICTIONS

PRIMARY PREDICTIONS

1. The development of the capitalist mode of production will create the international market.
2. All world economies, by threat of extinction, will adopt the capitalist mode of production.
3. The development of an international division of labor will produce a geographically segregated pattern for world production.

SECONDARY PREDICTIONS RELATED TO PRIMARY PREDICTION NO. 1

4. The falling rate of profit in the industrial economies will force the expansion of international capital movements.
5. The falling rate of profit in the industrial economies will force the development of the export industries and, consequently, international commodity exchange.
6. Credit institutions will accelerate the development of the capitalist

mode of production and, consequently, international commodity exchange and capital migration.

7. Transportation and communication facilities are constantly improved, so that the profitability of international trade will increase.
8. As capitalists' consumptions increase, foreign luxuries become a more important part of their mode of life.
9. The increasing capacities of advanced technology will force capitalists to seek new markets.

SECONDARY PREDICTIONS RELATED TO PRIMARY PREDICTION NO. 3

10. The incorporation of capitalist modes of production in colonial economies will produce corresponding changes in relations of production, that is, structural reorganization of their social and political orders.
11. The demand for raw materials, a consequence of expanding capitalist technology, will compel capitalists to develop the colonial economies.
12. The labor skills needed for the adoption of capitalist technology in colonial areas will be supplied by surplus populations migrating from advanced economies and also through the development of native labor skills through education.

A SPECIFIC PREDICTION RELATED TO PRIMARY PREDICTION NO. 1

13. Market expansion will end with the colonization of California and Australia and the opening-up of China and Japan.

SPECIFIC PREDICTIONS RELATED TO PRIMARY PREDICTION NO. 2

14. Russia and England must always be antagonists in the East.
15. Russia will break the English monopoly of Chinese products on the European market with the completion of her railway.
16. The United States will shortly break the industrial monopoly of Western Europe and England.
17. England will fulfill her double mission, viz., the destruction of Asiatic society and the regeneration of India on the foundations of Western society.
18. The railway system will become the forerunner of modern industry in India.

19. Modern industry will dissolve the hereditary division of labor in India, i.e., the caste system, and thereby destroy the impediments to Indian economic progress.
20. Without the acquisition of Louisiana, Missouri, and Arkansas by the United States, slavery in Virginia would long ago have been wiped out.
21. The expansion of the southern and northern economies in the United States will eventually lead to civil war.
22. The North will defeat the South in the civil war.
23. Without slavery, North America, the most progressive country, would be transformed into a patriarchal land.
24. If foreign trade in Japan leads to the development of money rents, the bases of the Japanese agricultural economy will undergo radical change.
25. The separation of Ireland from England is inevitable.

SPECIFIC PREDICTIONS RELATED TO PRIMARY PREDICTION NO. 3

26. The English feudal aristocracy will be destroyed by foreign competition in the international agricultural market.
27. The destiny of Ireland is to be an English sheep walk and cattle pasture.

A PREDICTION ON TARIFF PROTECTION

28. Once Ireland is independent, necessity will turn her to protection.

10

The increasing instability of the economy and the centralization of production and finance

IN THIS CHAPTER we examine Marx's predictions concerning the increasing instability of the economy, the growing concentration of capital in the hands of the few, and the transformation of production processes from atomistic capitalist units to joint-stock companies. These predictions, we shall discover, are derived principally from Marx's theories of capital accumulation and capital circulation, from his declining-rate-of-profit prediction, and from his analyses of innovation and credit institutions.

Marx's analysis of the inevitability of increasing instability will receive chief emphasis. This prophecy is pivotal, not only to his general theory of capitalist development, but also to the other forecasts considered in the chapter. Predictions of secondary and specific orders, twenty-five in all, that are associated with the inevitability of instability and with the concentration of capital in the hands of the few are also analyzed and are enumerated in the list of predictions at the end of the chapter.

(1) THE INCREASING INSTABILITY OF THE CAPITALIST SYSTEM

(a) DEFINITION OF INSTABILITY

Economic instability in Marx's analysis is described by the existence of the industrial cycle. Cycles, he notes, are the exclusive property of the capitalist system (C. IV, 380). Marx defines the industrial cycle as "a series of periods of moderate activity, prosperity, overproduction, crisis, and stagnation" (C. I, 495).

The period of overproduction emerges with the involuntary accumulation of commodity capital. This accumulation occurs when capitalists are unable to market the total supply of their commodity production.

131

The continuity of capitalist production depends upon the complete sale of commodities at their values. When involuntary accumulation of commodity capital occurs, capitalist production is checked. The period of crisis follows.

Marx describes the crisis as a period of intense competition among sellers, of declining market prices, wages, interest rates, and profits, accelerated depreciation of capital values, growing excesses in production capacity, and increasing unemployment. It is essentially in this period that the centralization and concentration of production and finance are heightened and the collapse of the credit institutions takes place.

The period of stagnation that follows the crisis is vaguely described by Marx as a period of relatively low production, contracting volumes of commodity capital, low product and factor prices, and an abundant supply of loanable funds and labor.

The period of moderate activity marks the turning point in the industrial cycle. Here exploitation of labor takes place under the most favorable conditions. Capital values having been depreciated, commodity capital having been depleted, and wages having been reduced to, and occasionally below, the value of labor power, the rate of profit on newly formed processes of production is higher than average for this period. This partial recovery gives rise to favorable expectations, to the reconstruction of the credit system, and to rising prices, profit rates, interest rates, and wages. The success of this recovery period leads directly into the period of prosperity.

Prosperity describes the highest level of production achieved in the industrial cycle. All the indicators of economic activity are high and rising. The end of prosperity occurs when the market capacity is unable to absorb the increasing quantities of commodity production. At this point overproduction of commodity capital emerges, and the industrial cycle is complete.

Although Marx describes the industrial cycle in terms of these five sequential periods, his analysis of economic instability is limited almost entirely to two periods: overproduction and crisis. To Marx, demonstration of the inevitability of the crisis is tantamount to demonstration of the cycle.

The cycle presented by Marx is characterized by the following properties: (1) it is multidetermined, (2) it is essentially endogenous, (3) it is recurring, and (4) it is of increasing intensity.

Consider the multidetermined nature of the cycle. Marx offers, as the core of economic instability, the real crisis, viz., the disproportionate allocation of production between the capital- and the consumer-goods departments in the economic system. Supplementing the real crisis are the credit crisis, the falling-rate-of-profit crisis, the innovation crisis, and the replacement crisis. Although these crises are independently determined, it is the real crisis that Marx sets down as the necessary and sufficient condition for economic instability under capitalism.

(b) THE REAL CRISIS

Marx explains the occurrence of the real crisis thus: "A crisis could be explained only by a disproportion of production in various branches, and by a disproportion of the consumption of the capitalists and the accumulation of their capitals" (C. III, 568).

(i) DISPROPORTION OF PRODUCTION IN VARIOUS BRANCHES

The term "various branches" refers to the individual production processes that are aggregated into capital- and consumer-goods departments. The Marxian term "disproportion" refers to disequilibrium in the interdepartmental market.

Recall that Marx's simple-reproduction model is set down in the form of a two-department input-output table whose production relations are described as

$$C_1 = c_1 + v_1 + s_1$$
$$C_2 = c_2 + v_2 + s_2 \tag{7.2}$$

The values of these equations are determined by the prevailing organic compositions of capital in the two departments, and these compositions are themselves aggregates of individually determined production processes.

Stability of the economy depends upon the ability of each department to market its commodities. In a two-sector model this means that the demands made by each department for the other's commodities must exhaust the supply made available by that other department. But since each department's production function is unrelated to the other's, the interdepartmental demand for, and the supply of, commodities are also unrelated. Stability, therefore, is pure chance.

The conditions for equilibrium in the economy take the form

$$c_2 = v_1 + s_1 \tag{7.4}$$

Net production in Department I (capital goods) after depreciation allowances are met is $C_1 - c_1$ or $(v_1 + s_1)$. Net production in Department II (consumer goods) after payments are made to its labor and capital is $C_2 - (v_2 + s_2)$ or c_2.

Equilibrium is achieved when the demands of each department for the commodities of the other are equal to the net production of the other. In other words, market capacity equals production capacity in both departments:

	Production Capacity		Market Capacity
Department I	C_1	=	$c_1 + c_2$
Department II	C_2	=	$(v_1 + v_2) + (s_1 + s_2)$

There is no reason to suspect that the capacities in both departments are, in fact, equal. Since the organic compositions of capital are constantly changing, the probability is very high that these capacities will not continuously be equal.

Consider, for example, a decrease in the organic composition of capital in Department II; i.e., its demand for capital goods, c_2, falls, while the capital composition in Department I remains unchanged. Then,

$$C_1 > c_1 + c_2$$

and

$$c_2 < v_1 + s_1$$

Disequilibrium, and consequently the crisis, results. Department I will be unable to sell the total value of its net production to Department II. Consequently, its purchases from Department II will be less than the value of $v_1 + s_1$. Assuming that the capitalists in Department I meet their wage obligations, the surplus value realized will be a composite of lower than expected consumer goods and unsold capital good, i.e.,

$$s_1 = C_1 - (c_1 + c_2) + (c_2 - v_1) \qquad (10.1)$$

The formula $(c_2 - v_1)$ measures the value of s_1 in consumer goods, and $C_1 - (c_1 + c_2)$ measures the value of s_1 that takes the form of unsold capital goods or involuntary accumulation of commodity capital. This overproduction of capital goods will result in a contraction of production, a reduction of employment, and a decrease in effective demand for commodities from Department II. The crisis emerges.

(ii) DISPROPORTION BETWEEN THE CONSUMPTION OF THE CAPITALISTS AND THE ACCUMULATION OF THEIR CAPITALS

Here Marx extends the analysis from simple reproduction to expanded reproduction. The expanded form is distinguished from the simple by the inclusion of accumulation.

Recall that accumulation, a, is measured by

$$a = g(s) \tag{7.5}$$

where g refers to the percentage of surplus devoted to accumulation. The production and market capacities under expanded forms of reproduction are changed. Demands for capital goods increase to

$$c_1 + c_2 + g_1s_1(c_1/c_1 + v_1) + g_2s_2(c_2/c_2 + v_2)$$

Accordingly, demands for consumer goods decrease to

$$(v_1 + s_1) + (v_2 + s_2) - g_1s_1(c_1/c_1 + v_1) - g_2s_2(c_2/c_2 + v_2)$$

The conditions for equilibrium therefore change from

$$c_2 = v_1 + s_1$$

to

$$\begin{aligned}
c_2 + g_1s_1(c_1/c_1 + v_1) + g_2s_2(c_2/c_2 + v_2) \\
= v_1 + s_1 - g_1s_1(c_1/c_1 + v_1) - g_2s_2(c_2/c_2 + v_2)
\end{aligned} \tag{10.2}$$

Thus, equilibrium in expanded reproduction depends not simply upon the correct technical proportions in the various branches of production but also upon the correct accumulation values for each of the individual capitalists.

The demand for consumer goods is initially reduced in the expanded form of production by increases in both the organic compositions of capital and the accumulative desires of the capitalists. The supply of consumer goods, on the other hand, entirely independent of the demand, increases with increasing organic compositions. Overproduction emerges and the crisis follows.

Marx thus states categorically that market capacity cannot increase as rapidly as production capacity. Departmental disequilibrium must occur through unavoidable structural disproportions, and these are further exacerbated by the accumulative nature of capitalists. Marx writes:

This last-named power [market capacity] is not determined either by the absolute productive power or by the absolute consuming power, but by the consuming power based on the antagonistic conditions of distribution, which reduces the consumption of the great mass of the population to a variable minimum within more or less narrow limits. The consuming power is furthermore restricted by the tendency to accumulate, the greed for an expansion of capital and a production of surplus value on an enlarged scale. *This is a law of capitalist production* imposed by incessant revolutions in the methods of production themselves, the resulting depreciation of existing capital, the general competitive struggle and the necessity for improving the product and expanding the scale of production, for the sake of self-preservation and on penalty of failure. . . . *But to the extent that the productive power develops, it finds itself at variance with the narrow basis on which the conditions of consumption rest* [C. III, 286–87; italics added].

What Marx presents here as a "law of capitalist production," as an inevitability of the capitalist system, is at best an estimated high probability. The proposition that production capacity must exceed market capacity does not follow from his analysis. True, as Marx aptly points out, long-run stability demands not only that multi-independent processes complement one another in the precise values needed, but also that the multiplicity of individual decisions concerning accumulation are also the correct ones for stability. The probability of this occurring is low and is increasingly lower for long-run considerations. But the probability is still greater than zero. While this may appear overly pedantic, it is of crucial importance to Marx's claim to scientific predictability. Contrary to the long quote above, the capacity differentiation simply does not emerge as a necessary consequence of capitalist development. Marx's prediction, therefore, is conditional.

Based essentially upon this "proof" of inevitability, Marx confidently predicts:

Notwithstanding California and Australia, notwithstanding the immense and unprecedented emigration, there must ever, and without any particular accident, in due time arrive a moment when the extension of the markets is unable to keep pace with the extension of British manufactures, and this disproportion must bring about a new crisis with the same certainty as it has done in the past. But if one of the great markets suddenly becomes contracted, the arrival of the crisis is necessarily accelerated thereby. Now, the Chinese rebellion must, for the time being, have precisely this effect upon England [MOC, 4].

The shrinking Chinese market, he further states, is not due to the lack of free ports in China or to the size of its protective tariff (MOC, 62, 69). The answer is found in the consumption habits of the Chinese. The belief, therefore, that through forceful penetration of the Chinese ports England will find an inexhaustible market "may help prepare a new crisis at the very moment when the world is but slowly recovering from the recent universal shock" (MOC, 52).

"For a crisis to be general," Marx predicts, "it is sufficient for it to grip the principal articles of trade" (C. IV, 393). When capitalists producing in principal branches of the economy are unable to sell their entire output, competition intensifies in that particular branch and drives market prices below their values. Profit rates accruing in these overproduced branches are reduced. Production, therefore, is contracted. This is the initial phase of the crisis. Other branches of production that depend directly upon the principal branches for their market, are, in the same manner, forced to contract production. And, since capitalist production is a complex of interdependent branches, what was once a crisis particular to one specific branch must, by the nature of the system, become general.

(c) THE CREDIT CRISIS

The introduction of credit in capitalist economies generates even more violent crises than those produced in noncredit economies. Credit aids the expansion of production by (1) reducing the time necessary to acquire the minimum capital outlays for production, (2) reducing the time of circulation, i.e., the time required to convert commodity capital to money capital, and (3) promoting the formation of entirely new production processes. Since the quantity of credit advanced in an economy is determined in large measure by the prevailing banking policies and general business confidence, new elements of potential instability are added to crisis considerations.

(i) BANKING AND PRODUCTION EXPANSION

The minimum capital requirement, we have seen (Chap. 6, sec. 1), varies directly with the organic composition of capital. Thus, as capitalism develops, the percentage of new capital formation that is financed by credit increases. Added to this is the formation, generally in periods of prosperity, of processes that are wholly dependent upon credit advancement. Marx writes that "those knights now appear in large numbers, who work without any reserve capital, or even without any capital at all and operate wholly on a credit basis" (C. III, 574).

Since all production processes are interrelated in the complex of sale and purchase, the elimination of credit-supported production units by banking policies, e.g., contraction of credit, can destroy not only those processes dependent upon credit but also those operating without it. And so Marx can predict that, as the credit economy evolves, the entire economy becomes subjected to the dictates of the money market.

This is also true for the effects of credit on the time of circulation.[1] Since reproduction necessitates immediate exchange, i.e., the transformation of commodity capital to money capital, the banking institutions intercede by discounting bills of exchange and extending the necessary credit to finance continuous production (see Chap. 4, sec. 2). Marx writes:

1. The time of circulation varies inversely with the development of the transportation industry and directly with the distance traveled (see Chap. 6, sec. 2).

For instance, the cotton passes into the hands of the spinner in exchange for a bill of exchange, the yarn into the hands of the manufacturer of cotton in exchange for another bill, the cotton goods into the hands of the merchant for another bill, from the hands of the merchant into those of the exporter for another bill, from the hands of the exporter for another bill into those of the merchant in India, who sells the goods and buys indigo . . . which is shipped to Europe and enters there into the reproductive process. The various phases of the process of production are here promoted by the credit, without any payment on the part of the spinner for the cotton, on the part of the manufacturer of cotton goods for the yarn, on the part of the merchant for the cotton goods, etc. [C. III, 565].

Marx can therefore predict:

Credit must grow in volume with the growing volume of value in production, and it must grow in the matter of time with increasing distance of the markets. A mutual interaction takes place here. The development of the process of production extends the credit, the credit leads to an extension of industrial and commercial operations [C. III, 565].

(ii) BANKING AND THE MERCHANTS

We have seen that as the modes of production become more capitalized there develops a subclass of merchants whose function it is to handle the sale of commodity capital (Chap. 8, sec. 4). The separation of commodity production and circulation is thus both temporal and functional. Industrial capitalists deal increasingly with the intermediary merchants and consequently are removed from any contact with the actual consuming market.

Reproduction of their capital, therefore, can be achieved by the accumulation of bills of exchange from the merchant class. To the industrial capitalist the reproduction of capital is complete once sale to the merchant is made. In reality no final sale has been made. During prosperity, the period preceding overproduction and crisis, a significant proportion of industrial and commercial capital is dependent upon this form of credit. If at any time, Marx writes, the return to the merchant from the consuming market becomes "so slow and meager, that the banks press for payment, or the notes for the purchased commodities become due before they have been resold," a crisis occurs (C. III, 359–60). The merchant class is forced to sell at whatever price to secure the means of payment. General market prices and consequently rates of profit decline. Credit becomes scarce, and all bills of exchange, securities, and commodities are forcibly converted into bank money (C. III, 674). The inability to transform the paper and commodity capital into money brings on the collapse of the credit system, the insolvency of the merchant class, and the beginnings of the real crisis.

The credit system may temporarily prolong the period of prosperity by discounting fraudulent bills of exchange. Marx writes:

> If the securing of advances on unsold commodities is facilitated more and more, then more and more of such advances are taken, and in the same proportion . . . the temptation [increases] to manufacture commodities, or throw already manufactured ones upon distant markets, for no other immediate purpose than that of obtaining advances of money on them. . . . Thus arose the system of mass consignments, by virtue of advances, to India and China, and this soon developed into a system of consignments purely for the sake of getting advances. . . . This had to lead inevitably to an overcrowding of the market and to a crash [C. III, 478–80].

Elsewhere he writes that

> the whole process becomes so complicated, partly by the making of bogus checks, partly by operations with commodities for the mere purpose of writing bills of exchange, that the semblance of a solid business and a smooth run of returns may persist even after returns come in only at the expense of swindled money lenders or swindled producers. . . . Business is always thoroughly sound and the campaign in full swing, until the collapse suddenly overtakes them [C. III, 569].

For example, the crisis of 1866 was signaled by the failure of a gigantic London bank, which touched off the collapse of countless swindling companies. Among its casualties was the iron shipbuilding industry (C. I, 733). The greater the employment of such fraudulent bills of exchange, the more intense is the inevitable crash (C. III, 480).

Thus Marx was able to predict that,

> So long as the social character of labor appears as the money existence of commodities, and thus as a thing outside of actual production, money crises are inevitable, either independently of crisis or intensifying them [C. III, 607]. The effects of mistaken banking legislation can intensify a monetary crisis, but no legislation can abolish it [C. III, 575].

(d) THE FALLING-RATE-OF-PROFIT CRISIS

While crisis was envisaged by Marx as being primarily the resultant of commodity overproduction, still a crisis may occur even with a prolonged accidental coincidence of production and market capacities. This form of crisis is attributable to the declining rate of profit.

Although profit is the "immediate purpose and compelling motive of capitalist production," there is a minimum rate of profit below which capitalists will cease production. "Its fall," Marx writes, "checks the formation of new independent capitals and thus seems to threaten the development of the process of capitalist production" (C. III, 283). Curtailment of production under this circumstance, as under conditions of excess commodity capital, must lead to general overproduction and crisis.

(e) THE INNOVATION CRISIS

Marx also considered the possibility of crisis resulting from a too rapid rate of innovation in the economy. Because of the competitive nature of capitalism, technological innovations produce declining commodity values and prices (see Chap. 3, sec. 4). Rates of profit, therefore, calculated on the pre-innovation values, will fall until the total depreciation of the pre-innovation constant capital has occurred. The higher the organic composition of capital, the greater will be the decline in prices, values, and profit rates. Also, the more rapidly the technological improvements are introduced into the system, the more difficult is it for capitalists to adjust to the new set of capital values. Therefore, the circumstance of increasing organic compositions of capital and rapid technological innovations may result in a complete destruction of capital values in principal branches of production, and this may set off the general crisis (C. IV, 388).[2]

(f) THE REPLACEMENT CRISIS

The turnover of advanced capital, Marx had shown, varies with the organic composition of capital. The circulating capital that enters the process of production transfers its entire value to the product and is continually reproduced in its natural form by the sale of the product (C. II, 208). The fixed-capital component of the composition, however, contributes only that portion of its value that is actually used up in the process, i.e., physical depreciation. Its reproduction, therefore, can take place only at one time, and all at once, at the end of its lifetime (C.

2. "Competition enforces the introduction of new machinery before the old is worn out, especially in the case of important modifications. Such a premature reproduction of the instruments of labor on a large social scale is generally enforced by catastrophes or crisis" (C. II, 194).

II, 209). Thus for a substantial part of the production process the values produced exceed the values demanded on the market. Only at the time of replacement of fixed capital does the market demand exceed supply. "The moments of prosperity," Marx writes, "are to the periods of crisis and stagnation in the 'true proportion' of 3 to 10" (PP, 113).

The duration of at least one aspect of the industrial cycle is therefore fixed by the timing of the replacement of the fixed capital. Marx believed this to be approximately ten years, although this duration will increase with the increase in the organic compositions of capital (C. I, 695). The relationship of this timing of replacement to the crisis is clearly stated by Marx:

So much at least is evident that this cycle comprising a number of years, through which capital is compelled to pass by its fixed part, furnishes a material basis for the periodical commercial crisis in which business goes through successive periods of lassitude, average activity, overspeeding, and crisis. It is true that the periods in which capital is invested are different in time and place. But a crisis is always the starting point of a large amount of new investments. Therefore it also constitutes, from the point of view of society, more or less of a new material basis for the next cycle of turnover [C. II, 211].

(g) THE UNDERCONSUMPTION CRISIS?

The real crisis, we have seen, occurs when production capacities exceed market capacities. In some of Marx's writings, one cause of the capacity gap may be interpreted as being the underconsumption of the working population. For example, he writes:

The last cause of all real crisis always remains the poverty and restricted consumption of the masses as compared to the tendency of the capitalist production to develop the productive forces in such a way, that only the absolute power of consumption of the entire society would be their limit [C. III, 568].

Yet, in a more complete explanation of the relationship between the underconsumption of the population and the inevitability of crisis, Marx clearly states:

It is purely tautology to say that crises are caused by the scarcity of solvent consumers, or of paying consumption. The capitalist system does not know any other modes of consumption but a paying one, except that of the pauper or of the "thief." If any commodities are unsalable, it means that no solvent purchasers have been found for them, in other words, consumers (whether commodities are bought in the last instance for productive or individual consumption). But if one were to attempt to clothe this tautology with a semblance of a profounder justification by saying that the working class receive too small a portion of their own product, and the evil would be remedied by giving them a larger share of it, or raising their wages, we should reply that crises are precisely always preceded by a period in which wages rise generally and the working class actually gets a larger share of the annual product intended for consumption. From the point of view of the advocates of "simple" (!) common sense, such a period should rather remove a crisis [C. II, 475–76].

Thus, whatever the statements to the contrary, it appears that Marx carefully avoided attaching any significance to the underconsumption theory of the crisis.

(h) THE RECURRING PROPERTY OF THE CYCLE

The critical phases of the industrial cycle, we have seen, are overproduction and crisis. Marx gives little more than scant treatment to the other periods, viz., stagnation, recovery, and prosperity. The forces which generate recovery originate in the latter stages of the preceding crisis.

Capitalists who, during a crisis, purchase the bankrupted production processes after the mass depreciation of their capital values advance a smaller outlay of capital in value terms than the physical assets represented by the process they purchase. For example, suppose that, prior to a crisis, a small capitalist had been operating with the production process $40c + 10v + 10s = 60$. In the period of overproduction the commodity price would fall below the commodity value of 60. The rate of profit consequently would decline. If price declines from its value of 60 to 55, profit rates would fall from 20 to 10 per cent. And further declines in commodity prices would produce further declining rates of profit. When price falls below 50, net losses are incurred. The owners of such small production processes are generally forced to sell out. The sale of the production process at bankruptcy prices will vary with the demand and supply conditions. If the fixed capital, $40c$, is sold at 50 per cent of its capital value, the new organic composition of capital, *measured by the purchaser,* will be $20c + 10v$. Therefore, even at a crisis price of 45, the rate of profit accruing to the new owner of the process will be positive, e.g., 50 per cent.

Rates of profit after insolvency, Marx observes, increase (C. III, 299). In such periods capitalists also strive to innovate further with "new machines, new and improved working methods, new combinations" (C. III, 299). These techniques are introduced to reduce individual values below their social values, thereby creating surplus profits (C. III, 303–4). "A crisis is always the starting point," Marx predicts, "of a large amount of new investment" (C. II, 211).

These forces of recovery, which originate in the crisis, tend to counteract the depressing effects of the crisis and produce the succeeding period of stagnation. While this vaguely defined phase is described as a period of low production, low profit, wage, and interest rates, and high levels of unemployment, the forces of recovery persist. Economic recovery, defined in terms of increasing production, follows stagnation. More intense exploitation of the old markets and the conquest of new ones lead to general increased production (CM, 17). Profit rates recover to their former levels, and the credit institutions, with increasing confidence, once more discount bills of exchange at low levels of interest. Increasing employment is also reflected in increasing wage rates. Capitals of higher organic compositions are introduced, and total production in periods of prosperity reaches peaks that surpass the levels attained in preceding periods (C. III, 575).

The inevitability of a new crisis is foretold in the overproduction that characteristically occurs in the later stages of prosperity. Once more, Marx claims, production capacity exceeds market capacity. With the continual expansion of both the modes of production and the credit system, the crisis must be more intense. "And in this way," Marx writes, "the cycle would run once more" (C. III, 299). So Marx prophesies: "The industrial cycle is of such a character, that the same cycle must periodically reproduce itself, once . . . the first impulse has been given" (C. III, 574). This prediction is often repeated. In the first volume of *Capital* he writes:

As the heavenly bodies, once thrown into a certain definite motion, always repeat this, so it is with the social production as soon as it is once thrown into this movement of alternate expansion and contraction. Effects, in their turn, become causes, and the varying accidents of the whole process, which always reproduces its own conditions, take on the form of periodicity [C. I, 695].

In the *Communist Manifesto* and in a pamphlet called *Wage-Labor and Capital* emphasis on increasing severity is added. For example, he writes: "And how does the bourgeoisie get over these crises? [They do it] by paving the way for more intense and more destructive crises, and by diminishing the means whereby crises are prevented" (CM, 17). Elsewhere he says that

the capitalists are compelled . . . to exploit the already existing gigantic means of production on a larger scale, and to set in motion all the mainsprings of credit to this end. . . . They become more frequent and more violent, if only because in the same measure in which the mass of production, and consequently the need for the extended markets grows, the world market becomes more and more contracted, fewer and fewer new markets remain available for exploitation, since every preceding crisis has subjected to world trade a market hitherto unconquered or only superficially exploited [WLC, 51].

(i) THE MIGRATORY PROPERTY OF THE CYCLE

(i) FROM DEVELOPED TO LESS DEVELOPED ECONOMIES

Capitalism, we have seen, not only creates the international market but divides the world into regions of industrial production and regions of raw-material supplies (Chap. 9, sec. 2). As these latter regions become capitalistic, they too become subject to the inherent instability of capitalist production. In addition to exhibiting these cyclical properties, their economic interdependence, made necessary by the increasing importance of the world market, subjects each economy to the fate of all others.

All economies, Marx writes, export and import too much (C. III, 577). Their credit institutions promote commodity exportation in the same manner as they attempt to expand domestic market capacity. Inevitably some of this exportation, the magnitude depending primarily upon the period of the cycle, cannot be absorbed by the foreign market. International overproduction occurs, and the industrial cycle follows. Therefore Marx predicts that, as the capitalist mode of production expands, industrial cycles must become international.

A crash in any one economy, Marx asserts, is generally transmitted to others. A contraction of credit in England may generate the international crisis. English exports to other economies will contract with curtailment of home production, and imports from these economies will also decline. The contraction of the other economies' exports to England leads to overproduction there, and the crisis results. This form of chain reaction works across all international borders where trade takes place.

Marx used the intricate trade patterns between China, India, England, the United States, and Australia to illustrate this interdependence. India has a favorable balance of trade with China, primarily as a result of the opium trade. England is on balance an importer from China, the United States, and Australia but is a major exporter to India. The foreign exchange earned by England in trade with India is essential to pay for her imports from the other areas. Therefore, Marx predicts that, if the Chinese government were to legalize the planting of opium in China, England and the entire international trade pattern would be thrown into chaos. India's opium market in China would be destroyed, preventing India from purchasing English commodities. The English trade with the United States and Australia would therefore collapse (MOC, 81).

Concerning the trade relations between England and the Continent, Marx predicts:

Just as the period of crisis occurs later on in the Continent than in England, so does that of prosperity. The original process always takes place in England; she is the demiurge of the bourgeois cosmos. On the Continent, the different phases of the cycle through which bourgeois society is ever speeding anew, occur in secondary and tertiary form. First the Continent exports incomparably more to England than to any other country. This export to England, however, in turn depends on the position of England, particularly with regard to the overseas market. Then England exports to the overseas lands incomparably more than the entire Continent, so that the quantity of Continental exports to these lands is always dependent on England's overseas exports in each case. If, therefore, the crises first produce revolutions on the Continent, the foundations for these is, nevertheless, always laid in England [CSF, 134–35].

(ii) MORE SEVERE CRISIS IN LESS DEVELOPED ECONOMIES

Marx predicts that the instability in the raw-material-supplying economies, once the capitalist mode of production is introduced, is more violent than it is in the manufacturing economies. Commodity prices rise during periods of prosperity. The derived demands for raw materials rise even more (C. III, 140). The much higher raw-material prices encourage both intensive and extensive investments in raw-material production and the general application of higher capital compositions in agriculture (C. III, 144). Total production of raw-material supplies therefore increases. In the succeeding period of overproduction the demand for raw-material supplies declines. This contraction, Marx writes, is more severe than the contraction in the commodity markets. Distant and poor areas that were brought into cultivation in response to the strong demand are immediately eliminated from the market, while the remaining areas, equipped to produce more raw materials as a result of mechanization and intensive cultivation, can market only a fraction of their supply. Marx therefore predicts:

The moral of this story, which may be also deduced from other observations in agriculture, is that the capitalist system works against a rational agriculture, or that a rational agriculture is irreconcilable with the capitalist system, although technical improvements are promoted by capitalism [C. III, 144].

And the revulsions increase correspondingly in frequency, so far as they are due to this violent fluctuation of one of the main elements of the process of reproduction (C. III, 141).

(2) THE INCREASING CENTRALIZA-TION OF PRODUCTION AND FINANCE

Marx defines centralization as "concentration of capitals already formed, destruction of their individual independence, expropriation of capitalist by capitalist, transformation of many small into few large capitals" (C. I, 686). The principal forces of centralization, he asserts, are the competitive market structure and the credit system.

The forces of competition, he writes, operate in three distinct spheres: among buyers, which tends to inflate price; among sellers, which tends to depress price; and between buyers and sellers, which establishes price (WLC, 24). Drawing an analogy to the military, Marx writes: "Industry leads two armies into the field against each other, each of which again carries on a battle within its own ranks among its own troops. The army among whose troops the least fighting takes place gains the victory over the opposing host" (WLC, 24). In periods of prosperity, when aggregate demand is strong, the competitive forces among buyers dominate the commodity market. The capitalist class as a whole tends to gain. In periods of stagnation and crisis overproduction prevails and the favorable position held by the sellers vis à vis the buyers deteriorates. "Except in periods of prosperity, there rages between the capitalists the most furious combat for the share of each in the markets" (C. I, 495).

While the capitalist class as a whole suffers net losses, the distribution of the loss among the individual capitalists depends upon their performance in the competitive market. It is in this competitive struggle, Marx predicts, that centralization becomes inevitable. He writes:

The battle of competition is fought by cheapening of commodities. The cheapness of commodities depends, *ceteris paribus,* on the productiveness of labor, and this again on the scale of production. Therefore, the larger capitals beat the smaller. It will further be remembered that, with the development of the capitalist mode of production, there is an increase in the minimum amount of individual capital necessary to carry on a business under its normal conditions. The smaller capitals, therefore, crowd into spheres of production which Modern Industry has only sporadically or incompletely got hold of. Here competition rages in direct proportion to the number, and in inverse proportion to the magnitudes, of the antagonistic capitals. *It always ends in the ruin of many small capitalists, whose capitals partly pass into the hands of their conquerors, partly vanish* [C. I, 686–87].

The process of centralization is cumulative. Large aggregations of capital provide for expanded scales of production, which permit greater divisions of labor, economies of scale in constant capital, and the application of innovations. Hence their probabilities of survival in the competitive market are enhanced. The weaker elements, i.e., the smaller capitals, are consequently forced out (C. III, 308). The nature of the capitalist process, therefore, makes the transition from small independent capitalists to giant industrial monopolies inevitable (C. I, 688). In *The Poverty of Philosophy* Marx describes the evolution of the monopoly structure in dialectic terminology:

We all know that competition was engendered by feudal monopoly. Thus competition was originally the opposite of monopoly and not monopoly the opposite of competition. So that modern monopoly is not a simple antithesis; it is on the contrary the true synthesis [PP, 169].

In the financial market, as in the productive, centralization is inevitable (C. III, 641). During periods of crisis and stagnation, with production organizations falling into bankruptcy, industrial security prices sharply decline. Individuals in possession of monetary funds are able to take advantage of this situation (C. III, 509). Mass purchasing of these securities during the crisis is one of the most effective means of financial centralization. "As soon as the storm is over," Marx writes, "the papers rise once more to their former level, unless they represent failure or swindles. Their depreciation in times of crisis serves as a potent means of centralizing money" (C. III, 550–51).

The increasing centralization in production, Marx writes, refers not only to the quantitative redistribution of production among capitalists but also to qualitative transformations in the capitalist mode of production. Joint-stock companies, the highest form of capitalist production, emerge with centralization and accelerate the centralization process (C. III, 517). This new form of enterprise, Marx states, represents an abolition of capitalist private industry in proportion as it expands and seizes new spheres of production (C. III, 519). The functions of ownership and control, united as we have seen in the industrial capitalist, are separated under the joint-stock organization. The industrial capitalist becomes a "mere manager," an "administrator of other people's capital," while the owners of the company are "mere money capitalists" (C. III, 516–17). Since the property under this form exists as shares in the enterprise, a class of speculators who specialize in stock-market transactions play with and precipitate stock-market fluctuations. In this game, Marx writes, "little fish are swallowed by the sharks and the lambs by the wolves" (C. III, 521).

The separation of property ownership from control is defined by Marx as the transition from private capital to social capital, the latter being the common property of the associates. Marx comments on the impact this separation has on the economy:

It establishes a monopoly in certain spheres and thereby challenges the interference of the state. It reproduces a new aristocracy of finance, a new sort of parasites in the shape of promoters, speculators and merely nominal directors; a whole system of swindling and cheating by means of corporation juggling, stock jobbing, and stock speculation. It is private production without the control of private property [C. III, 519].

(3) CONCLUSION

Economic stability in the Marxian system is held to be incompatible with the development of the capitalist mode of production. Cyclical fluctuations, Marx argues, are indigenous to the system and become increasingly severe with the application of higher capital compositions. The industrial cycle, he claims, follows the world market. Economies of predominantly raw-material production are susceptible not only to internal fluctuations but to fluctuations induced by the dominating industrial economies.

The critical variables in the Marxian analysis of cycles are the productive and market capacities. That productive capacities expand more rapidly than market capacities, he argues, follows directly from the laws of capitalist development. Overproduction results, and the crisis follows. The institution of credit merely intensifies the real-overproduction phenomenon. Although real overproduction is both a necessary and sufficient condition for cyclical movement in the capitalist economy, a continually falling rate of profit, a too rapid introduction of innovation, and the concentrated timing of fixed-capital replacement may also generate the cycle.

Increasing centralization of production and finance follows directly from the expansion of the capitalist mode of production. Forces of competition insure the supremacy of the more advanced productive processes. The introduction of centralization into the model intensifies the cyclical fluctuations by producing still greater productive capacities without extending the market.

While there is much to be said for Marx's analysis of economic instability and the predictions which follow therefrom, the *inevitability* of such instability cannot be logically derived from the model. Marx did not demonstrate that market capacity could not expand so rapidly as productive capacity or that the distribution of aggregate production between the two main departments of the economy could not produce stability. His analysis does, however, illustrate the *high probability* that cyclical instability would result. Given the structural disproportions of production, the predictions he sets down are in fact logical derivatives from his analysis.

PREDICTIONS

PRIMARY PREDICTIONS

1. The capitalist economy generates industrial cycles.
2. The expansion of the capitalist mode of production, which is dependent upon the competitive market, destroys, in the process of development, the competitive nature of the market. Concentration and centralization of wealth and production follow.

SECONDARY PREDICTIONS RELATED TO PRIMARY PREDICTION NO. 1

3. For a general crisis to occur, it is sufficient that overproduction grip merely the principal articles of trade.
4. The amount of credit outstanding in the economy increases with the development of the capitalist mode of production.
5. The credit economy will subject the entire economy to the dictates of the money market.
6. The institution of credit will generate more violent cycles than those in noncredit economies.
7. Business always appears sound just before a crash.
8. The use of fraudulent bills of exchange is inevitable, and it will intensify the crash.
9. Cycles become progressively more violent.
10. Cycles become more frequent.

11. Cycles become more violent in raw-material-producing economies than in industrial economies.
12. Cycles produce succeeding cycles.
13. Cycles become international by subjecting each economy to the instabilities of the others.
14. No legislation can abolish the crisis.
15. The continual decline in the rate of profit leads to crises.
16. The periodic replacement of fixed capital provides the material basis for commercial crises.
17. The crisis is always the starting point for large amounts of new investment.
18. Rational agriculture is irreconcilable with capitalist production.

SECONDARY PREDICTIONS RELATED TO PRIMARY PREDICTION NO. 2

19. Competition eliminates the smaller capitalists from production.
20. Centralization of money occurs in periods of crisis.
21. Joint-stock companies emerge with centralization and accelerate the centralization process.
22. Joint-stock companies produce a new aristocracy of finance, the nominal director.

SPECIFIC PREDICTIONS RELATED TO PRIMARY PREDICTION NO. 1

23. In England's attempt to exploit the Chinese market, her manufactures will outstrip the Chinese market capacity.
24. Cyclical fluctuations in England will occur every ten years.
25. If China were to legalize opium-planting, trade relations among the United States, Australia, India, China, and England would collapse and the international crisis would follow.
26. The crisis on the Continent always originates in England.
27. The Chinese rebellion will produce a crisis in England.

11
The increasing misery
of the proletariat and
the class struggle

MARX FORECASTS the workers' fate under capitalism. He predicts that their standard of living will decline and that this decline will create, then intensify, the class struggle. These predictions, like the other major forecasts he set down, are presented to the reader as logical derivatives of his theory of wages and employment; they are constructs from his theories of price, profit, and capital accumulation.

The logical derivation of the misery prediction is essentially this: The application of higher forms of technology under capitalism chronically displaces labor from production. This displacement swells the ranks of the unemployed, which forces wage rates to subsistence. Since subsistence is flexible downward, increasing misery is assured.

The inevitability of the class struggle is presented as a corollary of the misery prediction. Although economic in origin, it takes on the character of political activity in the later stages of capitalist development. Related to these two primary predictions are fifteen secondary and specific ones.

(1) INCREASING MISERY
OF THE PROLETARIAT

Marx's determination of wages under capitalism is reducible, on first approximation, to the simple analysis of supply and demand in the competitive labor market. Thus he can write that when the supply of labor exceeds demand, the excess supply—the industrial reserve army—exerts a downward pressure on wages. The larger the proportion of the labor force in the industrial reserve army, the more intense is the competition among sellers of labor, and, consequently, the lower is the wage rate. The downward movement of this wage rate is subject only to a subsistence restraint. The converse, Marx notes, is also true. As the

151

relative size of the industrial reserve army diminishes, the increasing competition among buyers of labor has a buoyant effect upon the level of wages. The upward movement of the wage rate, like its movement downward, is subject to a restraint. In the case of increasing wage rates, the restraint is the minimum rate of profit that capitalists will accept (C. I, 680). The analysis of wage determination in the Marxian system therefore rests upon an analysis of the formation of and changes in the industrial reserve army (C. I, 699).

(a) THE FORMATION OF THE INDUSTRIAL RESERVE ARMY

Consider here Marx's analysis of the effects of higher technology upon the size of the industrial reserve army. Marx's formulation of labor displacement due to the application of higher forms of technology or increasing compositions of capital, under conditions of constant capital outlay, can be expressed by

$$\Delta \text{IRA} = K_1[(c/K)_2 - (c/K)_1]/w \qquad (11.1)$$

where K_1 is total capital outlay, $(c/K)_1$ and $(c/K)_2$ are the organic compositions of capital before and after technological change, w is the prevailing wage rate, and ΔIRA gives the change in the industrial reserve army.

With K_1 constant, increases in the organic composition of capital displace laborers from production. This displacement augments the industrial reserve army. Marx uses the following example: $K_1 = \pounds 500$, $w = \pounds 1$, $(c/K)_1 = 40$ per cent, and $(c/K)_2 = 80$ per cent (C. I, 491). Displacement of labor, or the increase in the industrial reserve army, is 200. Marx also refers to this displacement as "relative surplus population."

Constancy of capital outlay in the above example is merely a first approximation. As we have seen in Chapter 7, the capitalist economy is characterized by capital accumulation. When mechanization of the production process occurs through the substitution of higher for lower organic compositions of capital, *additional* profits are forthcoming. Capital accumulation originating from this source of profit formation, in Marx's system, can be measured by

$$a = g(s_2 - s_1) \qquad (11.2)$$

where a is accumulation, g is the proportion of additional profits not consumed, and $(s_2 - s_1)$ is the change in profits accruing from the advanced technology.

With the value of a thus determined, additional demands for labor generated by capital accumulation via mechanization can be measured by

$$d = a(v/K)_2/w \qquad (11.3)$$

where d represents an additional demand for labor, $(v/K)_2$ is the inverse of the organic composition of capital, and w is the prevailing wage rate. For example, Marx supposes $a = £1000$, $w = £1$, and $(c/K)_2 = 80$ per cent, or $(v/K_2) = 20$ per cent. The additional demand for labor resulting from mechanization would therefore equal 200 (C. I, 491).

Since Marx assumes both changing technology and capital accumulation, the industrial reserve army remains stable only if

$$K_1[(c/K)_2 - (c/K)_1]/w - a(v/K)_2/w = 0 \qquad (11.4)$$

Under this condition, the prevailing wage rate remains unchanged.

In circumstances, however, where the result in equation (11.4) is greater than zero, unemployment occurs, the industrial reserve army expands, and the wage rate consequently declines.[1] Absolute as well as relative surplus population appears. On the other hand, if circumstances are such that the result is less than zero, the industrial reserve army diminishes, the intensity of competition among buyers of labor becomes greater, and the level of wages consequently increases. Absolute surplus population hence is negative. Marx concedes that such a situation may occur temporarily under capitalism. "A rise in the price of labor, as a consequence of accumulation of capital, only means, in fact, that the length and weight of the golden chain the wage-worker has already forged for himself, allow of a relaxation of the tension of it" (C. I, 677).

In the longer run, and for the much greater proportion of time, the worker's wage under capitalism, Marx asserts, is reduced to subsistence. In other words, according to Marx declining wages are a necessary consequence of capitalist development.

Even though Marx considered mechanization a necessary and sufficient condition for the expansion of the industrial reserve army, he incorporates into the analysis factors other than mechanization. These factors include centralization of production, net population changes, changes in the labor-population ratio, and changes in the incomes of surplus-receiving classes. Integration of these factors into Marx's completed model is illustrated in the accompanying diagram. The purpose

1. Marx did not suggest that wages fell to subsistence with a *positive* industrial reserve army. In the system Marx set it down that the "degree" of unemployment determines wage movements, although he never clarified this position. Was there a critical value of unemployment beyond which wage movements occur? Did this value change?

of setting down Marx's model in this form is to facilitate discussion of the question whether the complete Marxian wage model generates absolute surplus population under conditions of expanding capitalism. Marx's theory of declining wages, we have seen, is dependent upon such

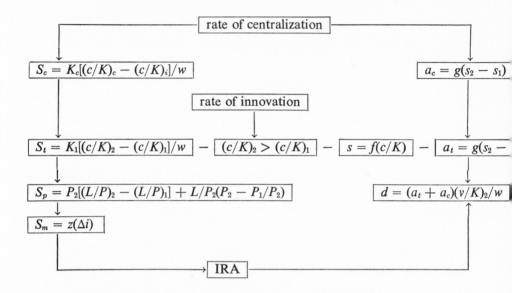

a demonstration. Consider the effects of each factor upon the size of the industrial reserve army.

(i) THE EFFECT OF INNOVATION

The degree of technological innovation, $(c/K)_2/(c/K)_1$, is independent of the model. The relative surplus population or the displacement of labor from current production is represented in the diagram by S_t. Innovation, however, is a double-edged sword. As we saw in Chapter 8, the productivity of labor resulting from the introduction of technological innovations increases in geometrical progression. Profits are augmented by $(s_2 - s_1)$, capital accumulation by $g(s_2 - s_1)$. Since there is no precise relationship between changing technology $(c/K)_2 - (c/K)_1$ and changing profits $(s_2 - s_1)$, no definite relationship can be made between the increased demands for labor generated by innovation, $a_t(v/K)_s/w$, and the increased technological displacement, S_t. The effects of innovation on the size of the industrial reserve army therefore are indeterminate.

(ii) THE EFFECT OF CENTRALIZATION

Centralization in the Marxian system is an independent variable.

The absolute decrease of the demand for labor necessarily following therefrom will naturally be so much greater, the more these capitals going through the process of rejuvenation have become accumulated in masses by means of the movement of centralization [C. I, 689].

Centralization of capital, Marx notes, releases not only laborers from the production process but small capitalists as well; "entire sections of the ruling classes are, by the advance of industry, precipitated into the proletariat, or are at least threatened in their conditions of existence" (CM, 22). Yet, here as in the case of innovations, centralization is executed with the conscious intention of augmenting surplus value from a given quantity of capital. Recall that, in the analysis of centralization, Marx showed that the productiveness of labor is a function of the scale of production (C. I, 680). If, therefore, a given quantity of independent small capitals is converted to one capital of higher composition, the surplus value derived from this centralized process should exceed the aggregate surplus value produced from the smaller capitals. Increasing accumulation due to centralization therefore follows, i.e., $a_c = g(s_2 - s_1)$. The demand for labor consequently increases by $a_c(v/c + v)_2$. As in the analysis of innovation, the amount of accumulation is contingent upon the change in surplus value. The net effect on employment due to centralization, that is, the relationship between S_c and $a_c(v/K)_2$, therefore remains indeterminate.

(iii) THE EFFECT OF POPULATION GROWTH

The rate of population growth, $P_2 - P_1/P_2$, is exogenous to the Marxian model. While Marx was aware of the population influx, he attached little significance to it as a cause of changes in the level of wages. Marx was interested in demonstrating that the capitalist system, not biological drives, created the excess supply of labor. None the less, he did recognize that part of the increased population, L/P_2, the labor-population ratio, augmented the IRA, S_p.

(iv) THE EFFECT OF CHANGES IN THE LABOR-POPULATION RATIO

Marx pointed out the direct relation between changes in technology and the bringing of women and children into the labor force (see Chap.

8, sec. 2e). As technology advances, the labor-population ratio, $(L/P)_2 - (L/P)_1$, increases, supplying additional members to the industrial reserve army, S_p.

(v) THE EFFECT OF FALLING INTEREST RATES

As we saw in Chapter 4, the supply of loanable funds increases with the development of the capitalist mode of production. Interest rates, Marx predicted, must decline (see Chap. 8, sec. 4). This decline, he further predicts, will decimate the money-capitalist class, who have no alternative but to join the ranks of the unemployed, S_m. He writes:

That the interest on capital decreases in the same measure as capital grows, as the mass and number of capital increase; that, therefore, the small *rentier* can no longer live on his interest but must throw himself into industry, and consequently, help to increase the ranks of the small industrialists and therefore of candidates for the proletariat—all this surely requires no further exposition [WLC, 51].

. . . the rate of interest diminishing in proportion as capitalists accumulate, the small investors who can no longer live on their incomes will be forced to embark in industry, and thus in the end to swell the number of the proletarians [DFT, 17–18].

The total *relative* surplus population resulting from the development of the capitalist system can therefore be described in the diagram on page 154 by $S_c + S_t + S_p + S_m$. It is this quantity that continuously supplements the industrial reserve army. The total increased demand for labor, or the "leakage" in the industrial reserve army, depends upon the value of capital accumulation and the prevailing organic composition of capital, that is, $d = (a_t + a_c) \, (v/K)_2/w$. To demonstrate that the industrial reserve army expands as capitalism matures requires proof that the capital accumulation forthcoming from the enhanced productivity is insufficient to compensate for the displacement of labor. Marx "proves" the inevitability of this consequence thus:

Since the demand for labour is determined not by the amount of capital as a whole, but by its variable constituent alone, that demand falls progressively with the increase of the total capital, instead of, as previously assumed, rising in proportion to it. It falls *relatively* to the magnitude of the total capital, and at an accelerated rate, as this magnitude increases. With the growth of the total capital, its variable constituent or the labour incorporated in it, also does increase, but in a constantly diminishing proportion. The intermediate pauses are shortened, in which accumulation works as simple extension of production, on a given technical basis. It is not merely that an accelerated accumulation of total capital, accelerated in a constantly growing progression, is needed to absorb an additional number of labourers, or even, on account of the constant metamorphosis of old capital, to keep employed those already functioning. In its turn, this increasing accumulation and centralisation becomes a source of new changes in the composition of capital, of a more accelerated diminution of its variable, as compared with its constant constituent. This accelerated relative diminution of the variable constituent, that goes along with the accelerated increase of the total capital, *and moves more rapidly than this increase* takes the inverse form, at the other pole, of an apparently *absolute increase of the labouring population, an increase always moving more rapidly than that of the variable capital or the means of employment.* But in fact, it is the capitalistic accumulation itself that constantly produces, and produces in the direct ratio of its own energy and extent, a *relatively* redundant population of labourers, i.e., a population of greater extent than suffices for the average needs of the self-expansion of capital, and therefore a *surplus-population* [C. I, 690–91; italics added].

In the passage just cited the vital distinction between relative and absolute surplus population is virtually ignored. The critical factor in the effects of mechanization, centralization, and changes in the labor force upon the size of the industrial reserve army, and consequently upon the level of wages, is *absolute* surplus population. Marx must prove that the demand for labor forthcoming from these factors via capital accumulation is insufficient to compensate for the labor displaced by the factors. It is here that Marx's argument concerning *inevitable* increases in unemployment breaks down. Why Marx stated that the relative decline in the employment of labor (variable constituent) "moves more rapidly" than the increase in total capital (accumulation) is never explained. Analysis here, following strictly Marxian thought, shows that the changes in the industrial reserve army that are caused by mechanization, centralization, and changes in the labor force are indeterminate. Actually Marx merely assumed in the statement of his proof what he set out to prove. The failure to demonstrate that absolute surplus population expands with mechanization invalidates the argument that real wages under capitalism must coincide with subsistence.

(b) THE INCREASING MISERY OF THE PROLETARIAT

Convinced that he had demonstrated the law of expanding unemployment under capitalism, Marx confidently predicts the increasing misery of the proletariat.

The modern laborer, on the contrary, instead of rising with the progress of industry, sinks deeper and deeper below the conditions of existence of his own class. He becomes a pauper, and pauperism develops more rapidly than population and wealth [CM, 25].

The greater this reserve army in proportion to the active labor-army, the greater is the mass of a consolidated surplus-population, whose misery is in inverse ratio to its torment of labor. The more extensive, finally, the lazarus-layers of the working-class, and the industrial reserve army, the greater is official pauperism. *This is the absolute general law of capitalist accumulation. . . .* It establishes an accumulation of misery, corresponding with accumulation of capital [C. I, 707–9].

Marx makes increasing misery of the proletariat synonymous with increasing pauperism (CM, 25; see also C. I, 482, 704, 707), agony of toil (C. I, 709), suffering (C. I, 470–71), starvation (C. I, 434, 516, 718), moral and intellectual degradation (C. I, 436, 432), physical deterioration of women and children (C. I, 434, 523), poorer living conditions (C. I, 722), fewer and inferior daily provisions (C. I, 739) —in essence, with the general decline in the laborer's real income. *Capital* (Vol. I, especially Chaps. 15 and 25) abounds with detailed "evidence" concerning the oncoming fate of the English proletariat.

Official paupers, Marx reports, increased from 851,369 in 1856 to 971,433 in 1865 (C. I, 717). Relatively higher and increasing infant-mortality rates in urban as compared with rural areas, he writes, bear further testimony to the effect of evolving capitalism (C. I, 434). Marx cites statistics on life-expectancy to show the dwindling of the English proletariat (C. I, 509, 704). Commenting on conditions of shelter, Marx states that "the greater the centralisation of the means of production, the greater is the corresponding heaping together of the labourers, within a given space; that therefore the swifter capitalistic accumulation, the more miserable are the dwellings of the working people" (C. I, 722).[2] The lot of the agricultural worker in the 1860's compared with his predecessor in the 1770's has changed to an extraordinary degree for the worse (C. I, 740). Detailing the tribulations of the proletariat under capitalism, Marx produces an excerpt from an official health report of 1864:

Long before insufficiency of diet is a matter of hygienic concern, long before the physiologist would think of counting the grains of

2. Marx continues, quoting from a health report of 1864, "Improvements of towns, accompanying the increase in wealth, by the demolition of badly built quarters, the erection of palaces for banks, warehouses, etc., the widening of streets for business traffic, for the carriages of luxury, and for the introduction of tramways, etc., drive away the poor into even worse and more crowded hiding places."

nitrogen and carbon which intervene between life and starvation, the household will have been entirely destitute of material comfort; clothing and fuel will have been even scantier than food—against inclemencies of weather there will have been no adequate protection—dwelling space will have been stinted to the degree in which over-crowding produces or increases disease; of household utensils and furniture there will have been scarcely any—even cleanliness will have been found costly or difficult, and if there still be self-respectful endeavours to maintain it, every such endeavour will represent additional pangs of hunger. The home, too, will be where shelter can be cheapest bought; in quarters where commonly there is least fruit of sanitary supervision, least drainage, least scavenging, least suppression of public nuisances, least or worst water supply, and, if in town, least light and air. *Such are the sanitary dangers to which poverty is almost certainly exposed,* when it is poverty enough to imply scantiness of food. And while the sum of them is of terrible magnitude against life, the mere scantiness of food is in itself of very serious moment. . . . These are painful reflections, especially when it is remembered that the poverty to which they advert is not the deserved poverty of idleness. *In all cases it is the poverty of working populations* [C. I, 721; italics added].

Quoting Ducpetiaux, a member of the central commission of Belgian statistics, Marx reports:

How comes it, however, that a great number, we might say, a great majority, of labourers, live in a more economical way? It is . . . by adopting expedients, the secret of which only the labourer knows; by reducing his daily rations; by substituting rye-bread for wheat; by eating less meat, or even none at all, and the same with butter and condiments; by contenting themselves with one or two rooms where the family is crammed together, where boys and girls sleep side by side, often on the same pallet; by economy of clothing, washing, decency; by giving up the Sunday diversions; by, in short, resigning themselves to the most painful privations. Once arrived at this extreme limit, the least rise in the price of food, stoppage of work, illness, increases the labourer's distress and determines his complete ruin; debts accumulate, credit fails, the most necessary clothes and furniture are pawned, and finally, the family asks to be enrolled on the list of paupers [C. I, 739].

(c) INCREASING RELATIVE MISERY?

In *Wage-Labor and Capital,* Marx distinguishes between relative and real wages. The critical variable, he suggests, is the relative wage:

Relative wages can fall although real wages rise simultaneously with nominal wages, with the money value of labor, [provided that the real wages] do not rise, however, in the same proportion as profit. . . . If capital is growing rapidly, wages may rise; the profit of capital rises incomparably more rapidly. The material position of the worker has improved, but at the cost of his social position. The social gulf that divides him from the capitalist has widened [WLC, 42].

The power of the capitalist class over the working class has grown, the social position of the worker has deteriorated, has been depressed one step further below that of the capitalist [WLC, 40].

The system of wage-labor is a system of slavery and to wit of a slavery which becomes more arduous in measure as the social productive forces of labor develop, *whether the worker receives better or worse payment for his labor* [CGP, 41; italics added].

Although the laborer's absolute standard of life would have remained the same, his *relative* wages, and therewith his *relative social position,* as compared with that of the capitalist, would have been lowered. If the working man should resist that reduction of relative wages, he would only try to get some share in the increased productive powers of his own labor, and to maintain his former relative position in the social scale [VPP, 103–4].

These statements imply that Marx's prediction concerning the increasing misery of the proletariat refers merely to the increasing inequality of income distribution. The real incomes of both capitalists and proletarians may actually increase. Misery is psychological. Interestingly, this implication still would be consistent with Marx's assertion that wages must fall to subsistence if he can demonstrate that subsistence itself rises with the development of capitalism. This Marx conveniently does. Consider these statements on the determination of the subsistence level:

The laborer needs time for satisfying his intellectual and social wants, the extent and number of which are conditioned by the general state of social advancement [C. I, 256].

His natural wants, such as food, clothing, fuel, and housing, vary according to the climatic and other physical conditions of his country. On the other hand, the number and extent of his so-called necessary wants, as also the modes of satisfying them, are themselves the product of historical development, and depend therefore to a great extent on the degree of civilization of a country, more particularly on the conditions under which, and consequently on the habits and degree of comfort in which, the class of free laborers has been formed. *In contradistinction there-*

fore to the case of other commodities, there enters into the determination of the value of labor-power a historical and moral element [C. I, 190; italics added].

A house may be large or small; as long as the surrounding houses are equally small it satisfies all social demands for a dwelling. But let a palace arise beside the little house, and it shrinks from a little house to a hut. The little house shows now that its owner has only very slight or no demands to make; and however high it may shoot up in the course of civilization, if the neighbouring palace grows to an equal or even greater extent, the dweller in the relatively small house will feel more and more uncomfortable, dissatisfied and cramped within its four walls. . . . Our needs and enjoyments spring from society; we measure them, therefore, by society and not by the objects which serve for their satisfaction. Because they are of a social nature, they are of a relative nature [WLC, 36–37].

When "needs and enjoyment spring from society," when the "historical and moral element" as well as the "intellectual needs" are incorporated into the concept of necessity, when the "degree of civilization" and "habit and custom" determine needs, then subsistence must represent something other than mere physical subsistence. Marx clearly points this out by describing minimal subsistence as "the value of the commodities, without the daily supply of which the laborer cannot renew this vital energy . . . ; those means of subsistence that are physically indispensable" (C. I, 192).

Although it may appear from the above analysis that Marx's prediction concerning the increasing misery of the proletariat refers to either absolute or relative misery, his claim of having derived the prediction from his wage and employment theory rules out the latter alternative. Marx, we have seen, believed that the industrial reserve army must increase with the expansion of capitalism. Thus, absolute wage rates decline. The minimum physical subsistence, therefore, becomes the lower restraint to wages. This conclusion, allegedly drawn from his wage and employment theory, denies the relative-misery hypothesis.

(2) THE INEVITABILITY OF THE CLASS STRUGGLE

(a) CLASS CONSCIOUSNESS AND THE CLASS STRUGGLE

The Marxian prediction concerning the inevitability of increasing class struggle follows directly from his misery prediction. The nature of the predictions, however, differs. The increasing misery of the proletariat, we have seen, is an economic phenomenon. The class struggle, on the other hand, is essentially a political process whose roots are found in the economic substructure. Classes relate to property conditions, i.e., to the owners and the nonowners of the means of production.

The evolution of the class struggle in capitalism presupposes the existence of *class consciousness* in the proletariat. The extent of this consciousness, Marx claims, is related to the mode of production. The institution of the factory system, the regimentation and intensification of labor, the leveling of skills, the misery of the proletariat, the increasing centralization and concentration of production, and the development of the market—all by-products of capitalist development—are considered prerequisite to the development of class consciousness.

In the *Communist Manifesto* Marx outlines a five-stage blueprint depicting the evolution of the proletarian class. Each stage, he notes, reflects the prevailing mode of production. In the precapitalist era, he points out, the conflict between the owners of the means of production and the original producers is carried on at a personal level, i.e., between the individual owner and worker. The primary goal of the capitalist in this relation is to maximize labor exploitation by extending the working day. The laborer, on the other hand, tries to reduce this exploitation to some reasonable limit. Hence, the origin of the conflict or struggle (see Chap. 3, sec. 3).

With the advent of modern industry and capital accumulation, the "little workshops" of the "patriarchal masters" become the great factories of the industrial capitalists. "Masses of laborers," he writes, "crowded into the factory, are organized like soldiers. . . . Not only are they slaves of the bourgeois class, and of the bourgeois State, they are daily and hourly enslaved by the machine, by the over-looker, and, above all, by the individual bourgeois manufacturer himself" (CM, 18–19). The class antagonism at this stage, while in essence the same as under premodern industrial conditions, is carried on at the factory level, i.e., between the industrial capitalist and the members of a factory. The laborers, reduced to the lowest of skills by the introduction of machinery and clustered together in a factory unit, recognize their common interests vis à vis the bourgeoisie. The centralization of industry augments the proletarian class with small tradespeople, shopkeepers, handicraftsmen, and peasants, as well as industrial capitalists who are eliminated from the bourgeois class by large-scale, low-cost production (CM, 19). As Marx wrote:

It is an inevitable phenomenon, rooted in the course of development, that people from what have hitherto been the ruling classes should also join the militant proletariat and contribute cultural elements to it [MEC, 375].

And he forecasts the ultimate polarization of the population: "Society as a whole is more and more splitting up into two great hostile camps, into two great classes directly facing each other: Bourgeoisie and Proletariat" (CM, 10).

The creation of the industrial reserve army has, Marx notes, both positive and adverse effects on the development of class consciousness. The growing competition among laborers breeds internal disunity, but there emerges from disunity the consciousness of common destiny. This consciousness, he claims, is the "real fruit" of the industrial reserve army (CM, 21). He cites the sporadic attempts at combinations (trade unions) and associations to bargain for shorter workdays and higher wages as evidence of this growing consciousness.[3] Thus, Marx prophesies that "the proletariat not only increases in number, [but] it becomes concentrated in great masses, its strength grows, and it feels that strength more" (CM, 20).

Marx's third stage is characterized by concerted activity on the part of the proletariat, e.g., by activity relating to the physical destruction of competing imports and by attempts to recover some status (CM, 20). Class identification at this level is generally associated with a particular trade in a particular locale.

The fourth stage in the evolution of the proletarian class follows upon the development of transportation and the expansion of the capitalist market. Marx writes:

This union is helped on by the improved means of communication that are created by modern industry, and that place the workers of different localities in contact with one another. It was just this contact that was needed to centralize the numerous local struggles, all of the same character, into one national struggle between classes [CM, 21].

The national proletarian class is thereby established. What took centuries for the capitalists to establish with miserable highways, he predicts, the modern proletariat can attain in a few years with the modern railway (CM, 21). The final stage of class consciousness, growing out of the establishment of the world market and the internationalization of the capitalist mode of production, Marx prophesies, will be the interna-

---

3. "The first attempts of workers to *associate* among themselves always take place in the form of combinations. Large-scale industry concentrates in one place a crowd of people unknown to one another. Competition divides their interests. But the maintenance of wages, this common interest which they have against their boss, unites them in a common thought of resistance—combination" (PP, 194).

tionalization of the proletariat. The modern subjugation of the laborer to capital, Marx writes, strips him of every trace of national character. Law, morality, religion, are now merely bourgeois prejudices. Marx explicitly refers to England, France, America, and Germany.

"Working men of all countries," Marx closes the *Communist Manifesto,* "unite!" (CM, 54). Yet, even here, the development of an international class consciousness is made a function of the complementary modes of production. The proletariat of each country, he cautions, must first settle matters with its own bourgeoisie (CM, 24). Interestingly, Marx states that the industrial proletariat can come into being only *after* the development of the industrial bourgeoisie:

Only under its rule the proletariat wins the extensive national existence, which can raise its revolution to a national one and itself creates the modern means of production, which become just so many means of its revolutionary emancipation. Only bourgeois rule tears up the roots of feudal society and levels the ground on which a proletarian revolution is alone possible [CSF, 43].

Although the roots of class identity are found in the economic exploitation of the worker, the class struggle ultimately becomes political. Marx writes that

the attempt in a particular factory or even a particular industry to force a shorter working day out of the capitalists by strikes, etc., is a purely economic movement. On the other hand the movement to force an eight-hour-day, etc., *law* is a *political* movement. And in this way, out of the separate economic movements of the workers there grows up everywhere a *political* movement, that is to say a movement of the *class,* with the object of achieving its interests in the general form, in a form possessing a general social force of compulsion [MEC, 318–19].

As the class develops, the political activity overshadows the economic:

If the first aim of resistance was merely the maintenance of wages, combinations, at first isolated, constitute themselves into groups as the capitalists in their turn unite for the purpose of repression, *and in face of always united capital, the maintenance of the association becomes more necessary to them than that of wages.* This is so true that English economists are amazed to see the workers sacrifice a good part of their wages in favor of associations, which, in the eyes of these economists, are established solely in favor of wages. In this struggle—a veritable civil war—all the elements necessary for a coming battle unite and develop. Once it has reached this point, association takes on a political character [PP, 195; italics added].

The trade-union movement plays a vital organizing, political, and educational role in the development of the class struggle (MEC, 189). For even though the working class may be unprepared for the decisive campaign against the political power of the ruling class, it must train for it by continuous agitation. Otherwise, Marx predicts, "it remains a plaything in their hands" (LTA, 94). At each stage in the economic struggle against the bourgeoisie, a political counterpart develops, e.g., socialist and semisocialistic sects. Marx explains the role of the utopian socialists. They are consciously aware, he states, of the proletarians' plight in bourgeois society. They attempt to rectify the evils by instituting reform. Reform, however, not on the basis of class conflict, but on the bases of society as a whole. Hence, they completely misconceive the origin of the evil. None the less, they are vital to the development of the proletarian class. They attack every principle of existing society. They enlighten the working class with critical literature (CM, 49). However, Marx writes,

The development of the system of Socialist sects and that of the real workers' movement always stand in inverse ratio to each other. So long as the sects are [historically] justified, the working class is not yet ripe for an independent historic movement. As soon as it has attained this maturity, all sects are essentially reactionary [MEC, 315; cf. CM, 50].

This type of socialism, Marx writes, passes from the proletariat to the petty bourgeoisie (CSF, 126).

But these political institutions are as transitory as the modes of production; their replacement by the International is imperative to the ultimate development of the working class.

(b) THE QUESTION OF INEVITABILITY

Unlike the economic forecasts, Marx's prediction concerning the emergence of class consciousness cannot be traced back to his theoretical construct of capitalism. It stands out simply as an article of faith. But even Marx seemed to have reservations concerning its veracity. In private correspondence he expressed grave doubts about the inevitability of proletarian class consciousness. Interestingly, these doubts are never revealed in his public writing. Here the working class is presented as a symbol of morality and determination. Yet, to charge Marx with outright intellectual dishonesty would be unjust. "Vacillating" would more accurately describe his thought in this connection. In many of his confidential letters his tributes to the working class are full of praise.

Writing to Kugelmann on working-class participation in the Paris Commune of 1871, he states:

What elasticity, what historical initiative, what a capacity for sacrifice in these Parisians: After six months of hunger and ruin . . . they rise, beneath the Prussian bayonets, as if there had never been a war between France and Germany and the enemy were not at the gates of Paris. History has no like example of a like greatness. If they are defeated, only their "good nature" will be to blame [MEC, 309].

In a letter to Engels, he recounts, in part, a conversation with Bruno Bauer. Bauer, Marx related, claimed that the proletariat could be bought off with a penny raise in wages. Marx dismissed this as mere "illusion" (MEC, 78). In articles to the *New York Daily Tribune* Marx glorified the English working-class reaction to the American Civil War:

At the present moment, English interference in America has accordingly become a bread-and-butter question for the working class. . . . The working class is accordingly fully conscious that the government is only waiting for the intervention cry from below, the *pressure from without,* to put an end to the American blockade and English misery. Under these circumstances, the obstinacy with which the working class keeps silent, or breaks its silence only to raise its voice against intervention and *for* the United States, is admirable. This is a new, brilliant proof of the indestructible excellence of the English popular masses [CWUS, 140–41].

Yet, on the very same issue, he wrote Engels:

What might be much more injurious in my view is the sheep's attitude of the workers in Lancashire. Such a thing has never been heard of in the world. . . . During this recent period England has disgraced herself more than any other country, the workers by their Christian slave nature, the bourgeois and aristocrats by their enthusiasm for slavery in its most direct form. But the two manifestations supplement one another [CWUS, 261–62].

Here the sterling qualities of the workers have become somewhat tarnished, and, commenting on a London skirmish between workers and police, he writes: "One thing is certain, these thick-headed John Bulls, whose brainpans seem to have been specially manufactured for the constables' bludgeons, will never get anywhere without a really bloody encounter with the ruling powers" (MEC, 213).

Engels' confidence in the emergence of class consciousness was, to say the least, not much stronger. Writing to Marx on the English election returns, he notes:

What do you say to the elections in the factory districts? Once again the proletariat has discredited itself terribly. . . . But it remains a hopeless certificate of destitution for the English proletariat, all the same. The *parson* has shown unexpected power and so has the cringing to respectability. Not a single working-class candidate had a ghost of a chance, but my Lord Tomnoddy or any *parvenu* snob could have the workers' votes with pleasure [MEC, 253–54].

Marx's doubts concerning the "growing class consciousness" keeps reappearing in correspondence. Of particular concern to him was the stubbornly nationalistic spirit of the workers, which, he thought, diverted them from class solidarity:

[The] English working-class . . . can never do anything decisive here in England until it separates its policy with regard to Ireland in the most definite way from the policy of the ruling classes. . . . And, indeed, this must be done, not as a matter of sympathy with Ireland, but as a demand made in the interests of the English proletariat. If not, English people will remain tied to the leading-strings of the ruling classes, because [they] must join with them in common front against Ireland [MEC, 278].

Marx expands on the Irish-English problem:

Ireland supplies its own surplus to the English labor market and thus forces down wages and lowers the moral and material position of the English working class. And most important of all: every industrial and commercial center in England now possesses a working-class population *divided* into two hostile camps, English proletarians and Irish proletarians. The ordinary English worker hates the Irish worker as a competitor who lowers his standard of life. In relation to the Irish worker he feels himself a member of the ruling nation and so turns himself into a tool of the aristocrats and capitalists *against Ireland,* thus strengthening their domination *over himself.* He cherishes religious, social and national prejudices against the Irish worker. His attitude towards him is much the same as that of the "poor whites" to the "niggers" in the former slave states of the U.S.A. The Irishman pays him back with interest in his own coin. He regards the English worker as both sharing in the guilt for the English domination in Ireland and at the same time serving as its stupid tool. This antagonism is artificially kept alive and intensified by the press, the pulpit, the comic papers, in short by all the means at the disposal of the ruling classes. It is the secret of the impotence of the English working class, despite their organization [MEC, 289–90].

Engels also expressed much concern about working-class nationalism. Writing on the Franco-German War, he showed that a German victory would free the French working class from the grip of Bonapartism: "Until this chauvinism is knocked on the head," he predicted, "and that properly, peace between Germany and France is impossible" (MEC, 245–46).

The prediction of increasing class struggle is thus made contingent upon the emergence of class consciousness. The development of this class consciousness itself depends upon certain basic assumptions concerning the political behavior of the various classes. As we have seen, Marx himself raised serious doubts about these political relationships. To say, therefore, as did Marx, that the economic conditions prepare for class consciousness is not sufficient. The behavior patterns of the workers must be definitely related to the economic change. Unlike the other predictions examined in this study, Marx makes no attempt to establish "laws" of political behavior. This, however, is understandable. The prediction of class struggle in the Marxian system is essentially political and therefore not amenable to the same rigorous analysis. While Marx presents a very plausible case for class struggle in his system, plausibility is not inevitability.

(3) CONCLUSION

Whatever may be said of Marx's theory of wage and employment determination under capitalism or of his prediction concerning the increasing misery of the proletariat, the latter cannot be said to follow logically from the former. And yet it was precisely "logical derivation" that Marx paraded as proof of the scientific merits of his prophecy.

The theoretical basis of the misery prediction which Marx set down in *Capital* may be summed up as follows. The subsistence wage under capitalism varies inversely with the progress of technology. Market wages depend upon demand and supply conditions on the competitive labor market. Two diverse consequences are manifest on this market as new forms of technology are applied to production. On the one hand, the labor requirement of the original capital outlay becomes smaller, thereby creating excess labor supplies (the industrial reserve army); and, on the other hand, capital accumulation, which follows from the enhanced profits due to mechanization, produces some degree of labor-recruiting. The laws of capitalism are such that the number of laborers displaced by technology always exceeds that number demanded by capital accumulation; to wit, the industrial reserve army must expand under capitalism. The level of wages, therefore, must fall; and since subsistence itself is flexible downward, no lower limit is known to market wages under capitalism. This process of capitalist production,

Marx declares, makes inevitable the increasing misery of the proletariat.

The salient defect in Marx's theoretical development of the prediction was that he treated a pure judgment of values of the variables as if they were logical derivatives of his model. Specifically, Marx stated that *because* higher forms of technology were continuously applied to production, the number of laborers displaced by technology must be greater than the number recruited by capital accumulation. This causality cannot be demonstrated in Marx's model. The excesses of labor displacement over recruitment emerge only when certain values are inserted in the model. The increasing industrial reserve army, therefore, is not *necessarily* the result of the operation of the model.

The nature of the Marxian prediction concerning the inevitability of class struggle is essentially political and lies outside the framework of the Marxian economic model. The basis for class struggle is the emergence of class consciousness. The degree of this consciousness is related to the economic substructure of capitalist society. As the modes of production develop, i.e., from small workshop units to the factory system, class awareness broadens. The internationalization of capitalism and the establishment of the world market generate a corresponding development of the international proletariat. Class activity, while at first economic, is soon directed to political objectives. The ultimate aim of proletarian political action is the overthrow of the ruling class.

Criticism of Marx's prediction concerning the inevitability of class struggle is leveled at the basic assumption concerning the emergence of class consciousness. But even Marx, it was shown, entertained serious doubts about the generation of this consciousness.

PREDICTIONS

PRIMARY PREDICTIONS

1. The misery of the proletariat increases as the capitalist modes of production develop.
2. The class struggle between the proletariat and the bourgeoisie will intensify.

SECONDARY PREDICTIONS RELATED TO PRIMARY PREDICTION NO. 1

3. The development of the capitalist mode of production leads to the development of the industrial reserve army.

4. Entire sections of the ruling class are drawn into the ranks of the proletariat.
5. As the interest rate falls with increasing capital accumulation, the small investors can no longer live on their income and are forced into the proletariat class.
6. The relative misery of the agricultural laborer increases more than his industrial counterpart.

SECONDARY PREDICTIONS RELATED TO PRIMARY PREDICTION NO. 2

7. The proletariat increases in number and grows in strength by developing class consciousness.
8. What took centuries for the capitalists to establish with miserable roads, the proletariat can attain in a few years with railways, namely, class cohesion.
9. The international proletariat emerges with the establishment of the world market.
10. The first attempt of workers to band together takes the form of combinations.
11. At every stage of capitalist economic development there will develop a corresponding political organization. When the world market is established, the International will supersede all previous forms of political organization.
12. The industrial proletariat can come into being only after the development of the industrial bourgeoisie.
13. Utopian socialism will pass from the proletariat to the petty bourgeoisie with the development of the world market.
14. As the class struggle develops, the proletariat will substitute political objectives for economic ones.
15. Unless the proletarians train for political activity, they will never succeed.
16. The proletariat will never get anywhere without a really bloody encounter with the ruling powers.

A SPECIFIC PREDICTION RELATED TO PRIMARY PREDICTION NO. 2

17. The English working class will never do anything decisive in England, as a class, unless it separates its policy toward Ireland in the most clear-cut way from the policy of the ruling class.

12

The inevitability of the proletarian revolution and the emergence of the communist state

THE PURPOSE OF THIS CHAPTER is to examine the Marxian predictions concerning the inevitability of the proletarian revolution and the emergence of the communist state. In section 1 major emphasis is placed on the development of the revolution as it evolves from the class struggle. In section 2, dealing with predictions about the communist state, attention is devoted primarily to prophecies concerning economic production and distribution.

(1) THE INEVITABILITY OF THE PROLETARIAN REVOLUTION

The ultimate objective of class struggle, we have seen, is the usurpation of political power from the bourgeoisie by the proletariat. However, Marx asserts, the proletarian class cannot rise without upsetting all existing relations of production (CM, 24). The state, identified in the Marxian system with the ruling class, will certainly not dissolve itself. Suicide, he argues, is unnatural (SE, 119). The abolition of the bourgeois relations of production, Marx therefore prophesies, can be effected only by revolution (CM, 24).

Marx's pronouncements on the "coming revolution" are not only vague but at times appear to be consciously directed more to political propagandizing than to scientific inquiry:

The rural population, the most stationary and conservative element of modern society, disappears while the industrial proletariat, by the very working of modern production, finds itself gathered in mighty centers, around the great productive forces. . . . Who will prevent them from going a step further, and appropriating these forces, to which they have been appropriated before? Where will be the power of resisting them? Nowhere! [OB, 375–76].

It is interesting to note that, with very few exceptions, Marx makes no mention, let alone analysis, of revolution in the volumes of *Capital*. His treatment of revolution is largely in generalities, and understandably so, for revolution is fundamentally a political activity and is subject to forces which fall outside the framework of model analysis. In this study Marx offers no prototype of revolution applicable to all nations. Indeed, the flexibility which he allows in his system concerning the instituting of revolutions is, as we shall see, surprising. None the less, certain general characteristics of the revolution are discernible. The analysis of Marxian predictions concerning revolution is here divided into two subsections which describe (a) the general characteristics of the revolution and (b) the flexibility of the revolution.

(a) THE GENERAL CHARACTERISTICS OF THE REVOLUTION

The proletarian revolution, Marx predicts, cannot occur until certain prerequisites have been established. Thus:

The working class movement itself is never independent, never is of an exclusively proletarian character until all the different factions in the middle class, and particularly its most progressive faction, the large manufacturers, have conquered political power, and remodelled the State according to their wants. It is then that the inevitable conflict between the employer and the employed becomes imminent, and cannot be adjourned any longer [RCR, 8].

In order that the revolution of a people should coincide with the emancipation of a special class of bourgeois society, it is necessary for a class to stand out as a class representing the whole of society. This further involves, as its obverse side, the concentration of all the defects of society in another class, and this particular class must be the embodiment of the general social obstacles and impediments. . . . In order that one class should be the class of emancipation *par excellence,* another class must contrariwise be the class of manifest subjugation [SE, 33–34].

The "concentration of all the defects in another class" includes the fulfillment of those predictions discussed in earlier chapters, viz., the declining rate of profit, the increasing concentration of industry and wealth, the increasing instability of the economy, and the increasing misery of the proletariat. Elsewhere Marx describes the prerequisites in more explicit terms, as follows:

If, therefore, the proletariat should overthrow the political rule of the bourgeoisie, its victory would only be temporary, only an episode in the service of the bourgeois revolution, *so long as the*

*material conditions which would render necessary the abolition of
the bourgeois mode of production,* and consequently the definitive
overthrow of political rule of the bourgeoisie, *had not yet been
created in the course of historical development* [SE, 137; italics
added].

In his analysis of the German proletarian revolution of 1848, Marx
discounted completely the influence of individual feats. The causes of
victory and defeat, he writes, "are not to be sought for in the accidental
efforts, talents, faults, errors, or treacheries of some of the leaders, but in
the general social state and conditions of existence of each of the
convulsed nations" (RCR, 2). German development, he concluded,
was not then conducive to revolution. This point is clearly demonstrated in Marx's essay "Moralizing Criticism" (SE, 134). Under such
circumstances, the proletarians, Marx suggests, should ally themselves
with the bourgeoisie in order to overthrow the feudal ruling class.
"They know," he writes, "that their own struggle with the bourgeoisie
can only break out on the day that the bourgeoisie triumphs. . . .
They can and must take part in the middle-class revolution as a condition preliminary to the labor revolution" (SE, 161). Concerning the
American political development, Marx wrote in 1852 that the bourgeoisie had not developed sufficiently to make class struggle obvious (MEC,
57). The Paris Commune of 1871 provides an interesting case of
contradiction. In his "Address to the General Council of the International Working Men's Association" (1871), Marx states that the Commune was "essentially a working-class government, the product of the
struggle of the producing against the appropriating class, the political
form at last discovered under which to work out the economical emancipation of Labor" (CWF, 43). Ten years later, writing to Domela
Nieuwenhus on the necessity of developing the conditions before the
revolution, Marx states, "Perhaps you will point to the Paris Commune;
but apart from the fact that this was merely the rising of a town under
exceptional conditions, the majority of the Commune was in no sense
socialist, nor could it be" (MEC, 386–87).

History, Marx confidently wrote, was on the side of the proletariat.
The downfall of the bourgeoisie and the victory of the proletariat, he
prophesied in the *Communist Manifesto,* was inevitable (CM, 25).
Revolution in the Marxian system, however, is a repetitive activity. The
class struggle, he claims, breaks into open conflict more than one time;
and more than once, he admits, the proletariat, however courageous,
meets defeat. None the less, he predicts:

But the battle must break out again and again *in ever growing
dimensions,* and there can be no doubts as to who will be the victor

in the end—the appropriating few, or the immense working majority [CWF, 62; italics added].

The *direct* causes of the proletarian revolution, Marx argues, are, in the main, economic. In every case, he writes, they are the consequence of the industrial crisis. During the period of crisis, mounting unemployment, arising from the curtailment of production, inflates the industrial reserve army. When the majority of the population are thus "put on the shelf," Marx assures the reader, the revolution must occur (C. III, 309). Reviewing revolutionary activity in eighteenth- and nineteenth-century Europe, Marx concludes that there had been no serious revolution which had not been preceded by a commercial and financial crisis (MOC, 9). The absence of revolution in France in May, 1850, Marx states, resulted not so much from the peaceful attitude of the press or the majestic calm of the petty bourgeoisie as from the commercial and industrial prosperity (CSF, 137–38). Extrapolating into the future, Marx predicts that "neither wars nor revolutions are likely to put Europe by the ear, unless in consequence of a general commercial and industrial crisis" (MOC, 9). In *The Class Struggles in France,* the Marxian prediction assumes a more explicit form. Analyzing the occurrences of revolution in a developed credit economy, Marx writes: "Public and private credit are the economic thermometer, by which the intensity of the revolution can be measured. To the same degree as they fall, the glow and generative force of the revolution rise" (CSF, 46).

In 1853, writing in the *New York Daily Tribune,* Marx stated that the next revolution in Europe would depend more on what was happening in China than in Europe itself. The contraction of the Chinese market will disturb, he writes, the delicate international trade relations among the European powers, setting off an industrial crisis and, consequently, a Continental revolution (MOC, 7). The English crisis of 1855, he predicts, will spark the working class, and "England will *at last* be compelled to share in the general social evolution of European society" (OB, 412; italics added).

Marxian predictions concerning England reveal an important and interesting inconsistency in his treatment of the class struggle and revolution. Most of Marx's analysis on revolution deals with the European continent directly. Yet Marx writes in 1870:

England, as the metropolis of capital, as the power which has hitherto ruled the world market, is for the time being the most important country for the workers' revolution, and moreover the *only* country in which the material conditions for this revolution have developed up to a certain point of maturity [MEC, 290].

How then can Marx say that England will be compelled to *share* in the social evolution of European society? Revolutionary leadership here has obviously been reversed.

Concerning the revolution proper, Marx had little to say. The classes involved are, of course, the bourgeoisie and the proletariat. The bourgeois class, he writes, is represented in the revolution by the "iron hand of mercenary soldiery," the working class by the proletarians themselves (CWF, 62). The proletarian class in periods of revolution includes not only the workers, conscious of their class objectives, and sections of the petty bourgeoisie but also the *lumpenproletariat,* a recruitment of "thieves and criminals . . . people without a definite trade, vagabonds . . . capable of the most heroic deeds and the most exalted sacrifices, as of the basest banditry and the dirtiest corruption" (CSF, 50). In the *Communist Manifesto* the lumpenproletariat appears as a threat to the stability of the proletarian society:

The "dangerous class," the social scum, that passively rotting mass thrown off by the lowest layers of old society, may, here and there, be swept into the movement by a proletarian revolution; its conditions of life, however, prepare it far more for the part of a bribed tool of reactionary intrigue [CM, 23].

None the less, he writes, they are an "unavoidable evil" and predicts that in time they "are shaken off" (CWF, 50).

The peasants, Marx claims, can play only a passive role in the overthrow of the bourgeoisie. In *Revolution and Counter-Revolution,* Marx examines their capacities, stating that

it is quite as evident, and equally borne out by the history of all modern countries, that the agricultural population, in consequence of its dispersion over a great space, and of the difficulty of bringing about an agreement among any considerable portion of it, never can attempt a successful independent movement; they require the initiatory impulse of the more concentrated, more enlightened, more easily moved people of the towns [RCR, 11].

While the misery of the peasant under capitalism exceeds even that of the proletariat, Marx none the less harbored a profound distrust for the peasant as a revolutionary. In *The Class Struggles in France* he described the peasant revolution of 1848 as "clumsily cunning, knavishly naïve, doltishly sublime, a calculated superstition, a . . . piece of buffoonery [bearing] the unmistakable features of the class that represents barbarism within civilization" (CSF, 71). The salvation of the peasant, he predicted, can result only from the institution of a proletarian government (CSF, 120). Yet, by contrast, in correspondence with Meyer and Vogt, Marx predicted that the moment the English army withdrew from Ireland, an Irish agrarian revolution would commence.

The passionate character of the Irish, he explained, makes them more revolutionary than the English (MEC, 288–89). Revolution in the Marxian system, it must be remembered, is a function of economic development, not "passionate character." The English proletarian revolution, he prophesied, would follow directly from the Irish overthrow of the landed aristocracy: "But the overthrow of the English aristocracy in Ireland, involves . . . its overthrow in England. And this would fulfill the prerequisite for the proletarian revolution in England" (MEC, 288).

For the proletarian revolution to be successful, Marx writes, political conditions must be so developed that the proletariat can take necessary measures for intimidating the mass of the bourgeoisie sufficiently to gain time for lasting action. Thus, Marx predicts the *revolutionary dictatorship of the proletariat* immediately succeeding the overthrow of the bourgeoisie (LTA, 45). In the *Critique of the Gotha Programme* this revolutionary dictatorship is defined as the institution of transition, the political equivalent of the economic transition from capitalism to communism (CGP, 45). In the *Communist Manifesto* Marx details the functions of the revolutionary dictatorship:

The proletariat will use its political supremacy, to wrest, by degrees, all capital from the bourgeoisie, to centralize all instruments of production in the hands of the State. . . . Of course, in the beginning, this cannot be effected except by means of despotic inroads on the rights of property. . . . These measures will of course be different in different countries. Nevertheless, in the most advanced countries the following will be pretty generally applicable:

1. Abolition of property in land and application of all rents of land to public purposes.
2. A heavy progressive or graduated income tax.
3. Abolition of all right of inheritance.
4. Confiscation of the property of all emigrants and rebels.
5. Centralization of credit in the hands of the State, by means of a national bank with State capital and an exclusive monopoly.
6. Centralization of the means of communication and transport in the hands of the State.
7. Extension of factories and instruments of production owned by the State, the bringing into cultivation of waste lands, and the improvement of the soil generally in accordance with a common plan.
8. Equal liability of all to labor. Establishment of industrial armies, especially for agriculture.

9. Combination of agriculture with manufacturing industries; gradual abolition of the distinction between town and country, by a more equable distribution of population over the country.
10. Free education for all children in public schools. Abolition of children's factory labor in its present form. Combination of education with industrial production, etc., etc. [CM, 36–37].

As we shall see in the following sections, once the transition is complete, the revolutionary dictatorship is assumed by Marx to disappear.

Concerning the nature of the proletarian revolution, i.e., the violent or peaceful overthrow of the bourgeois class, little debate is necessary. In the concluding paragraph of the *Communist Manifesto* Marx writes, "They openly declare their ends can be attained only by the *forcible overthrow* of all existing social conditions" (p. 54; italics added). The historical evidence that Marx presents in most of his other work indicates beyond question that, in the past, proletarian revolutions had been characterized by violence. And, as we observed in Chapter 11, Marx predicted that the English proletariat could never get anywhere without a bloody encounter with the ruling powers (MEC, 213). None the less, the general vagueness with which Marx treats revolution does leave room for speculation. In an essay entitled "Social Reform" Marx writes:

Every revolution dissolves the old society; in so far it is social. Every revolution overthrows the old power; in so far it is political. . . . The revolution as such—the overthrow of the existing power and the dissolution of the old conditions—is a political act" (SE, 132–33).

Is the revolution in the Marxian system merely a political act? Does the political act imply violence? It should also be noted that in the Preface to the first English edition of *Capital,* Volume I, Engels writes on Marx's prediction concerning the coming revolution that

surely . . . the voice ought to be heard of a man whose whole theory is the result of a life-long study of the economic history and condition of England, and whom that study led to the conclusion that, at least in Europe, England is the only country *where the inevitable social revolution might be effected entirely by peaceful and legal means* [C. I, 32; italics added].

The possibility of a peaceful proletarian revolution is also suggested by Marx. In 1872, at the Hague Congress of the International, he stated:

We know that the institutions, the manners and the customs of the various countries must be considered, and we do not deny that there are countries, like England and America, and if I understand your arrangements better, I might add Holland, where the worker may attain his object by peaceful means. But not in all countries is this the case.[1]

The special case of England reappears in an 1871 letter to Kugelmann:

I say that the next attempt of the French Revolution will be no longer, as before, to transfer the bureaucratic-military machine from one hand to another, but to smash it, and that is essential for every people's revolution on the Continent [MEC, 309].

The qualification "on the Continent" emphasizes the exclusion of England. But these quotations are exceptions to the rule. The overwhelming impression that Marx leaves with the reader is that proletarian revolutions will be characterized by some degree of physical violence.

(b) "REVOLUTIONARY FLEXIBILITY" IN THE MARXIAN SYSTEM

One of Marx's most interesting sets of predictions concerning revolution relates to Russia. As we saw in Chapter 9, he was well aware of the underdeveloped economic state of the country but still considered Russia a serious threat to English industrial supremacy. The political counterpart to this economic underdevelopment is the relatively underdeveloped political relations, i.e., the absence of a bourgeois class and the dominance of feudal aristocracy in state power. This situation, Marx concedes, characterized mid-nineteenth-century Russia (MEC, 348); and yet, concerning both revolution and economic growth, Marx predicts a political development in Russia that, according to his own theory, appears to run ahead of natural development. Almost ignoring his general prescripts for political development, which we have outlined, Marx writes in the Russian edition (1882) of the *Communist Manifesto:*

The question is now whether the Russian village commune—a form of primitive collective communal property which has indeed already been to a large extent destroyed—can pass immediately into the highest communist form of landed property or whether on the contrary, it must go through from the beginning the same process of disintegration as that which has determined the historical development of the West [CM, 104].

He answers:

1. In Karl Kautsky, *The Labor Revolution* (London: G. Allen & Unwin, 1925), p. 24.

If the Russian revolution becomes the signal for the workers' revolution in the West, so that the one supplements the other, then the present form of land ownership in Russia may be the starting point of an historical development [*ibid.*].

Even five years earlier, writing to the editor of *Otyecestvenniye Zapisky,* Marx predicts:

If Russia continues to pursue the path she has followed since 1861, she will lose the finest chance ever offered by history to a nation, [not] to undergo all the fatal vicissitudes of the capitalist regime [MEC, 353].

Engels' footnote to this statement explains that "chance" means "the finest chance of *escaping* capitalist development" (MEC, 353).

What is important here is not the path that Russia was pursuing but the acknowledged possibility that the proletarian revolution could occur without the development of capitalism. What becomes of the Marxian theory of social evolution? From whence do the revolutionaries emerge? Did not Marx himself assert that *only* through the application of machinery did the displaced workers form the industrial reserve army? If the Russian revolution is not proletarian, but peasant, did Marx not predict that the salvation of the peasant can only result from the institution of the proletarian government? Did Marx not state that the emancipation of the German proletariat could only be temporary so long as the material conditions were not present? How, then, does he reconcile this apparent inconsistency? One possible answer may be found in the letter to the editor of *Otyecestvenniye Zapisky,* quoted above, where Marx declares that his theory of social evolution is not a historic-philosophic theory of the *marche générale* imposed by fate upon every people whatever their historic circumstances (MEC, 354). Individual historical factors, he states, affect each country differently. Conditions unique to Russia may therefore explain this "flexibility."

The Marxian theory of class struggle and revolution thus appears merely as a sufficient, but not necessary, condition of proletarian emancipation. It is, in fact, difficult to assess the Marxian theories of revolution primarily because of the scant analysis Marx devotes to the subject. Obviously no reconciliation is possible on the Russian and German developments if we take Marx's statement seriously that *only* after the bourgeoisie have completed their revolution can the proletariat begin theirs. A period of 27 years, it should be noted, separates the Russian and German analyses. If Marx had recanted, the recantation was never made explicit.

Interesting on two counts is the qualification that Marx introduces in his prediction on Russia, i.e., "*if* the Russian Revolution becomes a signal for the workers' revolution in the West." Apparently Marx believed that the Russian revolution *would* occur. Writing to Sorge in the same year, Marx predicted, "This time the revolution will begin in the East, hitherto the unbroken bulwark and reserve army of counterrevolution" (MEC, 349). It should be noted that Marx cited as the immediate cause of revolution the Russo-Turkish war, not the economic crisis. This interesting deviation from economic causation is found in another of Marx's predictions:

What the Prussian fools do not see is that the present war is leading just as inevitably to a war between Germany and Russia as the war of 1866 led to the war between Prussia and France. . . . And a war No. 2 of this kind will act as the midwife to the inevitable social revolution in Russia [MEC, 301].[2]

The qualification also appears to solve the problem of world or piecemeal revolution—a problem that Marx had posed 18 years before this prediction:

The difficult question for us is this: On the Continent the revolution is imminent and will also immediately assume a socialist character. Is it not bound to be crushed in this little corner, considering that in a far greater territory the movement of bourgeois society is still on the ascendant? [MEC, 118].

But here, too, a contradiction emerges. In *German Ideology,* Marx predicts:

Empirically, communism is only possible as the act of the dominant peoples "all at once" or simultaneously, which presupposes the universal development of productive forces and the world-intercourse bound up with them [GI, 25].

Reconciliation is neither possible nor attempted.

The nature of the revolution, like that of the class struggle, is not amenable to the kind of rigorous analysis undertaken in the earlier chapters on Marxian economic predictions. All that can be said here is that, given the necessary economic and corresponding political conditions, the revolutionary character of the worker will force the antagonism between capital and labor into open and violent conflict. Yet, glaring contradictions confronted Marx, and where facts differed from theory, Marx had no alternative but to alter theory. "Flexibility" in his development of the prediction concerning revolution results primarily

2. In a letter to Engels 17 years earlier, Marx predicted the *reverse* of the qualification: "When the next [European] revolution comes, Russia will be so kind as to revolutionize as well" (MEC, 124).

from his concession that there is no *marche générale* which all countries must follow. However, to say that periods of gestation vary among animals is no justification for predicting birth without conception. And to say that individual historical circumstances may alter the form of revolution cannot be taken to mean that the socialist revolution can be achieved without the development of the bourgeoisie and proletariat. This, however, is precisely what Marx predicts.

(2) MARXIAN PREDICTIONS CONCERNING COMMUNISM

Marx's predictions regarding the communist state do not lend themselves to analysis. Scattered throughout his many volumes are references to communism, but they are in most cases incidental and often appear only in footnotes. Nowhere, however, does Marx *claim* to have examined communist society. As the title of his major work suggests, Marx's concern was primarily with the capitalist system. Indeed, more attention is devoted in his writings to precapitalist than to postcapitalist economies. The Marxian predictions concerning communism are divided here into two subsections: (a) predictions concerning political and social changes under communism and (b) predictions concerning the communist economy.

(a) SOCIAL AND POLITICAL CHANGES UNDER COMMUNISM

One of the most important predictions Marx makes about communism is the emergence of the classless society. The development of capitalism, we have seen, destroyed the landowner, the *rentier,* and the petty bourgeois. Populations, he predicted, would become polarized into the bourgeois and proletarian classes. With the advent of revolution and the consequent emergence of the revolutionary dictatorship of the proletariat, the function of the proletarian class, he points out, becomes not one of control but of the abolition of the bourgeoisie. And since the bourgeoisie represents personified capital, or the ownership of the means of production, destruction of private property by definition implies the abolition of the bourgeoisie. The proletarian class, therefore, becomes the only surviving class. But "class" in the Marxian system is merely a concept differentiating the propertied from the non-propertied individuals. Classes, therefore, cease to exist with the abolition of private property. Marx predicts:

If the proletariat during its contest with the bourgeoisie is compelled by the force of circumstances, to organize itself as a class, if, by means of revolution, it makes itself the ruling class, and, as such, sweeps away by force the old conditions of production, then it will, along with these conditions, have swept away the conditions for the existence of class antagonisms, and of classes generally, and will thereby have abolished its own supremacy as a class [CM, 37].

The classless society implies the abolition of the state. The state, Marx writes, is "nothing more than the form of organization which the bourgeois necessarily adopt . . . for the mutual guarantee of their property and interests" (GI, 59). It represents, in the Marxian system, the political organization of society. In the *Communist Manifesto* Marx predicts:

When, in the course of development, class distinctions have disappeared, and all production has been concentrated in the hands of a vast association of the whole nation, the political power will lose its political character [CM, 37].

Personal freedom can only be manifest, Marx asserts, with the elimination of the state (CGP, 43–44). In his *German Ideology* Marx predicts, "In order . . . to assert themselves as individuals, they [the proletariat] must overthrow the State" (p. 78).

The bourgeois family, which was reduced by the capitalist system to a mere money relation, vanishes under communism:

Bourgeois marriage is in reality a system of wives in common and thus, at the most, what the communists might possibly be reproached with, is that they desire to introduce, in substitution for a hypocritically concealed, an openly legalized community of women. For the rest, it is self-evident, that the abolition of the present system of production must bring with it the abolition of the community of women springing from that system, i.e. of prostitution both public and private [CM, 33].

Along with the bourgeois family, religion will disappear with the institution of the communist society:

The religious reflex of the real world can, in any case, only then finally vanish, when the practical relations of everyday life offer to man none but perfectly intelligible and reasonable relations with regard to his fellowmen and to nature.
The life-process of society, which is based on the process of material production, does not strip off its mystical veil until it is treated as production by freely associated men, and is consciously

regulated by them in accordance with a settled plan [C. I, 91–92].

In the Preface to *Capital* Marx reflects on the attitudes of the church. "The English Established Church," he prophesies, "will more readily pardon an attack on 38 of its 39 articles than on 1/39 of its income" (C. I, 15).

Marx's comments on the destiny of the Jews are most interesting in this context. The Jew, he claims, is essentially a "huckster"; his God, the God of practical needs. The social emancipation of the Jew is the emancipation of society from Judaism. The emancipation of society from Judaism, Marx continues, can only be achieved by the eradication of those conditions which foster Judaism, i.e., capitalist society:

As soon as society succeeds in abolishing the empirical essence of Judaism, the huckster, and the conditions which produce him, the Jew will become impossible, because his consciousness will no longer have a corresponding object, because the subjective basis of Judaism, viz., practical needs, will have been humanized [SE, 97].

(b) PREDICTIONS CONCERNING THE COMMUNIST ECONOMY

In almost every case, references made to the communist economic structure in Marx's writing have been subordinated to the examination of capitalism and are introduced into the analysis merely as comparative notes. For purposes of exposition, these notes on the communist economy are divided into (i) predictions related to production under communism and (ii) predictions related to distribution under communism.

(i) PREDICTIONS CONCERNING PRODUCTION UNDER COMMUNISM

The capitalist economy, we have seen, is characterized by the competitive market, which presupposes the existence of an industrial-capitalist class. Decisions by capitalists on what to produce and how much to produce are made independently, Marx claims, and therefore without knowledge of aggregate demand and supply. The very nature of capitalism, he pointed out, particularly in the credit system, subjects the economy to income instability (see Chap. 10, sec. 2). In contrast to this "anarchic" and "chaotic" production, production under communism, Marx predicts, will take the form of an organized social plan. The productive institution in the system is the workers' cooperative, an outgrowth of the joint-stock company (C. III, 521). In *Civil War in*

France, Marx writes that the united cooperative societies will regulate the national production by a common plan, putting an end to the constant anarchy and periodic convulsions (CWF, 44). He predicts:

Only when production will be under the conscious and pre-arranged control of society, will society establish a direct relation between the quantity of social labor employed in the production of definite articles and the quantity of the demand of society for them [C. III, 221].

The obvious question of who will direct the plan is given most superficial treatment. Society, employing "social intelligence," he states, will make the allocation decisions on investment and consumption (C. II, 261–62). Who this society is and how it makes decisions are questions never explored. Since production will be socially controlled and since "money-capital [will] be entirely eliminated, and with it the disguises which it carries into the transactions" under capitalism, the communist economy, Marx predicts, will not be subject to cyclical fluctuations (C. II, 361–62). In communism, the return to labor will not be determined by subsistence, as it is under capitalism, but by labor "needs." Thus Marx predicts that the final emancipation of the working class lies in the ultimate abolition of the wage system (VPP, 128). How these "needs" are to be determined is not considered.

Three observations of lesser importance are noted by Marx. Efficiency in the capitalist system, we have seen, depended upon the skills of the workmen and the discipline exerted upon them by their overseers. Under communism, Marx predicts, this discipline becomes superfluous (C. III, 100). The possibility that workers may shirk their social responsibilities under communism is dismissed by Marx:

It has been objected, that upon the abolition of private property all work will cease, and universal laziness will overtake us. According to this, bourgeois society ought long ago to have gone to the dogs through sheer idleness; for those of its members who work, acquire nothing, and those who acquire anything, do not work. The whole of this objection is but another expression of the tautology: that there can no longer be any wage-labor when there is no longer any capital [CM, 30–31].

The basis of ground rent, we have seen, is a function of quality variations in the soil. These variations, Marx admits, are independent of the economic system. None the less, he states, money rents and agricultural prices will differ under the communist system. Given the conditions illustrated in Table 10, market prices under capitalism, measured by the cost of production on the worst soil, would be 60 shillings (see Chap. 5, sec. 3). The total cost to society under capitalism would therefore be 600 shillings. Under communism, however, the total social or "actual" cost of the 10 quarters would be 240 shillings. The cost difference indicates, he claims, the "false social value" inherent in the capitalist economic system (C. III, 773). "The basis of a class of landowners," Marx predicts, "would thus be destroyed" (C. III, 773–74). This prediction, it should be noted, differs substantially from the Marxian prediction on rent developed in Chapter 8, where we noted that Marx predicted the elimination of the landowning class because of the introduction of new soils and the consequent reduction in differential soil fertility. Here Marx argues that the institution of communism creates a new system of pricing which eliminates the landowning class.

Table 10

Soils	Total Production	Cost of Production	Average Cost per Quarter
A	1 quarter	60 shillings	60 shillings
B	2	60	30
C	3	60	20
D	4	60	15
Total	10	240	24

While these predictions are not inconsistent, they do emphasize different causes; one is a natural result of capitalist development, while the other results from the conscious application of a new economic system.

"In a communistic society," Marx states, "there would be a very different scope for the employment of machinery than there can be in the bourgeois society" (C. I, 429 n.). As we have seen, the application of machinery under capitalism depends upon the costs of producing the machine and the costs of the labor it replaces. Since "costs of labor" are wages, which fluctuate with the industrial cycle, and since both the cycle and wage labor are abolished under communism, the quantity of machinery introduced into the economy should differ under the two systems. Marx, however, does not elaborate on this point.

(ii) PREDICTIONS CONCERNING DISTRIBUTION UNDER COMMUNISM

Distribution of income under communism, Marx claims, involves little analysis since labor is the only recipient of income. Not all the annual produce, however, goes directly to labor. Certain deductions, essential to economic growth and stability, are cited. The reproduction scheme, even under communism, Marx writes, is subject to accident, so that part of the annual income is neither consumed nor accumulated but is set aside for insurance (C. III, 987). In the *Critique of the Gotha Programme* Marx cites five additional "deductions" that must be made from labor's share of national income. These include (1) reimbursement for the replacement of the means of production used up, (2) an additional portion for the extension of production, (3) the general costs of administration, (4) the satisfaction of communal needs, i.e., schools and health services, and (5) funds for those unable to work (CGP, 27–28). Who is to decide how much income should be devoted to each category Marx does not say. Presumably it is "society"; certainly it is not the state, since the state no longer exists under communism. How society organizes to make decisions is nowhere analyzed.

Concerning the distribution of income among individuals Marx points out that, since individuals possess unequal endowments of physical and intellectual ability, "Rights must be unequal instead of equal" (CGP, 30). In the "higher form of communism," when the distinction between manual and intellectual work has disappeared, when the powers of production have so increased that "all the springs of co-operative wealth are gushing more freely," distribution will be determined, he predicts, by the rule "From each according to his capacity, to each according to his need" (CGP, 31).

(3) CONCLUSION

The revolution is presented in the Marxian system as the inevitable outcome of capitalist development. The analysis of revolution forms an integral part of his investigation of capitalism. Apart from the obvious contradictions which grow out of his attempt to relate theory to practical policy, the predictions on revolution—considered as resultants of "scientific inquiry"—have little foundation. His treatment of the proletarian organization is inadequate, particularly in view of his emphasis elsewhere on the disunity within the proletariat during periods of industrial crisis. No mention is made of trade-union activity, although in earlier chapters we have noted that he stressed the role of trade-union organization in the development of class struggle. Interesting also is the fact that Marx could not visualize any flexibility in administration of the state, i.e., class rule, although he never doubted that the revolutionary dictatorship of the proletariat would ultimately disappear after gaining possession of the power of the state apparatus. The most sympathetic criticism that could be leveled at Marx at this point are charges of naïveté or idealism, yet it was precisely this idealism or utopianism that

Marx himself criticized. Marx's comments on communism, it must be noted, however interesting, are void of "scientific" content.

PREDICTIONS

PRIMARY PREDICTIONS

1. The proletarian class cannot rise without upsetting all existing relations of production.
2. The proletarian revolution evolves from the class struggle.
3. The proletariat will ultimately defeat the bourgeoisie.
4. After victory, the revolutionary dictatorship of the proletariat will assume political power only to transfer the means of production from the private to the public domain and to suppress any attempt at reactionary counterrevolution.
5. Following the period of the dictatorship of the proletariat and the total abolition of the bourgeoisie, the proletarian class will become the only class, and consequently the purpose of the class structure will disappear. The classless society emerges.
6. The state will wither away.
7. Production under communism will be planned.
8. Distribution under communism will be according to needs.

SECONDARY PREDICTIONS RELATED TO PRIMARY PREDICTION NO. 2

9. The working-class movement can never achieve independence or anything of lasting importance until the bourgeoisie has consolidated its position in political power.
10. No proletarian revolution can take place until the basic material conditions for revolution have been created by the development of capitalist society.
11. The measures used by the proletariat to overthrow the bourgeoisie will differ in different countries.
12. Social reform will always be utopian until proletarian revolutions occur on a world-wide scale.
13. The proletarian revolutions will become progressively larger.
14. Revolutions will be initiated during periods of industrial crisis.
15. When most of the population is unemployed, revolution is inevitable.
16. The intensity of the revolution will vary inversely with the magnitude of credit.

17. During the revolution, part of the bourgeoisie will break away from the ruling class and join with the proletariat.
18. Lumpenproletarians join the revolutionary forces but are essentially reactionary.
19. The lumpenproletariat will be "shaken off" after the revolution.
20. The salvation of the peasant will occur only after the revolution.
21. The proletariat will forcibly overthrow the bourgeoisie from political power.

SECONDARY PREDICTIONS RELATED TO PRIMARY PREDICTION NO. 4

22. The centralization of credit will be taken over by the state bank.
23. Free education will be made available to all children.
24. Children's factory labor will be abolished.
25. Distinction between the town and country will disappear.
26. State industrial armies will be established.
27. A state factory system will emerge.
28. A heavy progressive income tax will be imposed.
29. All rights to inheritance will be abolished.
30. Emigrant and rebel property will be confiscated.
31. Landed property will be abolished, and the application of rents will be made for public purposes.
32. The transition to communism occurs as an act by people over the globe and all at once.

SECONDARY PREDICTIONS RELATED TO PRIMARY PREDICTION NO. 5

33. Individualism can be expressed only under communism.
34. All religions will disappear.
35. The bourgeois family will be abolished.
36. The system of wage labor will be abolished.

SECONDARY PREDICTIONS RELATED TO PRIMARY PREDICTION NO. 7

37. Society will make the allocation decisions on investment and consumption.
38. Production processes under communism will be workers' cooperatives.
39. Communist society will not be subjected to cyclical fluctuation.

40. Industrial discipline becomes superfluous.
41. Market prices for agricultural commodities will be measured by actual social cost of production.
42. There will be a different scope for the employment of machinery.

A SECONDARY PREDICTION RELATED TO PRIMARY PREDICTION NO. 8

43. Income, except for six necessary deductions for economic stability and growth, will be distributed directly to productive labor.

SPECIFIC PREDICTIONS RELATED TO PRIMARY PREDICTION NO. 2

44. England will be forced to join the Continental revolution (in 1885).
45. The moment English forces withdraw from Ireland, an Irish agrarian revolution will displace the English feudal aristocracy now in power in Ireland.
46. The English proletariat will get nowhere until the Irish revolution is accomplished. This will also destroy the power of the English landowning class in England and set the conditions for the proletarian revolution.
47. If the Russian revolution occurs, it may be the signal for the European revolutions, in which case Russia herself may join in the revolution and proceed immediately from primitive capitalism to communism without undergoing the tortuous developments of capitalism.
48. If Russia continues to pursue the path she has followed since 1861, she will lose the finest chance ever offered by history to a nation not to undergo all the fatal vicissitudes of the capitalist regime.
49. The European revolutions (1871) will originate in the East.
50. The Franco-Prussian War will lead inevitably to a war between Germany and Russia.
51. A Russo-German war will act as the midwife to the inevitable social revolution in Russia.
52. The proletarian revolutions in England, America, and Holland may be attained by peaceful means.
53. The next French revolution (after 1871) will smash the bureaucratic-military machine.

SPECIFIC PREDICTIONS RELATED TO PRIMARY
PREDICTION NO. 5

54. The Jew will be abolished with capitalism.
55. The English Established Church will more readily pardon an attack
    on 38 of its 39 Articles than on 1/39 of its income.

13

Further observations

IN CONCLUDING OUR ANALYSIS of Marxian predictions and theory, four further considerations are offered. First, a compendium of Marx's forecasts is constructed from the several lists of predictions, and here they are reclassified according to the more traditional economic categories of production, distribution, and exchange. In all, 153 prophecies are recorded; some, because they relate to more than one category, appear more than once.

Second, the use of *Capital* as a source of Marx's theoretical ideas is evaluated. What is suggested is not that any other source is more representative but that *Capital,* since it is an unfinished work, may not accurately reflect Marx's own thinking. Some of the logical defects we have found in his derivation of predictions from theory may be attributed to this incompleteness. This consideration is offered not as an apology for Marx but simply as a glimpse beyond the printed page.

Third, consideration is given to the interdependencies among the predictions. In earlier chapters emphasis was placed on deriving predictions from theory, and so, for the most part, the predictions were treated as isolated cases. Perhaps this dissecting technique detracted from a very significant quality of Marx's work—its unity. Prior to the appearance of *Capital* Marx wrote to Engels: "Whatever shortcomings they may have, the merit of my writings is that they are an artistic whole, and that can only be attained by my method of never having them printed until they lie before me as a whole" (MEC, 204). What Marx endeavored to produce was a general theory of social evolution. The dynamic model he constructed was intended to generate a network of interwoven predictions, which, in the process of fulfillment, are interdependent.

Finally, a classificatory system is designed to relate the predictions to the printed sources, i.e., the books, articles, and correspondence, from which they were derived.

(1) COMPENDIUM
OF PREDICTIONS

(a) PREDICTIONS CONCERNING THE DISTRIBUTION
OF OUTPUT

(i) PREDICTIONS CONCERNING THE SURPLUS-RECEIVING CLASSES

These prophecies include those affecting industrial capitalists, money capitalists, and landowners.

1. The distribution of the surplus among the three exploiting classes will change as capitalism expands.
2. The general rate of profit will tend to decline.
3. Competition will eliminate the smaller capitalists, forcing them into the ranks of the proletariat.
4. Joint-stock companies will emerge and produce a new aristocracy, the nominal director.
5. The moneylending class will, at first, increase with the general wealth of the economy.
6. The rate of interest will continuously decline.
7. As the rate of interest falls, investors will no longer be able to live on their incomes and will ultimately join the ranks of the proletariat.
8. The moneylending class will ultimately disappear.

Five predictions (9–13) relate specifically to the landowning class.

9. The rate of return to landowners will decline.
10. The large landowners will absorb the smaller ones.
11. All landowners will ultimately disappear, i.e., the distinction between the rural and urban areas will dissolve.
12. The English feudal aristocracy will be destroyed by foreign competition in the international agricultural market.
13. The moment English forces withdraw from Ireland, an Irish agrarian revolution will displace the English feudal aristocracy now in power in Ireland.

Predictions 14–17 relate to the oncoming struggle with the proletarian class.

14. The capitalist class will become increasingly involved in a class struggle with the proletarian class.

15. Entire sections of the ruling class will be drawn into the proletariat (see 3 and 7).
16. The proletariat will forcibly overthrow the capitalists from political power.
17. There is enough cultivated land in the underdeveloped areas to ruin the large and small landowners of Europe.

Marx's views on the objectives of the Church are reflected in the following prediction.

18. The English Established Church will more readily pardon an attack on 38 of its 39 Articles than on 1/39 of its income.

(ii) PREDICTIONS CONCERNING THE PROLETARIAT AND THE PROLETARIAN CLASS

19. Labor will be equalized by the developing modes of production and reduced to the lowest, commonest skill.
20. Mobility of the laborers will increase.
21. The labor of men will be superseded by that of women and children.
22. The value of labor power will decline.
23. The industrial reserve army of the unemployed will increase.
24. The misery of the proletariat will increase.
25. The relative misery of the agricultural laborer will be greater than that of his industrial counterpart.
26. The geographical relocations of labor will create the industrial urban centers.
27. The first attempt of the laborers to band together will take the form of trade combinations.
28. Utopian socialism will pass from the proletariat to the petty bourgeoisie with the development of the capitalist modes of production.
29. Entire sections of the ruling class will be drawn into the proletarian class (see 15).
30. Class consciousness among the proletariat will develop as they become more numerous and as the modes of production develop.
31. The world market will create the international proletariat.
32. At every stage of economic development there will develop a corresponding political development, e.g., the International will emerge with the international proletariat.
33. The working-class movement will never be independent nor will it achieve anything of lasting importance until the bourgeoisie has consolidated its position in political power.

34. The class struggle will lead directly to the proletarian revolutions.
35. When the majority of the proletarians are unemployed, the revolution will follow.
36. The proletarians will never get anywhere without a really bloody encounter with the ruling powers.
37. Unless the proletarians train for political activity, they will never succeed.
38. As the class struggle develops, the proletarians will substitute political objectives for economic objectives.
39. No proletarian revolution can take place until the basic material conditions for revolution have been created by the development of capitalist society.
40. The lumpenproletariat, although essentially reactionary, will join in the revolution on the side of the proletariat.
41. The lumpenproletariat will be shaken off after the revolution.
42. The proletarian revolutions will become progressively larger.
43. The proletarians cannot rise without upsetting all the relations of production.
44. The English proletariat will never do anything in England as a class until it will separate its policy toward Ireland from the policy of the ruling bourgeoisie.
45. The English proletariat will get nowhere until the Irish revolution is accomplished.
46. The salvation of the peasant must wait upon the revolution.
47. The dictatorship of the proletariat will emerge from the revolution.
48. The exploitative system of wage labor will be abolished under communism.

(b) PREDICTIONS CONCERNING PRODUCTION PROCESSES AND ACTIVITY

The basic prediction concerning processes to which all others in this subsection are related is No. 49.

49. Capitalists cannot exist without constantly revolutionizing the means of production.
50. Concentration and centralization of production will increase with the developing modes.
51. Joint-stock companies will emerge with centralization.
52. The developing modes will create the international market.
53. All economies will adopt the capitalist forms of production.

54. The international division of labor will produce a geographically segregated pattern for world production.
55. The destiny of Ireland is to become an English sheep walk and cattle pasture.
56. The separation of Ireland from England is inevitable.
57. The labor skills needed for adopting the new technology in the colonies will be supplied by the surplus populations in advanced economies.
58. Capitalist production will concentrate more on luxury items.
59. The productivity of labor will expand in geometrical progression.
60. The length of the working day will tend to be extended.
61. The number of capital turnovers will increase.
62. The value of moral depreciation will increase.
63. Increasing capacities will force capitalists to seek new markets.
64. The demand for greater raw-material supplies will make colonization inevitable.
65. The price of raw materials will decline.
66. The gap between the agricultural and nonagricultural organic compositions of capital will narrow.
67. Rational agriculture is irreconcilable with capitalist production.

Predictions 68–72 relate the effects of the changing modes of production on the social structures.

68. Modern industry will tear away from the family the sentimental veil and reduce it to a mere money relation.
69. Modern industry will alter the entire educational pattern in society toward the dominance of technical and vocational training.
70. The introduction of capitalism into the colonies will produce structural changes in their social and political organizations.
71. Capitalism will dissolve the hereditary division of labor in the Indian caste system and thereby destroy the impediment to Indian economic progress.
72. England will fulfill her double mission, the destruction of the Asiatic society and the regeneration of India on the foundations of Western society.

Property and slavery in the United States are recorded in Predictions 73 and 74.

73. Without the acquisition of Louisiana, Missouri, and Arkansas by the United States, slavery in Virginia would long ago have been wiped out.

74. Without slavery, North America, the most progressive country, would be transformed into a patriarchal land.

Predictions 75 through 94 relate to credit and crisis.
75. The capitalist system generates industrial cycles.
76. A credit economy will generate more volatile cycles than those in noncredit economies.
77. Cycles become progressively larger.
78. Cycles become more frequent.
79. The decline in the rate of profit will ultimately create a crisis.
80. The periodic replacement of capital will provide the basis for a crisis.
81. Overproduction of principal commodities will generally touch off a crisis.
82. The credit economy subjects the whole economy to the dictates of the market.
83. A crisis is always the starting-point for new investments.
84. Centralization of money will occur in crisis.
85. Credit accelerates the internationalization of capital and trade.
86. Cycles will become international in scope.
87. Cycles become more violent in raw-material-producing countries than in industrial countries.
88. Cycles, once started, will generate succeeding ones.
89. No legislation can abolish the cycle.
90. Business always appears sound just before a crash.
91. The greater the use of fraudulent bills of exchange, the more intense is the inevitable crash.
92. Cycles will occur in England every ten years.
93. The crisis on the Continent always originates in England.
94. The Chinese rebellion will produce a crisis in England.

Predictions 95–101 are made with respect to productive activity under communism.
95. A state factory system will emerge.
96. State industrial armies will be established.
97. Children's factory labor will be abolished.
98. Centralization of credit will be taken over by the state.
99. Society will make the allocation decisions concerning investment and consumption.
100. There will exist a different scope for the employment of machinery.
101. Industrial discipline under communism becomes superfluous.

(c) PREDICTIONS CONCERNING MARKET DEVELOPMENT

The basic prediction concerning market expansion is set down in Prediction 102. Predictions 103–115 specify this basic forecast.

102. The developing modes of capitalist production will create the world market (see 52).
103. Increasing capacities will force capitalists to seek new markets (see 63).
104. The falling rate of profit will necessitate market expansion.
105. The increasing demand for raw materials will result in greater emphasis on world trade (see 64).
106. Changing modes of transportation will facilitate the expansion of the market.
107. The class cohesion that took centuries for capitalists to accomplish with highways, the proletariat can accomplish in a few years with railways.
108. The railway and steam power will cut the time distance between India and England to eight days, so that India will become annexed to the Western world.
109. The credit economy subjects the whole economy to the dictates of the market (see 82).
110. Credit will accelerate the expansion of the commodity and capital markets (see 85).
111. As the modes develop, the marketing functions will be separated from the actual production organization.
112. Capitalist production will concentrate more on luxury items (see 58).
113. Once Ireland is independent, necessity will turn her to tariff protection.
114. If foreign trade in Japan leads to the development of money rents, the bases of the Japanese economy will undergo radical change.
115. Market expansion will end with the colonization of California and Australia and the opening-up of China and Japan.

The end of English domination and the continuing international fight for markets are seen in Predictions 116–121.

116. The United States will shortly break the industrial monopoly of Western Europe and England.
117. Russia will break the English monopoly of Chinese products on the European market with the completion of the Trans-Siberian railway.

118. England and Russia must always be antagonists in the East.
119. In England's attempt to exploit the Chinese market, her manufactures will ultimately outstrip China's market capacity.
120. If China were to legalize opium-planting, trade among the United States, Australia, India, China, and England would collapse and an international crisis would follow.
121. The English feudal aristocracy will be destroyed by foreign competition in the agricultural market (see 12).

(d) PREDICTIONS CONCERNING REVOLUTIONS, WARS, AND THE EMERGENCE OF COMMUNISM

Although essentially determined by economic forces, the predictions set down in this subsection reflect political behavior.

122. The intensification of the class struggle will produce the proletarian revolutions (see 34).
123. No proletarian revolution can take place until the basic material conditions for revolution have been created by the development of capitalist society (see 39).
124. As the class struggle develops, the proletariat will substitute political objectives for economic ones (see 38).
125. Social reform will always be utopian until proletarian revolutions occur on a world-wide basis.
126. When the majority of the proletarians are unemployed, the revolution will follow (see 35).
127. The proletarians will never get anywhere without a really bloody encounter with the ruling powers (see 36).
128. The lumpenproletariat, although essentially reactionary, will join in the revolution on the side of the proletariat (see 40).
129. The lumpenproletariat will be shaken off after the revolution (see 41).
130. The proletarian revolutions will become progressively larger (see 42).
131. Credit restriction will intensify the revolution.
132. The proletarians cannot rise without upsetting all the relations of production (see 43).
133. The English proletarian movement will get nowhere until the Irish revolution is accomplished (see 45).
134. The proletariat will forcibly overthrow the bourgeoisie from political power.
135. The European revolutions (1871) will originate in the East.

136. England will be forced to join the Continental revolution (1885).
137. The proletarian revolutions in England, America, and Holland may be attained by peaceful means.
138. The next French revolution (after 1871) will smash the bureaucratic-military machine.
139. The Franco-Prussian War will inevitably lead to a war between Germany and Russia.
140. A Russo-German war will act as the midwife to the inevitable social revolution in Russia.
141. If Russia continues to pursue the path she has followed since 1861, she will lose the finest chance ever offered by history to a nation, not to undergo all the fatal vicissitudes of the capitalist regime.
142. If the Russian revolution occurs, it may be the signal for the European revolutions, in which case Russia herself may in the revolution proceed immediately from primitive capitalism to communism without undergoing the tortuous developments of capitalism.
143. The salvation of the peasant must wait upon the revolution (see 46).

Marx makes two predictions concerning the American Civil War.
144. The expansion of the southern and northern economies in the United States will eventually lead to civil war.
145. The North will defeat the South in the civil war.

Predictions 146–172 relate to the emergence of communism.
146. The dictatorship of the proletariat will emerge from the revolution (see 47).
147. The measures used to overthrow the bourgeoisie will differ in different countries.
148. A heavy progressive income tax will be imposed immediately after the take-over.
149. All rights of inheritance will be abolished.
150. Emigrant and rebel property will be confiscated after the proletarian victory.
151. The centralization of credit will be taken over by a state bank (see 98).
152. A state factory system will emerge (see 95).
153. State industrial armies will be established (see 96).
154. Distinction between the town and country will disappear.

155. Children's factory labor will be abolished (see 97).
156. Free education will be made available to all children.
157. The bourgeois family will be abolished.
158. Landed property will be abolished, and the rents of the large landowners will be turned to public purposes.
159. Communism is only possible as an act of dominant people all at once.
160. Individualism can be expressed only after the institution of communism.
161. The exploitative system of wage labor will be abolished under communism (see 48).
162. There will exist a different scope for the employment of machinery (see 100).
163. Distribution will be according to need.
164. Production will be planned by social intelligence.
165. Production processes in communism will be in the form of workers cooperatives.
166. Communist society will not be subjected to cyclical fluctuation.
167. Industrial discipline under communism becomes superfluous (see 101).
168. All income, except for six deductions that provide for economic stability and growth, will go directly to productive labor.
169. The Jew will be abolished with capitalism.
170. All religion will disappear under communism.
171. The classless society will emerge.
172. The state will wither away.

(2) EVALUATION OF *CAPITAL* AS A SOURCE OF THEORY

In February, 1866, a year before the publication of the first volume of *Capital,* Marx wrote to Engels, "Although finished, the manuscript, gigantic in its form, could not be prepared for publication by anyone but myself, not even by you" (MEC, 205). In 1883 Karl Marx died, leaving behind the published first volume and reams of notes and unfinished manuscripts on economic theory which were later to become Volumes II and III of *Capital,* edited by Engels, and, after Engels' death, Volume IV, edited by Kautsky and retitled *Theories of Surplus Value.*

Upon reading Volume II, and particularly Volume III, one cannot help but feel that the comment Marx made in 1866 applies equally to the posthumous volumes. Indeed, no less a person than Engels himself substantiates this feeling. In his Preface to Volume II of *Capital* Engels wrote:

It was no easy task to prepare the second volume of *Capital* for the printer in such a way that it should make a connected and complete work and represent exclusively the ideas of its author, not of its publisher. The great number of available manuscripts, and their fragmentary character, added to the difficulty of this task . . . ; the thoughts were jotted down as they developed in the brain of the author. Some parts of the argument would be fully treated, others of equal importance only indicated. The material to be used for the illustration of facts would be collected, but barely arranged, much less worked out. At the conclusion of the chapters there would be only a few incoherent sentences as milestones of the incomplete deductions, showing the haste of the author in passing on to the next chapter. And finally, there was the well-known handwriting which Marx himself was sometimes unable to decipher [C. II, 7].

Similar testimony is given in the Preface to the third volume:

Nothing was available for the third volume but a first draft, and it was pretty incomplete. The beginnings of the various sections were, as a rule, pretty carefully elaborated, or even polished as to style. But the farther one proceeded, the more sketchy and in-complete was the analysis, the more excursions it contained into side issues whose proper place in the argument was left for later decision, the longer and more complex became the sentences, in which the rising thoughts were deposited as they came [C. III, 11].

Nothing was available for Chapter IV but the title. But as the point of issue, the effect of the turn-over on the rate of profit, is of vital importance, I have elaborated it myself. For this reason the whole chapter has been placed between brackets. It was found in the course of this work, that the formula of Chapter III for the rate of profit required some modification, in order to be generally applicable. . . . The main difficulty was presented by Part V, which treated the most complicated subject in the entire volume, and it was just at this point that Marx had been overtaken by one of those above-mentioned serious attacks of illness. Here, then, we have no finished draft, nor even an outline which might be perfected, but only a first attempt at an elaboration, which more than once ended in a disarranged mass of notes, comments and extracts [*ibid.*, 13].

These comments by Engels are particularly salient to the present discus-sion. The purpose here is to evaluate the predictions which Marx derives from his economic system. Marx's economic model is incomplete without Volume III. It is only in this volume that he examines the rate of profit, the critical variable in his system. It is primarily in Volume III that Marx analyzes rent, interest, and the credit system. Too, his important contributions to the theory of crisis are not fully developed until Volumes II and III. In a sense, therefore, an assessment of the Marxian system can only be an analysis of an unfinished work, a work that is incoherent, repetitious, and shot through with obvious omissions and errors which, given more time, the author might have corrected. Engels himself points to many ambiguities which, as editor, he decided to reproduce literally (C. II, 8). It is probably to these ambiguities, more than to any other factor, that one may attribute the variety of interpretations of Marx and the multiplicity of statements regarding "what Marx really meant."

One more comment must be made concerning the source of the Marxian predictions. Although sixteen years elapsed between the publication of Volume I and Marx's death, the book, during this period, received little recognition from academic circles.[1] Few scholarly journals reviewed the volume. Marx, in his Preface to the second German edition, explicitly notes the *Saturday Review*'s comment on *Capital* (C. I, 21). John MacDonnell, it should be noted, did review the volume in the *Fortnightly Review*,[2] but Marx surprisingly makes no reference to this journal. This general lack of response greatly disappointed him. Two years before he died, he wrote Engels:

> The English have recently begun to occupy themselves more with *Capital,* etc. Thus in the last October (or November, I am not quite sure) number of *Contemporary,* there is an article on socialism by John Rae. Very inadequate, full of mistakes, but "fair," as one of my English friends told me the day before yesterday. And why fair? Because John Rae does *not suppose* that [during the] forty years I [have been] spreading my pernicious theories, I was being instigated by "bad" motives [MEC, 397].

These facts are relevant to any evaluation of the Marxian system. They indicate an almost complete lack of communication between Marx and his academic contemporaries. Although much of his theoretical work was tried out on Engels, the latter was, without exception, a thoroughly convinced audience and hence a poor source for critical

1. It should be stated that *Capital,* Volume I, first published in German in 1867, was translated into Russian in 1872 and into French the following year. These translations, however, were undertaken by socialists and were distributed mainly within socialist circles.
2. "Karl Marx and German Socialism" *Fortnightly Review,* XVII (1875), 382.

suggestion. One can only speculate on what the finished product might have been had Marx himself completed the four volumes and had he been, throughout his creative years, in communication with the larger world of intellectuals and scholars.

(3) INTERDEPENDENCE AMONG PREDICTIONS

The pivotal prophecy that ties together the whole of the Marxian prophetic structure is the tendency for the rate of profit to decline. Its importance cannot be overestimated. Most of the other primary predictions, and, subsequently, most of the secondary and specific ones, derive from it.

First, consider Marx's prophecies concerning the development of international capitalism. Because capitalists seek the highest possible return on their capital investment, Marx is assured that capital will flow from the lower- to the higher-profit-yielding countries, i.e., from economies characterized by relatively low compositions. Principally upon the basis of this profit-rate differential, Marx predicts the creation of the world market, the internationalization of the capitalist modes of production, and the development of colonies. If, however, the rate of profit in the industrially advanced economies should not tend to fall, the justification for predicting the internationalization of capitalism would all but disappear.

Second, consider the interdependence of the profit-rate prediction and the prediction concerning the increasing misery of the proletariat. The misery forecast is predicated upon the inevitability of the increasing industrial reserve army. This inevitability depends upon the tendency for the rate of profit to decline. Recall the Marxian logic. As the capital compositions increase, laborers are displaced from production. But production carried on with the higher capital compositions yields greater surpluses, which, transformed into investments, provide for the reabsorption of laborers. But here's the rub. Since surplus becomes progressively smaller due to the declining rate of profit, the displacement of labor must ultimately be greater than the reabsorption of labor. The increasing size of the industrial reserve army of the unemployed will force wage rates to subsistence, and, since subsistence is flexible downward, the misery of the proletariat is assured.

But, by the same reasoning, if there is no tendency for the rate of profit to decline, there must also be no tendency for the industrial reserve army to increase. With a rising rate of profit and therefore a rising rate of investment, the additional demands for labor may actually create a labor deficiency. Under these circumstances, wage rates may rise to relatively high levels. The increasing-misery-of-the-proletariat prediction, therefore, holds no water.

Third, Marx's predictions of political unrest, the overthrow of the bourgeoisie, and the emergence of communism depend, in part, upon the increasing misery of the proletariat; without misery there is no class consciousness and consequently no class struggle. A proletariat without class consciousness cannot perform the historic role assigned to it. Because the inevitability of increasing misery is dependent upon the falling rate of profit, the entire set of forecasts relating to revolution and communism is linked to the rate-of-profit prediction. The link, however, is a necessary but not a sufficient condition for Marx's political prophecies. Although class consciousness cannot develop without increasing misery, it does not necessarily follow that it will develop with increasing misery. Marx's linking of class consciousness with misery is, whatever its merits, only an assumption in his system. True, in Marx's capitalism, the laborers, working with advanced technology, are grouped together into factory towns, are reduced to common skills, are subjected to the whims of chaotic capitalist competition, and are subsisting on minimal levels. But these factors can only suggest the possibility of class consciousness. They cannot, as Marx was wont to claim, make this consciousness inevitable.

But even if the forecasts of declining profit rates, increasing misery, and the development of class consciousness were fulfilled, Marx's predictions concerning the dictatorship of the proletariat and the subsequent production and distribution under communism would not necessarily follow. They are simply *non sequiturs*. However interesting, they are highly speculative forecasts whose roots go no deeper than wishful thinking.

Fourth, the prediction that is perhaps least dependent upon the falling rate of profit is the inevitability of increasing instability in the capitalist economy. Yet even here the break is not clean. The tendency for the rate of profit to fall was considered by Marx to be a necessary but still a sufficient condition for economic instability. And since he forecast falling rates of profit, the instability was assured on this account.

But whatever the rate of profit, increasing instability was to result. The proof rests upon his demonstration that, as the organic compositions of capital increase, market capacities expand less rapidly than the production capacities; this must result eventually in general overproduction, which will bring on the crisis. As an added insurance, the capital- and consumer-goods industries will expand at disproportionate rates, creating thereby sectoral imbalance, overproduction, and ultimately the crisis.

Fifth, Marx's prediction concerning increasing concentrations of production and finance is, in part, dependent upon the falling rate of profit and increasing economic instability. The ranks of the capitalists are decimated during periods of crisis and stagnation. Although their numbers decrease, aggregate production still increases in the ensuing periods of recovery and prosperity. The repetitiveness of this process leads to greater and greater concentrations. The continual applications of higher capital compositions also lead to the monopolization of production and finance. Capitalists are forced to innovate in order to survive. Those who cannot are eliminated by the force of competition. Production is further amalgamated.

Sixth, following upon the increasing concentrations of production and finance is the polarization of the world's population into two conflicting classes, the bourgeoisie and the proletariat. The inevitability of this polarization is re-enforced by the forecasts of the increasing misery of the proletariat, the declining rate of profit, the increasing economic instability, and the internationalization of capitalism. Several secondary forecasts also bear directly upon the polarization process. For example, the maximum rate of interest is fixed at the prevailing rate of profit so that, with declining rates of profit, the rate of interest will also decline. Eventually, the moneylending class will disappear. The elimination of ground rent follows upon the development of the world market. As colonies become the main suppliers of agricultural commodities for the advanced economies, differential and absolute ground rent will disappear. So, too, will the landowning class. In addition, the artisans, the handicraftsmen, the small tradespeople, the shopkeepers will dissolve into the proletarian class as the increasing technology renders their skills obsolete. The population polarization is thus continually sharpened.

In this manner Marx weaves an intricate pattern of social evolution. The secondary predictions, like the primary ones, are interdependent and reinforcing. They spell out in great detail the character and dynamics of Marx's capitalist system.

(4) THE PREDICTIONS AND THEIR SOURCES

While the foundations of Marx's economic theory are found primarily in the four volumes of *Capital,* the prophecies which he sets down are scattered through his economic, political, and historical volumes, as well as newspaper articles, political pamphlets, public addresses, and private correspondence. In quality as in content, Marx's predictions varied with the specific forms their expression assumed. The pattern is summarized in Table 11.

Table 11

Type of Prediction	Sources of the Prediction				
	Capital *	Books and Essays †	Articles ‡	Corre-spondence §	Total
Primary	12	4	1		17
Secondary	59	32	4	5	100
Specific	6	3	15	12	36
Total	77	39	20	17	153

* This category includes the four volumes of *Capital*.

† This category includes economic and political pamphlets as well as books. The volumes in this category include *Contribution to the Critique of Political Economy, Critique of the Gotha Programme, The Poverty of Philosophy, Economic and Philosophic Manuscripts of 1844, Value, Price and Profit, Wage-Labor and Capital, Selected Essays, The German Ideology, Class Struggles in France, Civil War in France,* and *The Communist Manifesto.*

‡ The articles referred to in this category are those included in volumes entitled *Revolution and Counter-Revolution, Civil War in the United States, Marx on China, Marx and Engels on Britain, The Eastern Question, Revolution in Spain,* and *The Russian Menace to Europe.*

§ The correspondence listed in this category includes *Marx-Engels Selected Correspondence, Letters to Americans, Civil War in the United States,* and *Letters to Kugelmann.*

Many of the primary and secondary predictions listed in the table are found in more than one source. Classification was made on the basis of two criteria: (1) the extent to which Marx developed the prediction in a particular source and (2) the number of times the prediction is repeated in a source. Thus, in the correspondence column, no prediction is listed as primary and only five are listed as secondary, yet almost every primary and secondary prediction is mentioned in Marx's extensive correspondence. They are, however, *developed* to a much greater extent elsewhere.

Of the 153 predictions cited here, 77 are developed in the four volumes of *Capital,* 39 originated in other of Marx's books and essays, 20 others appear in newspaper articles, and 17 are set down in his published correspondence. The importance of *Capital* as a source of predictions is thus clearly established. But equally significant is the distribution of the primary, secondary, and specific predictions among the four sources. The major economic predictions represent the highest level of abstraction in the Marxian system. All but one of the twelve primary predictions dealing specifically with the future of the capitalist system are to be found in *Capital.* The four primary predictions presented in his books and essays refer specifically to a future communist state and are found exclusively in the *Critique of the Gotha Programme*.

Whereas the primary predictions relate to the general development of the economic system, the secondary prophecies refer to particular aspects of the primaries and relate to social and quasipolitical as well as economic contexts, e.g., the bourgeois family deteriorates into a group bound solely by money ties, sections of the ruling class are drawn into the proletarian ranks, the uncultivated areas in underdeveloped economies are sufficient to ruin the small and large landowners in Europe, etc. The secondary predictions are more widely dispersed than are the primary predictions, yet even here most of them (59) are located in *Capital*. Thirty-two secondary predictions appear in books and essays, four in articles and five in correspondence. *The Communist Manifesto,* the celebrated document published in 1848 by Marx and Engels as a platform for the Communist League, deserves special recognition as a depository of prophecies. It contains within its few pages the rudiments of almost every one of the primary and secondary predictions which Marx later developed in *Capital*.

Marx's specific prophecies differ substantially from his primary and secondary predictions, for they involve no generalizations. They point to particular names, dates, and events in areas of politics, economics, and social and military activity. For example, in the *New York Daily Tribune* of September 25, 1858, Marx predicted that if China should legalize opium-planting, trade relations among the United States, Australia, India, China, and England would collapse and an international crisis would follow. Again, in a letter to Meyer and Vogt, written on April 9, 1870, he prophesied that if the English army and police should move out of Ireland, an agrarian revolution would immediately follow. Marx's specific prophecies suggest supporting evidence for his primary and secondary predictions. Of the 36 specific predictions analyzed in this study, 15 appear in newspaper articles, 12 in correspondence, 3 in books and essays, and 6 in *Capital*. This dispersion is not surprising. For letters and articles that Marx wrote were primarily concerned with the affairs of the day and necessarily took the form of specifically timed and spatially located forecasts.

Bibliography

THE WORKS of Marx and of Marx and Engels have appeared in many English editions and at the hands of many different translators. The editions listed here have been used in the belief that they are the most authoritative and are available in most libraries; page numbers cited in text and footnote references to Marx follow the pagination of these editions. The Modern Library edition of *Capital* follows the pagination of the Kerr edition.

1. WORKS BY KARL MARX

Capital, A Critique of Political Economy. Volume I: *The Process of Capitalist Production.* Edited by FREDERICK ENGELS. Translated from the 3rd German edition by SAMUEL MOORE and EDWARD AVELING. Revised and amplified according to the 4th German edition by ERNEST UNTERMANN. Chicago: Charles H. Kerr & Co., 1908.

Capital, A Critique of Political Economy. Volume II: *The Process of Circulation of Capital.* Edited by FREDERICK ENGELS. Translated from the 2nd German edition by ERNEST UNTERMANN. Chicago: Charles H. Kerr & Co., 1933.

Capital, A Critique of Political Economy. Volume III: *The Process of Capitalist Production as a Whole.* Edited by FREDERICK ENGELS. Translated from the 1st German edition by ERNEST UNTERMANN. Chicago: Charles H. Kerr & Co., 1909.

The Civil War in France. New York: International Publishers Co., 1933.

The Class Struggles in France. New York: International Publishers Co., 1934.

A Contribution to the Critique of Political Economy. Translated from the 2nd German edition by N. I. STONE. Chicago: Charles H. Kerr & Co., 1940.

Critique of the Gotha Programme. New York: International Publishers Co., 1933.

"The Discourse on Free Trade," *Pocket Library on Socialism, No. 50.* Chicago: Charles H. Kerr & Co., 1907.

The Eastern Question: A Reprint of Letters Written 1853–1856 Dealing with the Events of the Crimean War. Edited by ELEANOR MARX AVELING and EDWARD AVELING. London: Swan Sonnenschein & Co., 1897.

Economic and Philosophic Manuscripts of 1844. Translated by MARTIN MILLIGAN. Moscow: Foreign Languages Publishing House, 1959.

The Eighteenth Brumaire of Louis Bonaparte. Translated from the 2nd German edition by DANIEL DE LEON. New York: International Publishers Co., 1926.

A History of Economic Theories, The Physiocrats to Adam Smith. Edited by KARL KAUTSKY. Translated from the French by TERENCE MCCARTHY. New York: Langland Press, 1932.

Letters to Dr. Kugelmann. New York: International Publishers Co., 1934.

Marx on China, 1853–1860; Articles from the New York Daily Tribune. London: Lawrence & Wishart, 1951.

The Poverty of Philosophy. Moscow: Foreign Languages Publishing House, 1956.

Revolution and Counter-Revolution, or Germany in 1848. Edited by ELEANOR MARX AVELING. London: George Allen & Unwin, 1937.

Selected Essays. Translated by H. J. STENNING. New York: International Publishers Co., 1926.

Theories of Surplus Value. Translated from Marx's preliminary manuscript for the projected 4th volume of *Capital* by G. A. BONNER and EMILE BURNS. New York: International Publishers Co., 1952.

Value, Price and Profit. Edited by ELEANOR MARX AVELING. Chicago: Charles H. Kerr & Co., 1913.

Wage-Labor and Capital. Moscow: Foreign Languages Publishing House, 1947.

2. WORKS BY KARL MARX AND FREDERICK ENGELS

On Britain. Moscow: Foreign Languages Publishing House, 1953.

The Civil War in the United States. Edited by RICHARD ENMALE. New York: International Publishers Co., 1937.

The Communist Manifesto. Translated from the German by STEFAN T. PASSONY. Chicago: Henry Regnery Co., 1954.

Communist Manifesto, Socialist Landmark. Translated by SAMUEL MOORE. London: George Allen & Unwin, 1954.

Correspondence, 1846–95, a Selection with Commentary and Notes. Edited and translated by DONA TORR. New York: International Publishers Co., 1936.

The German Ideology, Parts I and III. Translated by W. LOUGH and C. P. MAGILL. Revised and edited by R. PASCAL. New York: International Publishers Co., 1939.

Letters to Americans. Translated by LEONARD E. MINS. New York: International Publishers Co., 1934.

Revolution in Spain. New York: International Publishers Co., 1939.

The Russian Menace to Europe. Edited by PAUL W. BLACKSTOCK and BERT F. HOSELITZ. Glencoe, Ill.: The Free Press, 1952.

3. WORKS BY OTHER AUTHORS

DOBB, MAURICE. *Political Economy and Capitalism*. London: George Routledge & Co., 1937.

KAUTSKY, K. *The Labour Revolution*. London: George Allen & Unwin, 1925.

LANGE, OSCAR. "The Marxian Economics and Modern Economic Theory," *Review of Economic Studies,* Vol. II, June, 1935.

LEONTIEF, W. "Marxian Economics for Present-Day Economic Theory," *American Economic Review,* Vol. XXVIII, 1938.

SCHUMPETER, J. A. *Capitalism, Socialism and Democracy*. New York: Harper & Bros., 1942.

VON MISES, L. *Socialism*. New Haven: Yale University Press, 1951.

Index

Accumulation, 81, 84; and crisis, 134; and profit, 152; and rate of profit, 111

Agriculture: in a capitalist system, 146; under communism, 185; under dictatorship of the proletariat, 177

Allocation decision, under communism, 183

Annenkov, P. V., 123, 124

Argentina, 113

Arkansas, 136

Asia Minor, 123, 124

Asiatic Society, 124

Australia, 121, 123, 124, 127, 136, 144, 145

Austria, 125

Average profit: and absolute rent, 69; definition of, 21; in land, 58

Average rate of profit: definition of, 21, 23; and general rate of profit, 166

Babbage, C., 45 n

Banking system, 47, 51; and bills of exchange, 52; and capital circulation, 71; and loanable funds, 50

Bankruptcy, and centralization, 147

Bauer, Bruno, 166

Bills of exchange, 52; discounting, 54; fraudulent, 139

Bookkeeping costs, 75

Bourgeoisie, 204–5; and crisis, 143; formation of, 163–64; and revolution, 174–75; and technological change, 93

Cairnes, J., 36

Calcutta, 124

California, 121, 136

Canada, 124, 127

Capital: advanced, 77; circulating, 77; commodity, 14, 72, 131–32; constant, 15; depreciation, 40, 132, 140, 142; employed, 77, 78; exports, 118; fictitious, 54–55; fixed, 77; industrial, 72, 73, 74; latent, 51, 52, 73; merchant's, 29; minimum requirement, 73, 85, 137, 146–47; money, 48, 72,

184; productive, 72; turnover of, 17, 76, 77, 78, 79, 107–9; variable, 15

Capital depreciation: and crisis, 132, 140; description of, 40; and rate of profit, 105–6; and recovery, 142

Capital goods sector, 81–88, 133–34

Capital turnover, 17; and capital employed, 78, 107–9; definition of, 77, 107; and organic composition of capital, 107–9; and rate of surplus value, 79; restricted in agriculture, 109; and working periods, 76

Capitalist, 13, 35, 39, 41, 44, 81, 84, 143, 183; and capital obsolescence, 106; and centralization, 146; claim to profit, 31; and income distribution, 160; and international market, 118; production, motive for, 84; and property, 28; share of social capital, 23; view of profit, 18–19. See also Bourgeoisie; Capitalist farmer; Industrial capitalist; Money capitalist

Capitalist consumption, 102; with capital accumulation, 31, 86–87; and international trade, 120

Capitalist farmer, 57–58

Capitalization principle, and land, 69

Catholic Church, 44

Centralization, 88, 157; and class consciousness, 162; and crisis, 147; and the industrial reserve army, 154; and misery, 158

Certificates of indebtedness, 54

Children, 37, 155; and industry, 104

China, 121, 124, 136, 139, 144, 145, 174, 207

Chinese rebellion, 136

Civil War, 117, 125–27, 166

Class consciousness, 204; and the industrial reserve army, 163; Marx's reservations concerning, 165; and modes of production, 164

Class struggle, 204; and increasing misery, 161–62; origins of, 162; political character of, 164; and trade unions, 165; ultimate objectives of, 171

Classical free trade doctrines, 122

211